C000063960

HIGH SPEED DIARY

This work is published with the assistance
of the
Michael Sedgwick Memorial Trust.

Funded in memory of the famous motoring researcher and author
Michael Sedgwick (1926-1983), the Trust is a registered charity
to encourage new research and recording or motoring history.

Suggestions for future projects, and donations, should be sent to
the Honorary Secretary of the Michael Sedgwick Memorial Trust,
c/o the John Montagu Building, Beaulieu, Hampshire SO41 7ZN, England.

HIGH SPEED DIARY

The Life and Times
of
Reginald Ellis Tongue

R E Tongue

AN ERIC DYMOCK MOTOR BOOK

D O V E   P U B L I S H I N G

First published in Great Britain in 2002

by

DOVE PUBLISHING
Old West Church Manse, 31 Argyle Terrace, Rothesay, Bute PA20 0BD

Text copyright © Eric Dymock 2002

Designed by Ruth Dymock
Jacket design Andrew Barron

ISBN 0-9534142-5-6

All rights reserved. No part of this publication may be reproduced,
stored in a retrieval system, or transmitted in any form
or by any means, electronic, mechanical, photocopying, recording or otherwise,
without the prior permission of the copyright holder.

British Library Cataloguing-in-Publication Data A catalogue record
for this book is available from the British Library.

This work is published with the assistance of the Michael Sedgwick Memorial Trust.

Origination by Colourwise Ltd
Printed in Slovenia by Printing House
Mladinska knjiga by arrangement with Presernova Druzba D.D.

To Elsie, Charles, Louise and Emma

Top: *Brooklands sunshine; The Motor photographer catches the garden party atmosphere of Britain's premier track on which Reggie Tongue was first a fascinated teenage spectator then a regular competitor. Junior Car Club (JCC) International Trophy Race, 1933, the first occasion on which the cars were handicapped by artificial chicanes, sharp turns that aimed to delay the faster cars, giving slower ones a chance to catch up. Mechanics, drivers, and hangers-on congregate on the grid, placed on the Finishing Straight on the clockwise "Double Twelve" course, with the Test Hill and Members' Hill behind. Assorted MGs foreground and No46 behind will contest the 250-mile (402.32km) race against the works Austins, including No34 on the right, and Freddie Dixon's Riley, No36. Whitney Straight, competing in a Maserati, sat an examination in Cambridge in the morning, then flew his own aircraft to Brooklands in time for the race's afternoon start.*

FOREWORD BY ELSIE TONGUE

Embarking on a second marriage at the age of 52 turned out to be exactly the challenge Reg needed after the death of his first wife Johnnie. It added two daughters to the son he already had and was a happy 30 years for all of us. Reg exercised an enormous influence on all three children, imparting some of his adventurous spirit and competitive streak. It had got off to a tricky start when I invited him to a family gathering in Devon. "But I was going to ask you to Paris for the weekend," was his response. Instead he found himself welcomed into a ready-made family, with two brothers-in-law-to-be in the motor trade, where much of Reg's heart and a lot of his business already lay. Despite our age difference we speedily decided to formalise our relationship.

Generous, hospitable, cheerful with a marvellous sense of humour, coupled with a zest for life, he had the ability as Kipling put it, "To talk with crowds and keep your virtue, Or walk with kings, Nor lose the common touch". Such was his unassuming nature that I only got to know of his experiences and achievements in motor-racing a couple of months after our engagement, through chance conversations with a colleague at work.

Our daughters were both under four when he decided to go on a sailing course, shortly thereafter acquiring a Halcyon 23 "Blue Dolphin", on which we all sailed about Anglesey and North Wales. Later we graduated to a Nicholson 35, which was kept at Beaucette Marina on Guernsey, an island encompassed by some of the highest tides and strongest currents in Northern Europe. Our experiences there added considerably to Reg's fund of tall stories.

This habit of regaling family and visitors with hilarious tales led Emma, our younger daughter, to give him a tape recorder for his birthday in 1985. He was urged by the family to record his life for posterity. He was hesitant at first, hardly realising the interest it could provoke, and it took him seven years. The last few sheets were typed after his first stroke and he dictated the final chapters on a convalescent trip to Madeira.

Reg's death left us with a strong determination to get all the mass of material – diaries, photo albums, correspondence and typed memoirs into a readable form, to be edited professionally. We were fortunate to be directed by two of his friends and associates, Rivers Fletcher and John Dugdale (both now alas departed) to Eric Dymock, whose invaluable knowledge of motors and motor racing has enhanced the interest which we hope young and old enthusiasts of this great sport will experience through these pages. We are grateful to both Eric and his wife Ruth for their meticulous and knowledgeable work, and advice with presentation and publication, also to the Michael Sedgwick Trust for financial assistance towards recording Reg's life and times.

I visited Emma in Western Australia shortly before the book was to be published. Looking out of the aircraft window I glimpsed the familiar Rolls-Royce emblem on the engine alongside, and could not help reflecting on the endeavours of Reg and his fellow test pilots with early jet engines all those years ago. They took risks that have brought the present world its increasing mobility. Now we take for granted the ability to fly to far-flung countries in under 24 hours.

Re-reading the manuscript I have been struck anew by the number of scrapes and near misses Reg survived. What good fortune he enjoyed, yet his attention to detail undoubtedly saved his life several times, especially during the war. What a good example of how to make the most of each day. "Thou wast not born for aye" might have been his motto. Let the story speak for itself, using many of Reg's own words.

Elsie Tongue

December 2001. Written in Western Australia.

HIGH FLIGHT

Oh! I have slipped the surly bonds of earth
And danced the skies on laughter-silvered wings;
Sunward I've climbed, and joined the tumbling mirth
Of sun-split clouds – and done a hundred things
You have not dreamed of – wheeled and soared and swung
Hung in the sunlit silence. Hov'ring there
I've chased the shouting wind along, and flung
My eager craft through footless halls of air.

Up, up the long, delirious, burning blue
I've topped the wind-swept heights with easy grace
Where never lark , nor even eagle flew –
And while with silent, lifting mind I've trod
The high, untrespassed sanctity of space,
Put out my hand and touched the face of God.

John Gillespie Magee

CONTENTS

Previous page: First sight of the chequered flag with the new ERA. In only its second outing Reggie wins the Cork 200-mile race at 85.53 mph on 16 May 1936. Photo Irish Times.

INTRODUCTION BY REGGIE TONGUE

I had thought of calling my autobiography Nine Lives, like the cat, because I seem to have spent a lot of time escaping doom and disaster. This was not by design. I enjoyed a challenge yet drew the line at anything really dangerous. I tried to remain as safe as possible when motor racing or flying, but there were times when the unexpected or the uncontrollable happened, and I would promise myself never to do that again. My close shaves continued even after I stopped racing and flying, so Somebody up there must have been looking after me throughout. In the end the book has been called High Speed Diary, the title of an article I wrote in 1936 for Speed, the magazine that evolved into Motor Sport. What a lot we of the 1930s owed to Motor Sport in the 1940s.

Often it was only when the danger had passed that I realised what close calls they were. I could have been killed at Oxford, where I was a medical student, coming back from the pub in a friend's car. We were in a hurry, because if we were late we could be gated or, more seriously, the driver could have his university driving licence revoked. In the rush to leave the pub I had not had time to relieve myself and my friends refused to stop the car. So I stood up in the back of the open four-seater Wolseley Hornet, facing rearwards, and did it over the back. I must have been oblivious to, or perhaps insufficiently aware of, the cool night air. Somebody shouted above the noise of the slipstream to attract the driver's attention so, foolishly I thought, he braked hard. I did a graceful (or disgraceful bearing in mind the circumstances) backwards somersault, flattening the folding windscreen as I went, and landing (as so often in life) on my feet. I was able to steady myself by holding on to a headlamp.

Another brush with danger was when Dick Theakston, who became a doctor, and I went to a party in Magdalen, in a room once occupied by the Prince of Wales. There was a performance of Oedipus in the gardens below, a noisy affair that we decided in our student way we ought to enliven. College windows had fire escape belts, attached by a cord, to a sort of centrifugal brake. The idea was that you would leap from a window in the event of fire, and this brake would lower you speedily, but without injury to the ground. We speculated that if I could stand on a windowsill wearing one of these belts and launch myself into space, the audience's concentration would be broken as I plunged earthwards. I had no real idea whether the apparatus was going to work properly, but I put it on under my jacket that conveniently had a split down the back, and confidently put it to the test.

I went out on the third floor windowsill, gradually drawing the audience's interest, so instead of looking at the play everybody was looking at me. I could see people nudging one another as they speculated on my imminent suicide. When I felt I had their full attention I gave a terrific shriek and launched myself downwards. My mistake was to launch myself also outwards. Straight down would have been better, and my trajectory swung me back in an arc, towards the wall I had just left. I saw the window of the room below coming to meet me and went straight through it. There was much shattering of glass and splintering of wood while I picked myself up, undid the belt, and made my escape.

I remember thinking that the room looked rather better than a student's. It turned out to belong to one of the tutors and there was a hue and cry to discover the culprit. With the collusion of the President of Magdalen Junior Common Room, it was decided that I should not give myself up, and the incident was considered a legitimate jape that had done nobody much harm. Magdalen students were gated for the rest of term, but showed a great spirit of comradeship, and nobody except people intimately concerned ever knew who it was until now.

The closest shave I had in motor racing was at Pescara, in a race called the Coppa Acerbo, when an Italian cadet driver caused an accident soon after the start. His car crashed into the crowd killing a number of spectators. The field was still bunched closely together, cars were cannoning off one another, and I recall vividly seeing one upside down above me with its driver still in the seat.

During the war in the Royal Air Force, I contracted malaria in Africa not once but twice, awaking on one occasion crying out that I did not want another night like that. A fellow-patient told me I had been like it for a week. I was despatched back to England much the worse for wear, but at least I was alive. The malaria prevented me being posted to Malta with the rest of my squadron, many of whom died there.

Another of my putative nine lives was nearly used up during a demonstration at Fairwood Common in South Wales for visiting Americans. I was showing that aerobatics were perfectly possible in a Hurricane equipped with a new interconnected throttle and airscrew control. Unfortunately I wound the tail trimmer the wrong way as I was rolling the aircraft on to its back close to the ground, and found that I could not get the nose up because it had altered the elevators. I was very frightened. Luckily I dived out, missed colliding with the control tower by a matter of feet, and feeling extremely chastened went round again and landed.

Right and overleaf: *Cambridge University Automobile Club Jack and Jill Trial, 1935. Reggie was disappointed with his Singer Le Mans, collecting it only a week before competing in the Alpine Rally in 1934. Singer team manager FS Barnes, perhaps unsurprisingly in view of his inexperience, refused Reggie a works-supported Singer but offered to prepare one for him and render whatever assistance he could on the event. The regulations stipulated standard cars, so it was Reggie's intention to use the Singer for the Alpine, then run it on the road and compete in the occasional trial during the winter. The works fitted the duo thermometer and spot lamp. Reggie proudly displays his recently acquired BRDC badge, taking part as a member of the Oxford team led by Kenneth Evans (MG Magnette), which finished fourth.*

As soon as the aircraft stopped everybody came out, cheering me on a marvellous display, especially the bit at the end where I beat up the control tower upside down. The Air Ministry was pleased, because it was persuaded that the interconnected throttle and airscrew was acceptable, and you could carry out fighting manoeuvres with it. I was absolutely shattered over what a stupid mistake I had made, and my knees were knocking so hard I could scarcely get out of the aircraft.

I test-flew a high performance Spitfire XXI in May 1943. It carried very little petrol, so had negligible range but it went extremely fast with a Rolls-Royce Griffon engine, one-third bigger than the V12 Merlin. It produced about 2000bhp (1491kW), and for test-flying carried auxiliary tanks. I carried out tasks at flight levels from 36,000 feet going down by 2000 foot intervals to

low level. I switched over to the auxiliary tanks above Nottingham and found no fuel was going through. They either had not been filled or were suffering a technical problem. The exact cause was academic because the engine was about to stop. Fortunately I was going exceedingly fast, and I had enough time and speed to get the nose up and climb before it petered out, and there was silence except for the wind rushing past the cockpit.

It was a clear day and I looked for a suitable place to land. Newton was within reach, but unfortunately it was out of use with trestles on the runways, designed to prevent German gliders from landing. However since I was now flying what was effectively a British glider, I summoned up all the skill accumulated in ten years of flying, and made for Newton's uninviting runway. The result was, in my view, a miraculous landing

avoiding all the obstacles and not damaging the aircraft. An irate and officious adjutant rushed out of a watchtower to remonstrate with me for landing at an out of use aerodrome. He could not bring himself to calm down, even when I told him why it had been necessary, but he found me some fuel and I managed to take off again and fly back to Hucknall.

The Handley-Page Halifax was one of the Second World War's outstanding bombers, and in the autumn of 1942 I was flying one as a test pilot with Rolls-Royce, four of whose Merlin XX engines it was using. We climbed W 7814 towards 20,000ft, carrying a lot of fuel, when it suffered an engine fire. It proved impossible to extinguish and there was nothing for it but for the three of us to bale out – J Steele a civilian from the manufacturers, my pilot SL (Roscoe) Turner, and me. The unfortunate civilian engineer had never baled out before and gripped the edge of the hatch so fiercely that I, next to jump, had to crush his fingers with my foot to make him let go. I was the only one to land without injury.

I once forced-landed in fog on an aerodrome strewn with laid-up Imperial Airways aircraft and twice led a squadron through the Liverpool balloon barrage as a result of an order by some desk-bound administrator. After the war things got safer, but I had some unnerving moments, such as one occasion when they were building a motorway across my farm. I got into quicksand and was going down quite quickly when, by the grace of God, Roy Mottershead saw my plight,

and was able to give me a hand to get out. He worked on the farm although he would not normally have been there at the time.

Another fortuitous encounter with a farm worker came when my horse fell on me. I was schooling it one morning when it reared and went over backwards. It was lying on my chest so that I could neither breathe nor get the animal off me. I was running out of air when a chance caller for a bale of hay brought help.

Late in life, recuperating from a serious operation, I reflected on times throughout my seventy-odd years when I had seemed to face mortal danger. I remembered running a high temperature as a child when it was still dangerous, before medical science was provided with antibiotics and careful monitoring. I was up half the night standing in a bath, being sponged down with vinegar and water to stop my delirium. I once even got away with cancer of the bladder, so when I was thinking about a title for my memoirs "Nine Lives Plus" seemed appropriate. It was only when I started counting, and found it added up to much more than nine, that I realised what a long and full life I had been spared to live. I resolved to put some of it on the record for my family, friends, and anybody else who might be reading.

Above: *Reggie at the controls of a Hawker Hurricane. By September 1940 he had 24 hours' flying time on Hurricanes. He flew them in the Battle of Britain, and on test flights, and forced-landed one spectacularly at Whitchurch.*

AN INTRODUCTION TO REGGIE TONGUE

Vintage doyen Peter Hull once wrote that there were two machines that had charisma in abundance, the English Racing Automobile (ERA) and the Spitfire, both of which evolved in the 1930s. Neither was perhaps overwhelmingly better than its contemporaries but both were products of enthusiasm and private enterprise. Both achieved and maintained eminence for years beyond their allotted span and their success far exceeded anything expected by their originators.

Reggie Tongue won his spurs with both.

Had it not been for the Second World War he would have been better known. He warrants more than a footnote in the histories of motor racing of the 1930s and the Battle of Britain in 1940. As an amateur driver he spent a good deal of money and effort flying the flag as he saw it, and his sporting career included trials, rallies, and racing. Accomplished and competitive, a successful amateur rather than an international star, he epitomised an essentially 1930s approach to sport in general, and motor racing in particular. This mind-set was understated, although not generally carried forward to 1940, and the conflict into which he was absorbed along with the rest of his generation.

Growing up in a privileged upper middle class Midlands family steeped in the culture of the 1920s, Reggie Tongue learned duty, responsibility, patriotism, and magnanimity

that might have appeared patronising to a later era of political correctness, yet it was not. It stemmed from principles of decency and religious propriety, even if the First World War overwhelmed its formality.

He exemplified the wealthy amateur sportsman of the 1930s. He could have settled for a languorous life after Oxford, a none-too-taxing business career perhaps, yet chose instead the demanding and dangerous world of motor racing. Transporting a racing car round Europe could be tiresome – petty frontier restrictions and the town-to-town tedium of the pre-motorway age (except in Germany), culminated in a few laps of adrenalin-inducing speed. He made his first flight in 1931 in a Tiger Moth from Barton Airport, Manchester, accumulating 40 hours by 1933, although some of his flying left a certain amount to chance. His logbook for a flight in an Avro 504N J9008 with a Lynx engine for 17 March 1933 records:

"Got to just south of Basingstoke when weather began to get damnable and likely that on reaching Tangmere they would not let me take off again. On turning rained like hell. Down to 700ft. Read sign on Kintbury railway station **(near Hungerford)**. Flew home by Bradshaw **(flying slang for following railway lines)**. Took wrong line out of Didcot and found myself at Steventon, eventually turned back to Didcot and Abingdon."

Reggie flew with the Oxford University Air Squadron until 1935. He gained more experience in 1936, then in 1937 bought his own Leopard Moth G-ACRJ, in which he flew into Brooklands on at least one occasion.

In the 1930s front rank motor racing was the preserve of the French, the Italians, and the Germans. America had a motor sporting code of its own. In Japan it had scarcely been invented. Reggie's era was well documented, and posterity dealt generously with Raymond Mays, "B Bira", Malcolm Campbell, Lord Howe, and SCH "Sammy" Davis. It dealt less well with Reggie Tongue and those who finished second, third or fourth as often as they won. It was much the same with Battle of Britain pilots. Stanford Tuck, Douglas Bader, and Adolf Galland were its high-profile heroes. Reggie Tongue was brave, determined and skilled, flying in combat during the crucial weeks between 10 July and 31 October 1940 with Fighter Command, but his exploits have up till now been obscure.

Previous page: *Reggie Tongue's ERA lifts a wheel on one of Brooklands' notorious bumps in the Junior Car Club's (JCC) 200 mile race in August 1938 in which he finished fifth.*

Top left: *Student pilots of the Oxford University Air Squadron grapple with parachute training under an RAF sergeant instructor at Eastchurch Camp, 1933. Reggie Tongue is the shorter of the two pilots with goggles seventh from the left in the group. Nine years later, he qualified for the exclusive Caterpillar Club, open only to those who have used a parachute to save their lives.*

Right: *OUAS Camp, Eastchurch 1932; Reggie Tongue is second from left in the second row.*

Reggie always wanted to put up a good show. In motor racing the highlights of his career were when he beat aces of the day such as Raymond Mays. He had been competitive from the moment he took the wheel, writing in his diary as a sixth former with his first sports car, a Riley Nine that he had "…managed to hang on to the heels of a Big 6 Bentley," and "… left a Morgan standing on the Chester Road." **More intriguingly on one occasion he had** "…a gorgeous day. Had a great scrap with a girl in a Bugatti Coupe from York to Harrogate. Won easily."

This was a spirit he kept throughout his life until, long after his motor racing and flying days were over, he rode and hunted and sailed with the same enthusiasm.

Reggie Tongue's custom of taking part, enjoying the experience and competing with vigour stood him in good stead throughout the 1930s in Alpine Trials, the 24 Hours of Le Mans, and great races up and down Europe driving some of the best cars of the time. He raced Aston Martin, MG K3 and R-type, ERA, and a 4CL Maserati, mixing his sport with a keen business sense. He went to America in 1939, as a director of Thomson and Taylor the Brooklands engineering firm that built John Cobb's successful Land Speed Record car. It was a visit that had to be cut short. Reggie hurriedly scrambled aboard a Pan-Am Clipper at the outbreak of war to join the Royal Air Force.

The rigours and dangers of competitive motor racing were in some ways a rehearsal for wartime flying and once again Reggie desperately wanted to put up a good show. He took part in the air war, even though at 28 in 1940 he was regarded as ten years too old for aggressive combat. His precise no-nonsense mind sometimes found service life irksome. He was twice ordered to take a squadron of aircraft through a fog-bound Liverpool balloon barrage. It was a Light-Brigade-Charge sort of command: a pointless exercise for which Reggie devised a typically

RECORD OF SERVICE

	UNIT	DATES FROM	DATES TO	TEST PILOT AT:- UNIT	DATES FROM	DATES TO
	OXFORD UNIVERSITY AIR SQDN	NOV 1931	JULY 1935	ROLLS ROYCE LTD: (M.A.P.)		
A/P/O	No 9. S.F.T.S. HULLAVINGTON	10.4.40.	27.7.40.	S.D.L. No 1 DEPOT UXBRIDGE) *	19.9.42	
P/O.	No 3 SQDN. WICK.	27.7.40.	2.9.40.	LATER A.M. UNIT HALLAM ST. W.1.		19.10.45
	ATTACHED No 5.O.T.U. ASTON DOWN.	3.8.40	17.8.40.	DEMOBILISED FROM:—	14.12.45.	
	No 3 SQDN. CASTLETOWN	2.9.40.	14.9.40.			
	No 3 SQDN. TURNHOUSE.	14.9.40	26.9.40.			
	No 504. SQDN. FILTON	28.9.40	10.11.40.			
	No 249 SQDN. N. WEALD	10.11.40.	16.11.40			
	No 46 SQDN. N. WEALD.	16.11.40	13.12.40.			
	No 46 SQDN. DIGBY.	13.12.40	28.2.41.			
	No 46 SQDN. CHURCH FENTON	28.2.41.	1.3.41.			
	No 46. SQDN. SHERBURN IN ELMET.	1.3.41.	7.3.41.			
ATTACHED	No 71.X SQDN. KIRTON IN LINDSEY	7.3.41.	9.4.41.	AMERICAN "EAGLE SQUADRON."		
	No 71. SQDN. MARTLESHAM	9.4.41.	14.4.41.			
	No 46. SQDN. SHERBURN IN ELMET.	14.4.41.	1.5.41.			
	No 1. P.D.C. WEST KIRBY.	1.5.41.	7.5.41.			
	H.M.T. F.6. (HIGHLAND PRINCESS)	7.5.41.	31.5.41.			
	TAKORADI. GOLD COAST.	31.5.41.	20.7.41.			
F/O.	M.V. "COPPACABANA".	20.7.41.	3.8.41.			
	H.M.S "CATHAY".	3.8.41.	28.8.41.			
	No 1 DEPOT UXBRIDGE.	29.8.41.	7.10.41.			
	P.M.R.A.F. HOSPITAL HALTON.	12.9.41.	23.9.41.			
A/F/L	No 55.O.T.U. USWORTH.	8.10.41.	5.3.42.			
F/L	ROLLS ROYCE LTD: (FIGHTER COMMAND) LIAISON.	7.3.42.	18.9.42			

X No 1 EAGLE SQDN.

* w.e.f. 9.11.42.

AIRCRAFT FLOWN

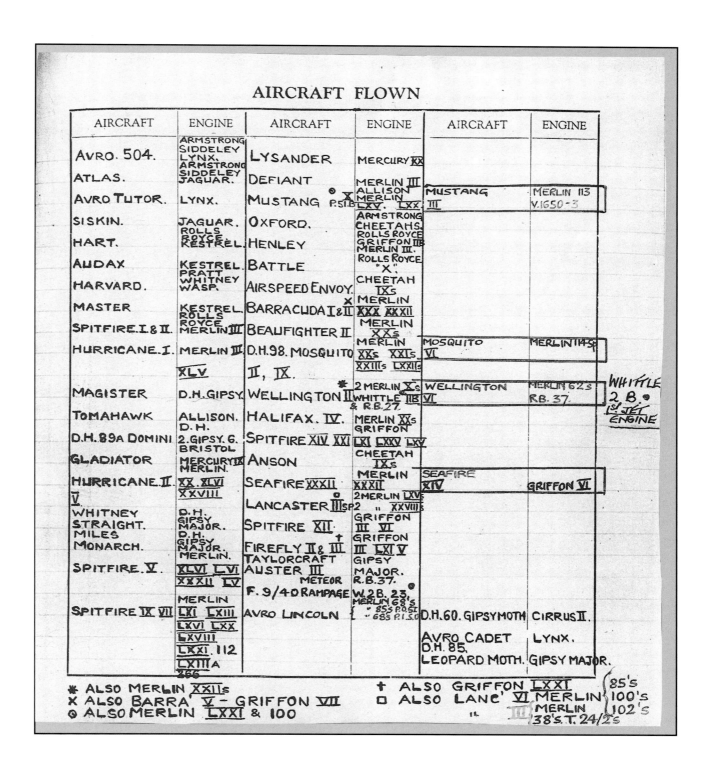

AIRCRAFT	ENGINE	AIRCRAFT	ENGINE	AIRCRAFT	ENGINE
AVRO. 504.	ARMSTRONG SIDDELEY LYNX.	LYSANDER	MERCURY XX		
ATLAS.	ARMSTRONG SIDDELEY JAGUAR.	DEFIANT	MERLIN III	MUSTANG III	MERLIN 113 V.1650-3
AVRO TUTOR.	LYNX.	MUSTANG P.51B	ALLISON MERLIN LXV. LXX.		
SISKIN.	JAGUAR.	OXFORD.	ARMSTRONG CHEETAHS.		
HART.	ROLLS ROYCE KESTREL.	HENLEY	ROLLS ROYCE GRIFFON IIB MERLIN III.		
AUDAX	KESTREL.	BATTLE	ROLLS ROYCE "X".		
HARVARD.	PRATT WHITNEY WASP.	AIRSPEED ENVOY.	CHEETAH IXs		
MASTER	KESTREL.	BARRACUDA I & II	MERLIN XXX XXXII		
SPITFIRE. I & II.	ROLLS ROYCE MERLIN III	BEAUFIGHTER II	MERLIN XXs		
HURRICANE. I.	MERLIN III	D.H.98. MOSQUITO II, IX.	MERLIN XXs XXIs XXIIIs LXXIIs	MOSQUITO VI	MERLIN 114 SP
	XLV				
MAGISTER	D.H.GIPSY	WELLINGTON II	2 MERLIN Xs WHITTLE IIB & R.B.27.	WELLINGTON VI	MERLIN 62s R.B. 37.
TOMAHAWK	ALLISON.	HALIFAX. IV.	MERLIN XXs		
D.H.89a DOMINI	D.H. 2.GIPSY.6.	SPITFIRE XIV XXI	GRIFFON LXI LXXV LXV		
GLADIATOR	BRISTOL MERCURY IX MERLIN.	ANSON	CHEETAH IXs		
HURRICANE. II. V	XX. XLVI XXVIII	SEAFIRE XXXII	MERLIN XXXII	SEAFIRE XIV	GRIFFON VI
WHITNEY STRAIGHT.	D.H. GIPSY MAJOR.	LANCASTER III SP 2	2 MERLIN LXVI " XXVIIIs		
MILES MONARCH.	D.H. GIPSY MAJOR.	SPITFIRE XII	GRIFFON III VI		
	MERLIN.	FIREFLY II & III	GRIFFON III LXI V		
SPITFIRE. V	XLVI LVI XXXII LV	TAYLORCRAFT AUSTER III	GIPSY MAJOR. R.B.37.		
		METEOR F.9/40 RAMPAGE	W.2.B. 23.		
SPITFIRE IX VII	MERLIN LXI LXIII LXVI LXX LXVIII LXXI. 112 LXIIIA 266	AVRO LINCOLN	MERLIN 68's *855 P.O.S.1 * 68S P.I.S.O	D.H.60. GIPSYMOTH	CIRRUS II.
				AVRO CADET D.H. 85.	LYNX.
				LEOPARD MOTH.	GIPSY MAJOR.

WHITTLE 2.B ⊙
1st JET ENGINE

* ALSO MERLIN XXIIs
X ALSO BARRA' V – GRIFFON VII
⊙ ALSO MERLIN LXXI & 100

† ALSO GRIFFON LXXI
□ ALSO LANC' VI MERLIN III { 85's 100's 102's
MERLIN 38's. T. 24/2s

robust solution. He suffered from plenty of none-too-bright orders, yet disliked indiscipline, and was exhausted emotionally by the never-ending waste of young lives. Frustrated by a system that denied him higher rank in the RAF, he nevertheless exercised a lot of control and responsibility, to tasks that included applying RAF standards of discipline to the sometimes less than respectful personnel of the American Eagle Squadron.

Reggie had been put on the Special Duties List on 11 November 1942 and applied the same care he had exercised as a racing driver to being a test pilot with Rolls-Royce. He may not have been belligerent enough to be an outstanding combat pilot, in any case, aged 30 he was of more value to the air force for his experience. The analytical quality he applied to motor racing flourished in the air. Tony Rudd, a contemporary Rolls-Royce engineering boffin who became chief engineer at BRM, met him at Rolls-Royce's Hucknall establishment, and affirmed that he would never have graduated to such an exclusive role had he been anything but an outstanding pilot.

His version of events is part of Britain's social, industrial and wartime history. His era of motor sport was one when it was still essentially sport not a stressful mixture of show business and technology and, like his war, still a conflict between individuals. In each case, if they could not quite see the whites of one another's eyes, they could still look into an opponent's cockpit.

His collection of memorabilia was an epitaph on a full life. It included telegrams and correspondence from Richard Seaman the British driver who died in a works Mercedes-Benz, and dinner menus autographed by the great and the good of 1930s motor racing. He cherished congratulatory letters from Cecil Kimber, the founder of MG, and chortled over cuttings from foreign newspapers that regularly mis-spelt his name Tingue, Tongué, or Tong.

Individuals who spent their money on yachts, racing cars, record cars, aeroplanes, or golf tours were called "sportsmen" in the 1930s, a term often, though not invariably, prefixed by "rich". Reggie Tongue was a sportsman by any definition and his diaries and the tape recordings of his reminiscences formed the core of this biography. The author filled in gaps, occasionally administering a corrective for historical accuracy. Reggie recorded his "Nine Lives" from 1989 at the age of 77, during the three years before he died, demanding it be put right on matters of fact. One's response to reading his diary chronicling narrow escapes on the racetrack and in the air is "only nine?"

This account of his life is based on those diaries, records, cuttings, photographs, pilots' log-books, memorabilia and other accounts of his motor racing and flying between 1930 and 1945.

The Tongues were an old family, taking their name from their locality, "of Tone" or "Tong", and there are parishes of the name in Shropshire, Kent, the West Riding of Yorkshire and, significantly, two in Lancashire. Most of these take their name from the shape of the land, a tongue on a bend in a river, or hillside. The earliest reference is Wluricus Tunge in 1188. He was followed by John de Tonghe of Shropshire (1279) Nicholas Tonge (1279) of Bucks, Peter Tonge shoemaker of Chester, Charles Tonge and Mary Hancocke who were married in London in 1659. There were Irish Tongues of whom one, Miles Tonge, was in the gang that cut the boom at the siege of Derry in 1689.

Reggie Tongue was born at Flixton near Manchester. His parents Anne Mudd and Cyril Ellis Tongue married on 15th February 1911 and he arrived at the house called Amcet (an acronym of his parents' initials) on 17 July 1912. His father was a chartered accountant and to young Reggie the small semi was thoroughly fitting for what he regarded as his modest start in life. It was a well-kept home with fields on one side, and farm buildings on the other. He enjoyed an idyllic country childhood, chasing rats out of harvesting corn to stop them coming into the house, a classic rural North of England upbringing although never far from the industrial shadow of Manchester.

Reggie's description of his grandfather "developing some ability in accountancy" may be something of an understatement. His grandfather founded the family fortune, and the trust he set up looked after Reggie following the deaths of both parents, later providing the money for his motor racing. Reggie's mother died in January 1920 at the age of only 34 when Reggie was seven. A solitary child, Reggie had been distraught even when she went shopping, and had to be consoled by the domestic staff.

Reggie and his father moved to Whitecroft, a big house with garaging for two cars, a large garden, and a housekeeper who would cuff him behind the ear, as Reggie put it, whenever she thought it necessary. The village postman worked for the family, as gardener and handyman, and helped with the cars. He started his postal round at five in the morning, and since he had not much to do afterwards, spent the rest of the day on domestic duty. Reggie's father was shocked to discover he shared his bed with the housekeeper even though they were not married. Innocent times. Reggie's preoccupation however was with the postman's AJS motorcycle and sidecar.

When I was a child there seemed to be no background noise in the country, so you could hear the bells of Flixton Church, loud and clear across the fields on Sunday morning. It must have been a mile and a half away. By family tradition my great grandfather had been a lamplighter, and my grandfather Alfred Tongue took a job as a cotton mill clerk, as soon as he left school. He developed some ability in accountancy and was among the founders of the Chartered Accountants' Institute. Lloyd George's government engaged him to conduct a study on how power would be generated in Britain after the 1914-1918 War.

During the fuel shortage in the First World War one of my grandfather's Daimlers was converted to run on gas. It had a huge bag on the roof and had to be driven along to the gasworks to be filled. Johnson, the long-suffering chauffeur, was at the mercy of Grandmother's speaking tube. He could not speak back; he could only listen. She had a speedometer in the rear and constantly monitored what speed she was going at. Her upper

limit was 25 or 30mph, so if Johnson was overdoing it, at about 32mph she spoke firmly down the tube, "Johnson, have you looked at your speed? Do you know you are doing 32mph? We go at 30mph. Please slow down." Johnson would slow at once but after a while would get bored and drop to 26 or 27mph. Grandmother would then demand, "Johnson, come along, wake up. You are only doing 27mph. We travel at 30mph please speed up."

I went to prep school aged eight; I was proud of my Raleigh bicycle with a chain that ran in an oil bath. It was old fashioned but I was an old fashioned child. Elsie the housekeeper and Jack the postman eventually married and father and I joined aunts and cousins for summer holidays at Cleveleys near Thornton north of Blackpool. A furnished house at Rossall Beach was taken for the month, and became the base for outings with domestic staff, who dispensed sixpenny tickets for Blackpool Winter Gardens.

I learned to drive at Rossall Beach. Like many middle-class children this was achieved with the connivance of good-natured servants, in my case at the wheel of my aunt's Bullnose four-seat Morris tourer, propped up on cushions by grandfather's chauffeur. The roads near the beach were well out of sight and mercifully empty enough to allow a nine- or ten-year-old driver to try his hand.

Grandfather's Double Six Daimler was an aristocratic car of almost unbelievable size and complexity. To a small boy the twelve-cylinder sleeve valve engine had the majesty of a railway locomotive. Each bank of cylinders had its own water pump, magneto, and Daimler four-jet carburettor. The crankshaft ran in seven main bearings, and chains drove the shafts carrying the eccentrics, operating the sleeve valves almost silently. It was a masterpiece of precision demanding the utmost care in maintenance. For the most part it ran beautifully, although like the Double Sixes used by the Royal family, the haze

Previous page: *From Reggie's album. Top, at Scorton, 1923, and bottom with postman Jack Thompson and possibly the coveted AJS and sidecar.*

Below: *With bicycle on holiday at Rossall Beach.*

of blue smoke it trailed was a legacy of the Knight sleeve valves' lavish lubrication. A Double-Six was not cheap; in 1930 the bare short chassis alone cost £1850 and a seven-seat limousine was £2800 when a top five-seat Hillman was £285 and you could get a good 6-cylinder Rolls-Royce for £3,000.

The Daimler was never an easy car to start. It was equipped with a self-starter, but in winter when the oil was thick and the sleeve valves sluggish, the chauffeur had to half-open the compression taps on each cylinder, pour in a drop of ether from a bottle he always carried, then crank it by hand. If he miscalculated, the starting handle could break his arm, but provided he got it right the engine started with a reassuring bang.

In 1924 for my twelfth birthday treat I had a memorable visit to the Wembley British Empire Exhibition. A four-course dinner and cabaret at the Trocadero cost a formidable twelve shillings and sixpence (62.5p). Jointly with a cousin I mortgaged five weeks' pocket money on a knickerbocker glory in a tall glass with cream and a cherry. Impressionable age, twelve. I may not have decided there and then that the acquisition of wealth was crucial, but the experience established a certain fondness for life's knickerbocker glories.

Right (top): *Cyril Tongue gazes fondly at his Bentley. Reggie's father was a keen driver and would have liked to race. The car was a 3-litre, and Bentley factory records show that TD9501 was delivered new to CE Tongue in April 1927 with a 4-seater body by Vanden Plas No1187. The car survived into the 21st century.*

Right (bottom): *Reggie was as much at home on the water as in a car or an aircraft. Here he rows on Maelog Lake around 1923.*

As soon as I arrived at The Ryleys, my first school that took me to age thirteen, I was taken to meet the headmaster. Mr McCulloch, rarely glimpsed without gown and mortarboard, seemed to use his cane almost on principle. All my life the smell of stale whisky brought back school mornings and the whiff of McCulloch's morning tipple, seemingly necessary to enable him cope with unruly small boys.

The Ryleys seemed bereft of carpets or linoleum. The floors were bare wood so that you got splinters in your knees when you knelt. The day began with Assembly when we sat behind long desks, said the Lord's Prayer, and McCulloch read out the leading article in the Daily Mail. He seemed to think that it would give us a deeper understanding of the world but I cannot say it ever meant much. My cousin Philip was supposed to be looking after me, but as soon as I arrived he absconded, went back home and after hiding outside became hungry and was caught stealing food. His father drove him straight back to school; not a very good example for me, I thought.

My school reports were not altogether unkind. "His soccer would be improved, if he could stop charging around like a bull in a china shop." "Not the brightest boy in the school but certainly the noisiest". I was also "the only boy we have had here able to sing 'Hearts of Oak' on one note throughout." School years were crammed with firm friendships such as that with Dick Bickerton who lived in some style near Macclesfield. Thorneycroft Hall, Chelford had a huge dining room, and I thought it rather grand when staying for weekends, that people came in for meals at half past eight in the evening. I was also struck by the beauty of Dick's sisters, and longed to be old enough to marry one of them. The highlight of staying at Thorneycroft however, was the Bickertons' large tiller-steered electric limousine. It was smooth and comfortable although not very fast with a top speed of about 25mph. Its batteries only lasted from Thorneycroft to Alderley and back again. Dick went into the family diesel-engineering firms Mirlees Bickerton and Day, and National Gas Engines, at Ashton under Lyne near Manchester.

My father nourished my interest in cars and motor racing, recounting tales of the Bentley Boys at Le Mans. British motor racing seemed supreme and as a small boy how I admired Sir Henry "Tim" Birkin, Sammy Davis, Woolf Barnato, Dr Benjafield, George Duller, JF Duff, Frank Clement, Jean Chassagne, Bernard Rubin, and the memorable victory after the White House crash, in 1927, of Davis and Benjafield.

Father's 12/60 Fiat of 1921, and a 20/70 Crossley a couple of years later, whetted my appetite. I never drove the Fiat although it seemed immensely fast and was the first car in which I saw 60mph on the speedometer. What thrills; a mile a minute. Its pistons had cast iron tops and aluminium skirts but unfortunately they were prone to failure, so a spare set had to be carried, ready to be fitted on the spot if necessary. The Crossley was a different proposition, just as fast but wholly reliable. It was strongly made and could be driven like a modern off-road 4x4 over the Yorkshire Fells; the real fells not just fell roads. The ground clearance was generous enough for crossing moorland streams, and it could be dug out, brought home, washed and polished, then driven to Brooklands in Surrey more than 200 miles away at an average of over 40mph (64.2kph).

I was still at school in 1925 when my father had a 3-litre Bentley and a 1924 Talbot 10/23 two-seater, a beautiful car capable of 50mph; developed from the 8/18 with a 1074cc engine it was built like a watch, and one of the first cars I ever drove. Among other early driving experiences were a Standard 9 and a Morris Chummy. When my father was away in Ireland I drove the Talbot round the lawn, flat out in second gear, delighted to discover that despite its small radiator it did not boil. However it did have a solid rear axle so the lawn was a real mess. I thought he had overlooked the incident until I wrote home asking for pocket money. A frosty reply came back, to the effect that I would be paying off the damage to the lawn until my school days were over, and pocket money was not immediately forthcoming. Still I could not have started my driving career on a finer car. I remember a beautiful gearbox, a sweet-running engine, excellent steering and how precisely all the switches worked. The quality of the accessories and instruments made later cars seem shoddy.

Far left: Cyril Tongue's Standard 9.5HP Ranalegh Coupe is an electric-headlamp post-war version of a car that came out in 1913 with acetylene lighting. Known as the SLS with a 1328cc engine, it was produced until 1921. As a gesture of support for local Manchester car-maker Crossley, Cyril Tongue bought a 20/70, a much modernised 3.7-litre sports version of the Royal Flying Corps' staff car of World War I. Although a side-valve it had slipper-type pistons, a lightweight polished aluminium body, and could do 75mph (120.4kph). Photographed at John o' Groats (top left) it does not look as though Tongue Snr specified the Perrot four wheel brakes optional in 1924.

Top right: Ever an aficionado of the Lake District, in 1930 Reggie photographed a Rover Light Six at Hawkshead for his album. The Rover basked in the reflected glamour of having just beaten the crack French Blue Train between Calais and the Riviera.

It was surprising how fussy car owners of the time were. Grandfather's Daimler was washed down and leathered every day, then put away in a dry garage; it was just like the coaching era. Father's chauffeur Blackwell washed my aunt's Bullnose Morris Cowley at Rossall Beach with the wheels jacked up, playing the hose on the spokes, setting the wheels spinning to throw the dirt off. The speedometer drive came from the offside front wheel, and although usually quite adept, he put his finger through the spokes and caught it between the teeth of the gear wheels. I thought that as a former Grenadier Guardsman, Blackwell would be impervious to pain, so I was amazed at the state he got into. Somebody had the presence of mind to wind the wheel backwards to release his finger, but not before the cogs had punched a hole right through it. He was brought into the house and fainted clean away before being taken to a doctor. He managed to keep his finger but it must have been excruciatingly painful.

Grandmother would not allow my father and his brothers to be sent away to school. She wanted to influence their upbringing, so they went to Manchester Grammar School where she could make sure they had dry shirts, and were properly looked after and fed. In point of fact she never did any of that sort of thing at all, the housekeeper did it, but she had the satisfaction of acting as supervisor.

As a result I did not go to Manchester Grammar and instead became one of the first

members of the family to go away to public school. Shrewsbury was first choice but unfortunately I did not get through the Common Entrance Examination. Father was very severe about it, demanding to know what I was going to do: "You're thirteen and a half. Your life is finished before it has started. You won't get any education now. I suppose you could go to work and learn a trade or something."

He had no intention of my education finishing, but he wanted to bring me up short, and demanded to know what career I intended to follow. It seemed to me that Blackwell enjoyed life, always excepting the hole in his finger; he looked after the cars, and did a bit of gardening, so I said I would like to do a job like that.

"Do you mean you would like to be a chauffeur-gardener?"

I couldn't think of anything more congenial, so he promised to try and get me fixed up. He really was less concerned about what I did, as long as I was happy doing it – advice I have always passed on. His ambition had been to be a surgeon, but grew up in a generation accustomed to doing what it was told, and had been frustrated. He

never got on well with my grandfather and found it difficult to work in the family accountancy practice. He was always in demand for intricate assignments, yet he was never made a partner, and the omission rankled. He had good connections with industry, and performed delicate tasks with great diplomacy, yet never felt appreciated despite showing skill as a receiver. He worked on Vulcan, Lea-Francis, and many other carmakers that fell on hard times in the 1920s.

I grew close to my father after mother's death. We went on holidays to the Lake District and the West Riding of Yorkshire, and walked on the fells. He loved organising

impromptu nights at the theatre, booking a table in the Midland Hotel and arranging the best seats. We visited Brooklands, the banked track near Weybridge, laid out in 1906 by Hugh Fortescue Locke-King on his Surrey estates. Brooklands was designed in the style of the only racecourses its creators knew, those for horses, as a closed loop with a finishing straight in the middle. It never became the prototype for motor racetracks as Locke-King hoped, but for years it was the heart of British motor racing. At Brooklands I discovered the passion my father had for the sport. He would have liked to be a racing driver, but the dangers were only too apparent in the 1930s, and concern for what would happen to me if he were killed or injured dissuaded him.

Thus were sown the seeds of a motor sporting career. I was already a keen motorcyclist riding a Matchless TE 2304, and my diary entry for 13 April 1929 reads: "I entered for the Schoolboys Motor Cycle Trial but unfortunately sprained my ankle a few days before so missed it..."

Far left, top: *Birthday treat, 1928, Brooklands. Reggie photographed paddock scenes for his album. The historic clubhouse is on the right and, visible in the distance, the finishing straight and Vickers sheds. On the left of the paddock is the "telegraph" used to display runners and riders and one end of the 1926 finishing straight bridge.*

Far left, below: *One of the two "flatiron" Thomas Specials, sophisticated straight-8 1.5-litre cars with which JG Parry Thomas took the Class F hour record at 112.7mph (180.92kph).*

Left: *Reggie with his Matchless in 1929 with which he hoped to commence his motor sporting career.*

Right: *Sedbergh School, Winder House. Inconvenient for school but greatly loved.*

Top: *Reggie poses outside Winder House.*

Failing Common Entrance turned out to be no bad thing. Sedbergh (motto *duro virum nutrix* – a hard nurse of men) said it would be prepared to take Reggie and he spent some of the happiest years of his life in the Yorkshire dales. His housemaster Neville Gorton proved a lasting influence and many years later he went back to the house "Gorty" lived in at Hartsop, between Patterdale and Brotherswater, his fondness for it undimmed. Prominent Old Sedberghians include Will Carling the England rugby captain and one of a number of other former pupils who played for their country; Lord Bingham of Cornhill the Lord Chief Justice; Sir Christopher Bland Chairman of the BBC; and Sir Jock Slater the First Sea Lord.

I went to Sedbergh in a bi-term in January joining Winder house. This was made up of three semi-detached dwellings, inconveniently placed so that you often had to queue for breakfast. Tail-enders waited in the rain for their bowl of porridge and syrup, followed by a slice of bacon on fried bread, and a mug of tea. My father believed in toughness and cultivated something of a spartan existence. Once on the Isle of Man we met a member of Shackleton's Polar support team, whom he regarded as the perfect example of somebody healthy, tough, and clean. Sedbergh fulfilled his requirements in this respect, and it was not long before I was setting myself strenuous targets, trying to run further and faster than anybody else.

Except for a miserable first few days I loved every minute of it. I started as a fag (when the word still meant a schoolboy's orderly), and on only my second day was told to make the house prefects' coffee. Unfortunately on my way to their study before afternoon school I tripped and threw the coffee all over the floor. Retribution came at six o'clock when Alan Bell, a senior prefect, gave me six of the best on my behind. I refused to allow him to write a note to the housemaster, fearing it might get me into further trouble, so really Sedbergh began disastrously. Spilling the coffee also made me late for school, so as a further punishment I had to write out a hundred times on red lined paper, "I must not be late for my lessons". The housemaster initialled this so he did know I had misbehaved, and although such a

punishment may sound excessive, in due course when I became a prefect and head of house, I looked on it as perfectly right and proper. Still, Alan Bell and I remained friends long after we had left school and university.

The physics master, Mr Woodhouse, was generally lenient but when he discovered me reading *The Autocar* in class, demanded to know if I was more interested in it than I was in him. There was only one answer and I confessed to looking at the classified advertisements. His response was a demand that I write, on red lined paper, an entire page of second hand car advertisements. It was small print, very detailed, and took ages.

Dormitory windows at Sedbergh were invariably kept open. It was part of the toughening regime; when the rain blew in I woke up with water on the floor and cold wet bedding. The morning routine included a cold bath, a walk up to school often in rain (Sedbergh is east of Kendal, Cumbria in the Lake District, one of the wettest places in Britain) and sometimes the boys (girls were not admitted until 2001) sat in damp clothes through lessons. It did not seem to do much harm until my cousin caught rheumatic fever and died.

Top left: *Reggie on the beach at Scarborough with grandparents and Aunt Lucy on his right.*

Top right: *The most deeply respected car of the middle class, an Alvis. The Tongue family's 1928 16.95HP Silver Eagle sports saloon.*

Right: *Among the bizarre home-built machinery of Reggie's youth was a lightweight and largely tubular land-yacht that achieved great speed on the beach on Anglesey.*

I detested cricket. They always put me in the deep and I stood there all afternoon in the sun; nobody ever had the strength to hit a ball that far, and they were unlikely to lob one up into the sky so that I could catch it. As soon as I could I gave it up, spending my days wandering around the beautiful fell country, having farmhouse teas at half a crown a time, and bathing in the river.

My housemaster Neville Gorton bought his old Lake District cottage in Hartsop at the end of our last summer term. He asked Peter Bell and Dick Bickerton and me to spend a week there hill walking. We began well, walking all the way from Sedbergh, as usual following our noses rather than using maps. We went first to Lowgill, then on to Tebay where we climbed over Shap Fell, finishing up in Kentmere on the other side, tired and thirsty. We stopped at a cottage where they had one of those big school teapots with handles at both ends.

We did not have proper walking boots, hiked in our ordinary gym shoes and shorts, yet still managed over the top near Kirkstone Pass, and down to Brotherswater. By then we were so tired we could not complete the short distance to Hartsop. At around thirty miles it sounds a lot, but in the 19th century the Wordsworths thought nothing of walking that far in the Lake District, even after dark. Dickens walked thirty miles round London at night. Nowadays only keen ramblers walk more than ten miles a day.

Neville Gorton had a lovely little 10.9hp Talbot and kindly indulged my enthusiasm for driving. He telephoned the headmaster from his sitting room: "You know I suffer from arthritis and

rheumatism, headmaster. Well, I'm not feeling at all fit and I've got some business in Windermere. Would it be all right for Tongue to drive me?" As we later reached Windermere I asked where he wanted to go for his business appointment. "Business, boy?" he said. "The business is taking you for tea at the Old England Hotel."

Gorty was a keen car enthusiast and later exchanged the Talbot for an old Rolls-Royce tourer that, according to a godson Sir Hugh Cortazzi, he drove at breakneck speed. There was one hill up which Gorty found his Rolls could only go really fast in reverse. Astonished people would see this tall figure, in extraordinary clothes, standing upright in his car facing backwards roaring up the hill at hair-raising speed. Things did not improve later in life when he was headmaster of Blundell's. Gorty's biographer recalled an occasion when six members of the music club were taken to Exeter for a lute concert. It was a boring event relieved by the ride back, which was described as breathtaking. "Every so often he would turn round to talk to one of us in the back, leaving the car to its own devices while the others cried 'Sir!' in an attempt to prevent our demise in the hedge or the River Exe."

I was robustly sporting at Sedbergh, academically bright enough to read medicine at Oxford, although I failed to graduate through a combination of conflicting interests and what I could only describe as ineptitude. My schooldays were dominated by the deaths of my parents, that of my mother cruelly broken to me by my father one morning when I was only seven years old.

The memory haunted me throughout my life, as did the torment of my father's final illness.

He drove open cars in the severest weather, had a cold bath every morning, and thought he was pretty well indestructible. He enjoyed visits to the Lake District and in his active way did vigorous gymnastics. He could even manage an unsteady handstand in his forties. He fell ill after a visit to the Royal Oak at Keswick and the Blencathra Hunt Ball, and that evening as usual without wearing a coat or hat, had gone out to Friar's Crag.

The following Monday he telephoned his secretary, Miss Grainger, to say he was not coming to work. The doctor called next day, but by Wednesday father had gone into serious decline with pneumonia. On Friday I was sent home from school and found him delirious. Watching him being restrained was heartrending. I have often felt it would have been kinder if I had not been called back. My presence did not seem to do a lot for my father, by the end of the week he was dead, and I was in a terrible state.

When I got back to school Neville Gorton was marvellous and from then on he became a sort of second father. "Gorty" never made demands and treated me with great kindness and understanding. In effect I then had two fathers, the other my dear Uncle Tom Stephens, married to my father's sister Mab. They seemed to reassign the affection they had for him to me, and even though they had a lot to put up with, they never complained and supported me staunchly.

They set a marvellous example. They knew what life was about, and I never forgot their kindness, bestowed often when I did not deserve it. After my father's death, I think perhaps I somehow took his place for Aunt Mab, and later on even filled the breach left when she lost her own son.

2 GETTING STARTED IN CARS

Cars were not allowed at Sedbergh, but after a lot of effort Reggie managed to get the rules changed. Pupils were allowed to bring cars and garage them, but had to promise only to maintain and admire them. Cars were not on any account to be taken out on roads, which prior to the 1930 and 1934 Road Traffic Acts that brought in driving tests and urban speed limits, were the most dangerous of the century. The school authorities decided that they would be useful educationally, but adventure was on every boy's mind and fascination with mechanical things knew no bounds. Sedbergh pupils were encouraged to work on their cars up to the level of a decoke, the tiresome process of removing the carbon deposits in combustion chambers. It was a pious hope. Temptation to break the restrictions on driving proved irresistible.

Reggie was driving his late father's MG. Given the task of administering the estate until Reggie came of age the trustees decided his Bentley was unsuitable for a schoolboy, and sold it. They let him keep the 1926 MG MkIV 14/40, an early featherweight fabric saloon with an upright flat radiator instead of the rounded bullnose inherited from Morris. The front was enhanced with an appliqué cutout MG octagon, one of the first of the emerging make to carry a strong MG identity. The 14/40 was based on the Morris Oxford with flattened rear springs, remounted steering box, and raked column. MG guaranteed the model, the chassis plate said MG and it was registered as an MG, but its speed and specification was not far removed from a Morris. The difference was largely one of style and a slightly racy quality.

My father had owned some striking cars, and although the MG had a good pedigree, it never quite lived up to the others. Tall and elegant, it was a step up from the Morris it was based on, it was well engineered and could do 65mph (104.3kph) but the body left a lot to be desired. The engine suffered from heavy cylinder wear, and water dripped on to the occupants' legs, through the ship-style scuttle ventilators of which Cecil Kimber of MG and William Lyons of SS Jaguar were so fond.

The bonnet catches chipped paint off the wings, and when the front door blew open its handle punched a hole in the rear door. My cousin later bought the car and fitted strong straps connecting the front doors to pins, but the wind still blew them open and although the strap held, it pulled the hinges out of the doorframe. Still the 14/40 had a lovely-sounding exhaust, it was nippy, and it looked good.

The trustees thought the MG would be convenient for carrying luggage to and from school. They were not to know that cars were like drugs to me; I simply had to drive them. At that age you do not always stick to rules no matter how solemn your undertakings, and soon after we were allowed our cars at school, we did take them out. We seized the opportunity of a Scout camp to drive two cars to Morecambe in the dead of night. Gabriel Carex, whose father was Bishop of Liverpool, was in mine and Tom Arnison who became a solicitor in Appleby was in the other with Bill Jebb from Newcastle. Bill accompanied me many times on trials, went up to Clare College Cambridge, and became a doctor. The aim on our nocturnal expedition was to swim in Morecambe public baths on the sea front. It was about three o'clock in the morning, pitch dark, and as we stripped off ready to take the plunge I felt a firm hand on my shoulder. It was the police: what were we doing? "Just going for a swim."

"I shouldn't do that. They've let all the water out."

We were very lucky. We might have dived into the empty pool. As it was I thought we were going to be run in for indecent exposure or something. There was nothing for it but to own up to coming from Sedbergh and having broken the rules. The policeman could see that we were in big trouble. He knew we could get expelled, and sensibly (and fortunately for us all), decided we had learned our lesson. He never even asked to see our licences. All he said was "Get back into your cars and go back to school. And don't be so stupid again."

We did so, and we weren't. A policeman of a later age might have wanted to make an example of us and it would surely have made good headlines for the tabloids. But this was policing of an older gentler time when a good wigging was just as effective as a heavy hand. The Headmaster GB Smith was a kind, considerate, helpful man, and it was appalling that we broke faith with him. Fortunately he never knew. I was forever grateful to those masters who did find out but did not report us.

My aunt persuaded my trustees to let me trade the MG for a Brooklands Riley, because poor dear, she thought I drove her 1928 2-litre Ballot DH Coupe so well. The Ballot was built like a lorry, yet despite its weight it had a lively turn of speed. She sportingly argued that an eighteen year old should not be encumbered with a saloon car, and even though it was a toss up against a 1½-litre

TT Lea-Francis, the Riley won. Awaiting me, with small aero screens and close-fitting wings on my return from school at the end of my sixth form, was VM 4723. What a marvellous car. It had been developed by JG Parry Thomas just before his death at Pendine in 1927, and his work was carried on by Reid Railton who had been connected with the Thomas Inventions Development company at Brooklands.

Previous page: First car. Reggie's caption in his album says only K + MG. K was Karen Borgens, a 1931-1932 girl friend, 17-year old daughter of Danish family friends. "We got on like a house on fire." She survived to go with Reggie to the Lake District in his next car, a Riley, at weekends. The MG was his father's 1926 MkIV 14/40, a featherweight fabric saloon but a disappointment.

Top: The Riley 9. Classic Post-Vintage Thoroughbred, archetypal British sports car with firm springing, spartan bodywork, and striking appearance.

Right: The Riley on the Windermere ferry.

My Sedbergh housemaster Neville Gorton sent for me: "You have to start thinking about your further education. I understand you would like to go to Oxford and read medicine but you're weak in Latin. You'll either have to get a Credit in School Certificate Latin or take Responsions, which is the Oxford Exam." In 1931 they still insisted that everyone had to do Latin to get in so I had extra coaching. I could manage all right on the rest of my work; sciences, maths and everything else were excellent, but I had to get tuition in Latin at nights.

Despite my best endeavours I still failed. It was deeply shocking but I had to have another shot and after still more coaching I felt confident. The Latin translation was from Caesar De Bello Gallico, Chapter 46 and I virtually learned it off by heart. I went into the exam and sure enough there was Caesar De Bello Gallico Chapter 46. I could do it with my eyes shut and I sailed through without any problems.

Accordingly it was no longer a question of getting in so much as which college I was to go to. Neville Gorton said I could go to Balliol and be a little fish in a big pond or go to Exeter College and be a fairly big fish in a little pond. I said I would rather be a big fish so it was arranged that I should go to Exeter. I still had to get through the entrance exam, although it helped that the former Master Dacre Balsdon had been a master at Sedbergh, and was sub rector of Exeter College. A number of Sedberghians were already there, like Kelly who got an Oxford Blue for rugby.

The Latin entry requirement was eventually dropped, but at the end of the first year you were faced with an exam in Divinity, known as Divvers, dating back to when the college was a religious foundation. The popular ploy was to find a freshman that had done a year and already taken Divvers. For half a crown he would sell you the papers for the last five years, so it was easy to find out which questions came up most often. A day or two beforehand you put the coffee pot on and stayed up all night with your head between your hands learning as much as you could. One question that came up year after year was, "Give a list of the Kings of Israel." If you learnt that off by heart, you were a third of the way to your pass mark. Fifty per cent was necessary, and with the Kings of Israel you already had 33 per cent, so you only needed to scrape through some of the others. The arrangement worked quite well until for the first time in living memory the questions were different. There was no longer the one about the Kings of Israel, but students were instead faced with, "Discuss the merits of Elijah and Elisha as prophets".

It was the year the Conan Doyle brothers, Adrian and Dennis, were taking the exam and one of them wrote: "Far be it for a man of my limited knowledge, to consider expressing a personal opinion on the merits of Elijah and Elisha as prophets, when it is going to be read by such erudite gentlemen as yourselves. But to show that I have some knowledge of my subject I will do a list of the Kings of Israel." Needless to say he failed. And the penalty of failure in those days was that you were sent down.

I went up to Exeter College in October 1931, and loved every minute of it, even though cars were forbidden for a student's first year. I thought of Exeter as just an extension of school until I realised the amount of work I had to do. My tutor was John Wolfenden from Manchester, whose family were stockbrokers, and as things turned out perhaps he was too easygoing. I turned up without having worked for tutorials. He was never irate; he just let me get away with it. I played a lot of rugby and in the summer rowed although not altogether successfully.

I already had some flying experience so I was accepted for the Oxford University Air Squadron. I also became involved with what had been the Oxford University Car Club, which had been badly administered and was bankrupt. The proctors refused to reissue its authority until I talked things over with the creditors, and after being appointed secretary, set out to put the club to rights. It had to be called Oxford University Motor Drivers' Club because the proctors, to say nothing of the creditors, would not allow the old name to be reused.

I did some clinical work in the Radcliffe Infirmary in Oxford and also in Newcastle with Bill Jebb my old Sedbergh companion. The port medical officer gave us jobs. He would write down names and addresses and say, "See what you can do with that lot". It seemed rather rough and ready and one mother thought I was a poor sort of doctor when her little boy had tonsillitis. I was trying to look at his throat, with a sterilised spoon handle to hold his tongue down, but he would not allow me and I chased him round the room trying to see his wretched tonsils.

Another memorable case that betrayed my inexperience occurred when I went to see an elderly lady who was undoubtedly dying. Her relations were standing round the bed looking extremely grave. I quite liked being called doctor, and after I had examined her, they asked how long I thought she'd got. I suppose I must have seemed professional, and I well knew what was likely to happen, so I told them. "When I come around tomorrow I think she will be dead, so sadly you must brace yourselves for this event." I called the following day and sure enough she had died. They thought that I had been most prescient, and I was feeling pretty good about it myself, until the senior member of the family said to me, "Could we now

have the death certificate, Doctor." Well of course I was not qualified. I could not sign a death certificate. I quickly made an excuse about not having the forms with me, and had to go and get the Port Officer to sign one and took it round.

Harry Carleton was Professor of Histology at Oxford University and although I was never really interested in the subject I was obliged to do it. Harry sportingly never tried to force it on me; he was far keener to come motor racing in the long vac. Curiously motor racing was still rather looked down upon at Oxford. It was regarded as not quite a proper sport, and anybody who supported me was frowned upon as well, which may not have done their careers much good.

Far right: *Oxford University Air Squadron Avro 504s over the South Coast. Reggie flew all aircraft in the squadron during 1932-1934, before OUAS moved on to Avro Tutors and Armstrong Whitworth Siskins. He first flew K2367, second aircraft from the camera, on 26 June 1933 from Eastchurch near Sheerness in Kent, with RAF instructor Sergeant Kirkland practising turns and landings, "not very well," according to his logbook. Eastchurch became a key airfield in the Battle of Britain. The 1918 Avro trainer was re-engined with the Lynx radial in 1937, and as the 504N remained in production until 1933. Both Oxford and Cambridge University Squadrons used it.*

Below: *Exeter College, Oxford.*

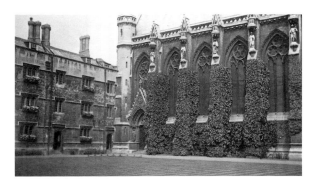

My medical career effectively ended with failure in my physiology finals before Professor Sir Charles Sherrington. A lot of hypodermics had been set out for candidates to give injections to a cat, which was tied up, with muscle recorders connected to a revolving drum. It took a long time to set these animals up with the various strings and levers and muscle attachments, a job done beautifully by laboratory technicians not by us, and I am sorry to say the result in my case was a complete disaster.

I was to administer an injection to the unfortunate animal and describe its reactions, to show that I recognised the effects of various doses of different drugs. However instead of picking up the one that would start the process, which I think was adrenalin, I chose to give it the final *coup de grace* one. This was a fatal dose of strychnine, and when I gave it the animal went into a paroxysm. All the strings broke, the pen flew off the drum, and that was the end of that.

Professor Sherrington did not much like what he had seen, and when I came to take my viva I was asked: "Is it your intention, if you get through these exams and qualify as a doctor, that you will practise?" I felt I could scarcely say I would not, even though it was still unclear whether motor racing was to be an absorbing business. Anyway I did not hesitate. I said yes, that I intended to practise. Many years later I got to know one or two of the dons in the medical school, and they told me that they were going to let me through if I had said no. Their conscience got the better of them however and they decided that in the interests of the great British public it was safer to fail me.

I nevertheless decided to remain at the University because I was enjoying it so much, and do contract law which I passed, and French, which I did not. Then I did a thing called Hakluyt's Voyages, a study of the work of Richard Hakluyt the Elizabethan geographer who recorded the expeditions of English explorers. He regarded the American colonies as relieving England of its unemployed poor, and prophesied no civil peace, until new lands were found for victims of over-population.

However as time passed I grew more and more

The Brooklands Riley Nine was produced from 1927 to 1932. Developed from the Nine family saloon, it was shown as a prototype at the 1927 motor show, with an engine typical of Percy Riley design. It had twin underhead camshaft-operated inclined overhead valves, and although efficient, at 1087cc it was quite small. With two Solex or SU carburettors it developed about 50bhp (37.3kW) at 5000rpm despite having only a two-bearing crankshaft. The fully developed Brooklands Nine of 1927 won a race at 98.62mph (158.3kph) in the hands of Reid Railton, later a close collaborator of Reggie's at Thomson & Taylor with the ERA. The production car could reach 80mph (128.4kph) fully road equipped. Reggie's 1930 Speed Model cost £420 and its specification included a dropped chassis frame, underslung at the rear, although the ride was harsh and weather equipment rudimentary. Despite the low ground clearance it was a strong performer in trials, and Riley developed from it a 6-cylinder, which evolved into the 1½-litre ERA Reggie would drive in 1936.

At the end of 1930 Reggie took his Riley on the London-Exeter Trial, leaving home at Eccles with the battery already flat. He was to pick up Bill Jebb in Newcastle, so drove up the A6 towards Carlisle through fog and falling snow, and with no lights of his own to speak of, was guided by the taillights of lorries. Unfortunately, after leaving the A6 and crossing the Pennines on the A69 east towards Newcastle, there was no lorry traffic and he was soon lost. He was not only driving blind but worried lest he be apprehended for being without lights. Reggie found a farmhouse whose occupants were already celebrating Christmas, used their telephone, and Jebb came in his father's car to tow the Riley into Newcastle.

interested in motor racing. My father's ambition had been to be a doctor. But since he would also have liked to race I decided that if I could not make it as a doctor, the next best thing was for me to be involved with cars. He would have liked that.

My first sports car was also to be my first competition car, and although it was nominally only nine horsepower, I did adore my Riley. It performed well and caused quite a stir when I was allowed to take it to University in my second year. There were not many like it. Reliable and fast, it never had a major failure and any misfortunes it suffered were mostly the fault of the driver. With hood and sidescreens erect the maximum speed was not as high as Riley liked to claim, but the roadholding, braking, and steering were ahead of other cars.

Bill Jebb's father bought him an MG Midget, with a fabric body, in which we did the Land's End Trial in April 1930. Bill drove throughout and we won a gold medal. We had decided on the London-Exeter as the next stage in our motor sporting career, but learned a number of useful lessons in car preparation when I arrived in Newcastle on the end of a towrope.

The following day we got the battery charged and set off for London where the Exeter started. Bill was driving, the roads were covered in snow, and just after Scotch Corner the car skidded and hit the kerb. The Riley had a low centre of gravity for good handling, but tended to skid unexpectedly in the wet. If it got completely out of control there was not much you could do to retrieve it. We were doing about 50mph, and although Bill corrected four of the skids he hit the kerb several times, breaking a wheel as well as the axle casing. He was all for driving on, but the wheel accompanied by its half shaft was coming out of the axle casing, so we had no choice but to stop. We had to be towed back to Northallerton where the axle was rebuilt. A completely new casing was needed and I did not get the car back for some time.

My trustees forbade racing but, on the grounds that I was unlikely to come to much harm in road events, I was allowed to drive in the great Motor Cycling Club (MCC) classic Land's End Trial at Easter 1931. We found to our delight that Sammy (SCH) Davis the talented driver, artist, and as "Casque" sports editor of *The Autocar*, was also driving a Riley. The start was at Virginia Water and we competed for much of the night with FJG Jefferiss in his Alfa Romeo TT car, and later with HJ Aldington (Frazer Nash) who failed to finish. It was a fine night but started to rain at about 6.30am. We climbed the first two hills satisfactorily although hit the bank on the second. On the third and fourth hills the radiator boiled and oil pressure dropped to zero.

We were congratulated in *The Autocar* for managing the climb in second gear, but this was not quite the case. It may have sounded like second but it was really first as a result of a gearbox modification I had made. The Riley was unsuitable for trials and MCC veterans thought it would not get very far with its low ground clearance. I could not do much about that but I could do something about its inappropriate gearing and an engineer in Eccles made me a new gear cluster. This was installed for trials, and while it limited top speed to only about 50mph (80kph), the car would go up hills like a rabbit. The change was kept secret to disguise how a Riley, usually geared for maximum speed, did so well in trials, and the normal gearbox was restored for road driving.

By March 1932 we had built up a lot of trials experience at club level, and persevered once again in major events, such as the Land's End.

FJG Jefferiss came as passenger on this occasion, and as we arrived at the start, the car began to boil. It then oiled up plugs during the night, but otherwise it was a steady and fairly uneventful run, and we climbed all the hills before Launceston without excitement. After Ruses Mill

a tyre went down, and we had to change it for a poor spare, so we had one good competition tread and one bad one. This might have been responsible for skidding on Blue Hills Mine, sending the crowd running, yet we managed to the top and gained a premier award.

Some of the press coverage was less than flattering. *The Motor* said, "RE Tongue was amongst the wildest and, just to make sure that the crowd should witness his display, approached the corner with much 'peeping' of his hooter; after narrowly missing the bank on the outside and the fence on the inside, he scattered the crowd beyond and roared victoriously to the top."

The Light Car was no more generous: "The 1½-litre class numbered 12 failures, all due to insufficient lock or bad judgement. One of the most wild was RE Tongue (Riley) who shot from side to side in such an alarming manner after nearly hitting the bank that the crowd took to its feet and ran. Being an expert in the art of wheel twiddling, however, Tongue got away with it."

The London to Scarborough Trial at the end of July started at South Mimms, on the Great North Road, with a short circuit in the headlamp wiring. Lucas carried out repairs efficiently and we climbed all the hills but suffered a great deal of plug trouble. The Riley boiled on White Horse Hill but so did nearly every car. *Motor Sport* called the hill "a longish affair albeit not very difficult." The car ran well but some gulleys were deep, and there was so much mud towards the end, that it smothered the screen faster than I could wipe it off. I had to look round the side of the screen so got absolutely drenched in filthy splashes. By the

Overleaf: *London-Land's End Trial, March 1932. Spectators turned out in their hundreds to watch mud-plugging trials. Here Reggie supplies the excitement as he runs wide in the Riley, its secret gearbox modification helped on sharp hairpins and steep climbs.*

39

finish in blazing sunshine, on Royal Albert Drive Scarborough, the mud was caked on nevertheless I was able to claim a Premier Award.

The Autocar: "There was the atmosphere almost of a concours d'elegance as the cars came in, and only the mud, especially on the sports cars, reminded one that this had been a very good MCC Trial, not too difficult, certainly not too easy but fair, well organised, and an excellent prelude to a holiday weekend. This indeed was what many people made it, the equipment of the various machines ranging from spare plugs and tins of fuel and racing oil to bathing costumes and beach pyjamas, of which latter incidentally there was no lack at Scarborough all adding to the gaiety of things. Against that the navigator of a Brooklands Riley finished in blazing sunshine in a flying suit with a fur collar, his driver covered in mud in true trials fashion. Excellent amusement, it seems probable that the Scarborough will become an MCC feature."

In November 1932 came what The Autocar called "the annual students' race", otherwise known as the Oxford and Cambridge Reliability Trial, held over a very sporting course in the Chilterns starting from Marlow. Competitors were allowed chains or competition tyres but if they were able to get under way without such aids they received a bonus of five marks, equivalent to starting with one hill's advantage, since a failure counted for five marks. Only seven cars used competition tyres, a soft damp November mist was falling and the hills were at their very worst.

The lack of Oxford support was regrettable but the attitude of the authorities at 'the other place in the Midlands' was shown by a telegram received by the Cambridge secretary on Friday. 'Please get responsible person to wire senior proctor today giving assurance no danger to life or limb in trial.' This was a poser, but Cambridge was fortunate in having a high official of the university as its president, and a suitably baffling reply was concocted.

"Maurice Falkner entered a Targa Florio Itala but the connection with the Sicilian race was obscure. He failed on the first hill and retired on the second with something called camcreek or oleaginous bake, acute lack of oil pressure, or in this case lack of any oil at all as the drain plug had fallen out.

"All the motorcycles failed on Alwe but Thorpe's MG, the first car got up clean, with the passenger perched out on the luggage grid, Goosens' passengers similarly well aft were not so lucky and were bounced right out of his rumble seat into the mud. Leaf mould was a problem on Crowell on the steep portion near the top. Still it was agreed that the trial had been a Good Thing and Cambridge won by 56.8 against 30.6 but Andrew Fairclough the Cambridge secretary won his own cup, which was decreed a Bad Thing. L Butler-Henderson (Frazer Nash) got a first class award just ahead of R E Tongue's Oxford Riley."

In February 1933 The Autocar reported the Inter Varsity Speed Trials:

"A pretty problem faced A M Laing, secretary of the Oxford University Car Club last Friday night, for snow was falling thick and fast over the dreaming spires, and a good entry had been obtained for the Speed – sorry Acceleration – Test on the morrow. Should he send out notices cancelling the event or should he trust that the Eynsham by-pass would be in fit condition on Saturday? Courageously he made his decision. Blow wind! Come, wrack! At least we'll die with harness on our back." This is from Macbeth. Near the end I think when he comes over brave. It starts, "Ring the alarum-bell!"

The snow turned to rain, but apart from a certain amount of slush in places, the kilometre-long stretch of the by-pass was reasonably clear. What a day. Snow falling heavily in other parts of the country caused a number of intending competitors to abandon the attempt to reach the startline. One unhappy group comprising a 2.3 Bugatti and a Montlhéry MG Midget gave up at Stokenchurch. We were sorry that Oliver Bertram's latest acquisition the 12-cylinder Delage, Thomas Fothringham's Bugatti, Robin Jackson's supercharged Magnette, and RGJ Nash with his fearsome The Spook were absentees. Eric Bass could not turn up with his beautiful new Speed Twenty Alvis because he had overturned it in a ditch near Bicester. There was some trouble with the

Inter-Varsity Trial: *Passenger Tom Cross. First Class Award with score 95% including a five-mark bonus for not using competition tyres. Start wet and misty, no difficulty until Alwe Hill, where through loss of horsepower we failed like everybody else. Went on to lunch check - nearly late but got there in 15 minutes extra time limit. After lunch bounced down Kimble Lane, sliding and jumping with all four wheels in the air at once, then crashing down on the undershield. Failed Cromwell due to skidding off. When we checked in we found that we had missed the last hill, so we went back and did it in company with Gough's bodyless Morris Minor. Skidded again, at 50mph on the last downhill on the way to the finish, once more due to mud on brakes and tyres. Fortunately the time limit was abolished due to the long wait at Crowell.*

timing apparatus, so somebody had to be sent to Oxford to buy a whole counterful of cotton reels, nearly fifty being needed to operate the clocks. I was officiating on this occasion and when I found frost-bitten marshals skulking like Achilles in their tents (actually a hired bus), I had replacements sent round the course in an ambulance.

Oxford won the class for semi-sports cars up to 850cc whereupon Andrew Fairclough won the next up in his Salmson. The runs were separated by ten minutes sometimes to take account of the traffic, the cotton-thread timing device, and the weather. Next class up saw an Alvis Silver Eagle, lose out to a Ford V8 with a similar car third. Bickford and Powys-Lybbe won the 1500cc class but claimed some misunderstanding on the grounds that their engine was 1646cc, but the organisers told them that they could keep the trophy because they were such thoroughly good chaps. Great sporting spirit.

Kenneth Evans found that using funny-smelling dope in his supercharged MG was a positive disadvantage because it clogged the carburettor. He removed the instrument, setting fire to the float chamber, and reassembled it, which seemed to frighten the little car into making ftd at 33.6 seconds crossing the finishing line at over 100mph. Oliver Bertram's old red grand prix Sunbeam was entered by the Duke of Grafton, who had just gone up to Cambridge, but it was suffering from clutch slip.

I had no mechanic at the Inter-varsity Speed Trials at Gopsall Park in March 1933 and won nothing, finishing eighth. RVC Bolster competed in a Frazer Nash, Whitney Straight (Bentley) Oliver Bertram (Vauxhall), and Kenneth Evans (MG) also took part. Bolster won the class for racing cars up to 1100cc in a GN. The Riley ran in two classes but was not very fast because the foot brake jammed on. Still, it was an enjoyable day having entered as "A Vincent", a *nom de guerre* I used in an effort to conceal my motor sporting activities from the family trustees. They had given permission for me to enter in a few road events but not in speed trials. They were after all *in loco parentis* in almost all aspects of my life. They not only administered the cash my father had left, but also had the responsibility of looking after the investments in my grandfather's Trust.

In April 1933 I was a passenger in Bill Jebb's Morgan for the Land's End as my Riley still had its high gear ratio in from the Inter-Varsity Speed Trial and I was too broke to have it changed back. The Trustees paid me an allowance, and if I used it all up before the end of the month, I had to make do as best I could. The event started from Heston, the aerodrome close by what would become Heathrow, and I seized the opportunity of going for a pleasure flight at night in a cabin machine, a closed aircraft as opposed to one with the customary open cockpit.

One of the most notable drives I ever had in the Riley was with Edgar Hickling, when we went from Land's End to John o'Groats. A friend of my father's, Edgar was an accomplished engineer who among other things helped us make our first canoe on Anglesey. We decided to drive from Lands End to John o'Groats in twenty-four hours. It was an adventure that would have appealed to my father, so we went off ostensibly for a holiday, laying up a cache of petrol for the midnight part of the journey to Eccles since all-night filling stations were few and far between. We sent a telegram to the family from Penzance Post office establishing the time and date. It read, "Weather not good Cornwall Stop Propose trying North of Scotland."

The Riley's seats were so close that if Edgar nodded off I could steer it from the passenger's side. It was even possible to change gear from there without using the clutch, although there was no synchromesh. We got as far as Inverness before taking a wrong turning. Edgar was tired, I was not paying attention, and instead of going north he pointed us down the Great Glen alongside Loch Ness, where the splendid A82 from Inverness to Fort William was under construction. The detour delayed us by about two hours, because it was not until I woke up in the passenger seat that we discovered what had happened. We were half way to Fort William before the mistake could be put right, and arrived in John o'Groats just twenty-six hours after we left Lands End. Had it not been for our blunder we would have just about managed it in twenty-four hours.

We decided not to stay at John o'Groats, but went on to Thurso some 20 miles along the coast, past the Castletown aerodrome where I was to be stationed briefly during the war. We arrived exhausted wearing Sidcote suits, bulky flying gear, because the Riley was draughty and wet and had no heater. With goggles and the heavily padded one-piece clothing I went into a hotel to ask for a room. I was desperately tired but went upstairs, the proprietor helped me off with the Sidcote suit, and turned the taps on for a hot bath. It had been an arduous trip and I was beginning to doze off in the warm water when I suddenly remembered Edgar still in the car outside. I rang down to reception: "…would you please tell the gentleman asleep in the grey Riley 9 outside to come in. I have got a hot bath waiting for him". We had covered 2,000 miles and never so much as removed a spark plug.

Breakfast at Taunton. Tyre blew on the first hill (Doverhay). Bent rear axle so had to be pushed down backwards. We waited until all the other Morgans had got out before being able to get back to Porlock to change the tyre and repair the axle. Lost two hours. Climbed the next three hills (including Beggar's Roost) but failed three following, two because of insufficient left lock and Hustyn due to wheelspin. Finished two hours late with bent front axle and broken T-Bar.

James went to St Ives and I went back to his flat by train overnight. He wrote me a letter a few days later telling how driving from St Ives to Totnes he had burst the rear tyre on a corner and finished up in a hedge. He felled a tree in the accident and it landed in the passenger seat. Lucky I went home by train I think.

3 MOTOR RACING 1932

In 1932 I became motoring editor of Isis, like many an enthusiast before and since, in order to obtain cars from manufacturers for road test. One of the first was the new J2 MG, which for its size and type had quite a lot to commend it. It was beautifully proportioned, well finished, and carefully made in a world of mass-produced rivals. It was a car of some distinction. We felt mass produced cars were made with less care and were deeply suspicious of pressed 'tin' bodies.

It was an extremely wet and windy day when we tested the MG. After leaving the works the first thing that came to our notice was the fierceness of the clutch, but after a few miles we became accostomed to the short travel, and found it very pleasant, the getting away from a standing start being excellent.

The car, although not capable of very high speeds, attained 72mph, with the windscreen in the upright position under difficult conditions. This speed was rather on the low side, but the car had been in use for some time and had not received even the normal servicing, even the plugs had not been cleaned. In third gear 55mph was attained.

Even if the car had only been capable of 70mph the higher speeds would not have been missed, as we felt that the car would run at 55mph indefinitely, which together with the uncanny road-holding capabilities and the light steering made it possible to maintain a high average speed with complete safety and comfort. Such averages are possible over indifferent roads, as the springing for so small a car is exceptional, which with the low centre of gravity imparts an amazing stability to the car. The braking is excellent even on wet roads.

For some the steering may be too low geared, but this maintains the light movement, and there is not the slightest tendency to wander even when a bend is misjudged at fairly high speed.

The gear change itself

is very simple, and it is impossible to miss the silent selection of a gear within wide limits of the throttle. The gears must be used to obtain the best results, especially as the gearbox is of the twin-top type. The gear change itself is by remote control, and is one of the few we have noticed to be free from rattles. In fact the sturdy build of the car gave us the impression that, even with hard use, rattles would not easily develop.

The bodywork has been vastly improved on this year's model by larger wings and a neat running board, which give the car a pleasing appearance, as well as keeping it clean. The entrance and exit of the car is made easy by two large doors, which is not the case with many sports cars of today.

The windscreen may be folded flat on the scuttle, in which position two wind-cowls protect the driver and passenger.

The excellent finish and complete equipment of the car is exemplified by such details as the tinted driving mirror, which prevents the driver being annoyed by the reflection of the sun or the lights of a following car at night. Another example of the excellent equipment is the spare plug and holder under the bonnet.

The car is in every way ideal for those wanting a cheap two-seater sports car capable of a lively performance. In brief: Price £199.10s. Engine, 850cc 8HP. Weight, 11½cwt laden. Petrol consumption 35mpg (min) petrol supply 12 gallons."
RET

(Isis)

The J2 Midget two-seater was the first MG for which the makers claimed 80mph (128.75kph), but this was a speed of which early production examples at least were scarcely capable. *The Autocar's* road test recorded 80.35mph (129.31kph) with the windscreen folded flat, but owners were sceptical. There was deep suspicion that the press test car had been carefully tuned.

The 4-cylinder overhead camshaft engine of only 847cc was wonderfully efficient, and at a chassis price of £199.10.0 (£199.50p) the car was something of a bargain. After MG discontinued the J1, J3 and J4, the cycle-winged J2 was re-equipped with swept wings and running boards to complete the style and specification of the classic two-seater. It had a close-ratio gearbox, centre-lock wire wheels, and a large octagon-backed dial served as both speedometer and tachometer. The engine revs were marked off on the face for third and top gears. For an extra 12 guineas (£12.60) de luxe equipment included an electric clock, Ashby steering wheel, stone guards on the headlamps, oil thermometer, bonnet strap, racy-looking cam-and-lever-type fuel fillers, stop tail and reverse lamp, and water temperature gauge. Leather upholstery and pneumatic cushions were standard although *The Autocar's* opinion that thanks to the cutaway doors both driver and passenger had unlimited freedom of movement was unconvincing. Reggie's road test of the 1934 J2 MG was unequivocal.

I had been in a quandary. I took the J2 to the top of a hill on the Benson by-pass, dived down on to the straight, but it would only reach 65mph (104.3kph). Perhaps it was off-colour. I gave it the benefit of some doubt and said it could do 72mph (115.6kph) and awaited the wrath of MG's founder the great Cecil Kimber.

I was not motoring editor for long. I had more

or less implied that the J2 did what the manufacturers claimed for it, provided it was taken to the top of a steep hill, and enjoyed a following wind. Kimber told me off and said that he never wanted anything more to do with me. He would certainly never let me have a test car again.

A good deal changed when in due course I became an MG customer. Neither of us could foresee how well we would come to know one another, and that I would race two MGs, the K3 Magnette and the R-type all over the Continent.

Right: *GX 72, Reggie's first Aston Martin that led to his involvement with the works team and eventually Le Mans. Cycle-type wings that steered with the front wheels and stylish 2-seater body made it the archetypal sports car of the 1930s. GX72 had already taken part in rallies with a previous owner C Anthony, finishing 11th in the 1932 Royal Scottish Automobile Club Scottish Rally.*

Below: *November 1933, Inter-Varsity Trial. Reggie relaxes with the Aston Martin at the foot of Crowell, one of the hills that had to be climbed non-stop to gain marks towards an award. Car 22 behind is Kenneth Evans's MG J2 in a scene that epitomises a branch of motor sport almost unknown outside Britain.*

In the end Lord Nuffield held a function at the Savoy to present me with an inscribed tankard thanking me for what I had done for the marque. All was in the end forgotten or at any rate forgiven. Later I often met Cecil in London for convivial lunches at the Steering Wheel Club, from at least one of which I had to drive him home.

I bought a beautiful blue two-seater Le Mans model Aston Martin, GX 72 for the Alpine Trial in August 1933. I decided against the Riley, because I thought the cooling might not be up to it, but in the event Donald Healey put up a brilliant show with his. The Alpine regulations demanded

sealed radiators; so frequent replenishment was impossible, and I feared the little Riley would overheat on long climbs at high altitude. I was sorry afterwards that I forsook the Riley, because although the Aston was superbly reliable it was heavy, and often lost time because the turning circle was too wide for the sharp bends.

Edgar Hickling was the obvious choice to accompany me in my first real competition with GX72. The Aston was no racing car, and although it looked like one, it was essentially a sports car. The start was at Merano in the Northern Italian Dolomites, the finish at Nice on the French Riviera, and how I enjoyed the timed climbs up mountain passes on gravel roads, long before they were metalled and modernised and widened.

Excitement prevailed from the moment we left the Aston Martin works on a bright autumn Sunday afternoon. Not much of importance happened during the preparation of the car, or on the run to Manchester and back, running-in low compression 7:5:1 pistons. There was no room for luggage, and although we thought we

Aston Martin and the Alpine Trial

In 1933 Reggie decided to take up motor sport seriously, beginning with the Alpine Trial. The pedigree of the *International Criterium des Alpes* went back to the Austrian Alpine trials of pre-1914, organised by well-to-do clubs, for the encouragement of car development and design. Competitions, it was believed, helped manufacturers to improve their products, and public trials represented a shop-window for the successful. The route of the Alpine lay across the mountain frontiers of France, Germany, Austria, Italy, Switzerland, and Yugoslavia and besides spectacular scenery encompassed some of the highest roads in Europe.

Even modern engines lose three per cent of their power for every 1000ft (305m) of altitude, so the modest output at sea level of 1930s cars was seriously curtailed at the top of the Stelvio Pass, 9048ft (2758m) high. A J2 MG Midget produced 36bhp (26.84kW) at sea level. At the top of the Stelvio this was reduced to a feeble 26bhp (19.4kW) or so, about the same as the superseded M-type that would take nearly half a minute to reach 50mph (80.2kph) and had a top speed of about 60mph (96.3kph). A lot of low-speed high-revving climbing in the intermediate gears brought the risk of overheating. In the 1930s there was no outright winner of the Alpine. Competitors strove for a Coupe des Alpes, or in 1931-1934 a Coupe des Glaciers for a penalty-free run.

were taking the absolute minimum, we had to construct a sort of wooden tray on the back to carry spares for any eventuality. We took too much of course, making the car unduly heavy, so it did not go as well as it should have.

We had an anxious period worrying that something vital had been forgotten, but as soon as we left Feltham, we seemed to leave our cares behind us. We set out for Dover ahead of the second car LM8, a former works car that had been bought by CH Wood, with Leonard Hill co-driving. Wood was a wealthy individual whose everyday car was an Alfa Romeo, and was known as "Happy", largely because he always appeared so miserable. He worked at Aston for the fun of it; he had a substantial private income and had been an apprentice at Dennis, taking over the service department when LG Hornsted left. Apart from a change of plugs, all went well until we stopped for tea near Farningham, about half way to the ferry. Here Edgar discovered that he had lost a coat with his passport and driving licences in a pocket. Back we went to Feltham to see if it had been left in the Aston works.

On the way we stopped at Kingston Police Station, since it was in Kingston that we had changed the plugs, but the coat had not been brought in. When we got to the factory of course it was closed, and we had to find George from the Service Department, which we did by going round all Feltham's pubs. This still produced no coat. We called at Staines Police Station and also CH Wood's hotel, the Red Lion at Hounslow, to no avail. It was now 11.30pm so we set off rather hopefully perhaps once again for Dover. It was foggy and when we arrived we slept on the promenade to the accompaniment of hooters and fog signals. We found a hotel at 7am, had a bath and breakfast, and telephoned Staines Police Station.

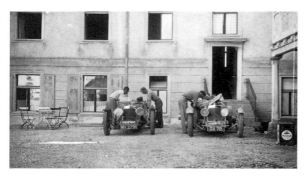

Previous page: *For the Alpine Trial GX72 had lightweight mudguards that did not shroud the brake drums. Air circulation round the brakes was crucial on Alpine descents. Checking in at St Moritz, officials are joined by a crowd of schoolboy spectators.*

Left, top:*Adventure on the way to the Alpine. Running repairs carried out, including replacing much of the wiring. By the following morning both cars were ready to resume their journey to the start of the rally.*

Left, bottom: *Reggie to the rescue at Santa Maria after finding LM8 crashed with Leonard Hill in cap and Edgard Hickling Reggie's co-driver with goggles and pipe on right.*

Top right: *Humphrey Symons, motoring correspondent of The Sunday Times and keen driver, took part in the Alpine in the first-ever works team from SS-Jaguar. Rough roads had already cost his SS1 a headlamp as he refuelled at Guillestre near Briançon. Two of the three team cars failed with warped cylinder heads.*

1ST STAGE: *Successful despite wheelspin and a jammed throttle due to ignition lever coming off. Lost five marks on the Pordoi. On the* **2ND LEG** *lost 37 marks on the Stelvio, after having had to reverse about eight times due to Aston's bodyshop replacing the steering arm the wrong way round, reducing our steering lock. The gear ratios were not well spaced for climbs.*

3RD STAGE: *Manfred Schicht in a Röhr, a lively little German car with an opposed 4-cylinder engine and independent suspension like a Volkswagen, got between the two Astons and we made up our mind to catch him tomorrow.*

4TH STAGE: *Two punctures, but gained 4 points on the Röhr, which put me 2 points ahead. The two Astons were together again and we had to run to time to finish fourth and fifth. Lost 12 marks on the Galibier. Valve rocker almost broken.*

5TH STAGE: *OK Arrived Nice: We were mostly on bad roads but the car stood up to it. We needed different gear ratios and lighter bodywork. Edgar was a marvellous passenger and skilled mecanicien. When we stopped in Turin I was surprised to see most of the competitors draining their sumps in the main road. We did at least drain ours out in the country. We were able to pass Donald Healey's Riley going into Grenoble late. He finished second in Group V, up to 1100cc, behind WE Belgrave's MG. There was only one penalty point in it. Coupes des Alpes for manufacturers' teams won by Ford, Hotchkiss, Adler, Riley and MG and Coupes des Glaciers by Ford, Bugatti, Alfa Romeo, Riley, and MG. Other fine performances by Daimler-Benz, Frazer-Nash, Vauxhall, Singer, Aston-Martin, and Triumph.*

We awaited the arrival of Wood and Hill, on the chance that they might have the missing coat and its vital contents, but they had not.

I decided I would take the ferry to Calais leaving Edgar behind to go to London and get a new passport. On his way he took the precaution of phoning the RAC from Dover Station. It was good news. Its London office had been told a workman had found the coat and papers. The bad news was that the man was working and could not bring them in until 5pm.

The RAC put them on a train, and Edgar had them by 9pm, arriving in Calais by cargo boat that evening. We arrived in Langres just short of Dijon next day, after only one mishap, when a back wheel locked solid due to an Aston mechanic having left a bolt loose. It was fortunately not serious and the car did not skid. We had marvellous rooms in Davos Platz on the second day, then ran out of petrol at the top of the Flüelapass and sat wondering what to do next, when the other Aston came up.

We thought they would have been a long way ahead of us. We continued on our way soon afterwards behind them, until just after the Italian Swiss Border at Santa Maria, on a particularly sharp corner we noticed the wooden barricade on the outside was badly out of shape. Sure enough, there in a field was LM8 badly bent, with CH Wood and Leonard Hill looking unhappy. We stopped to help, and I felt obliged to point out, that they no longer seemed likely to do the Alpine in that car. It was terribly battered and a short circuit had burnt out all the wiring.

After manhandling it back on to the road, we

took it to a farm further down the valley, which turned out to have an elaborate hot water system. It had a boiler furnace, a huge fire with chains and valves and weights and all sorts of things attached. It was like a smithy and just what we needed. We got the bellows going, and with the fire roaring, bit-by-bit we straightened the bent pieces as best we could. To our great delight the Aston went through the whole of the Alpine Trial without further attention, and was not only classified as a finisher, but also came third in its class.

Next day we arrived in Merano, drank Gancia Spumante until the garage was available, then worked hard getting the cars ready for technical inspection and scrutineering on Sunday. With the help of the garage owner who interpreted, we swapped autopulses, filters, drained the oil and did a thousand and one things to pass the inspection. I was sent away to cut all but one coil off the condenser. So on Monday we started.

The Motor said British light cars were overwhelmingly superior and a team of Vauxhalls came second in Group III although a long way behind the winning Adlers. Curiously the Vauxhalls scarcely merited a mention in press reports of the rally, probably because they were a General Motors entry and driven by foreigners, HS Wiwell, L Mallemann, and AB Buertin. One of the Hotchkiss drivers was WF Bradley the veteran journalist, and one of the Daimler-Benz team was Alfred Neubauer, the Mercedes-Benz team manager. We were fourth with 56 penalty points in Group IV 1100cc to 1500cc behind Jack Hobbs (Riley) with 3 penalty points,

AG Gripper (Frazer-Nash) with 7 penalties, and Wood and Hill in the other Aston Martin with 37 penalties. The rival Röhr, driven by Schicht, was fifth in the class with 56 penalties. It was a good result although disappointing not to beat the Riley, having forsaken it in favour of the Aston. Went to Aston when we got back. Everyone including Bertelli was pleased with the show put up by the two cars.

I pulled up at a filling station during the Alpine and found a car with the wheels jacked up. The owner was carefully moving each wheel round until all the hubcaps were exactly in line, with the makers' name showing where it should be. He told me he had seen other cars with their hubcaps going any old how and wanted his to be straight and matching. I had not the heart to tell him that by the time he cameto the next corner they would be higgledy piggledy again. If he had a Frazer Nash of course at least the back wheel hubs would remain in step.

Top left: *Alpine idyll. Loose surfaced hairpin on the Pordoi, one of the classic Alpine Trial passes with Beris Wood driving Leonard Hill's Aston Martin. The 1933 event was one of the toughest Alpines for years, and only three out of 121 cars completed the course unpenalised.*

Bottom left: *Below. Hill (driving) and Wood celebrate their arrival at Pontresina near St Moritz after tackling the Bernina Pass.*

The 1933 Nice Grand Prix took place on 6 August, the day after the finish of the Alpine. From the stands Reggie and Edgar Hickling watched former champion driver Felice Nazzaro drop the starter's flag for a memorable race, along the Promenade des Anglais, then through the palm-lined gardens amongst the houses and out again to the seafront. Nuvolari, having just left Scuderia Ferrari with Borzacchini, was at the height of his powers racing new Maseratis and older 2.9 Alfa Romeos as independents.

The heat was intense and the racing close. During a keen duel with Philippe Etancelin (Alfa Romeo), Nuvolari overheated his brakes so much that he had to stop and adjust them, leaving him 34 seconds behind Marcel Lehoux (against whom Reggie would race and befriend until his fatal accident in ERA R3B at Deauville in 1936) and nearly a minute behind Etancelin. Nuvolari caught up with Lehoux and with 45 of the 95 laps gone, pressed Etancelin into a spin on a hairpin, gaining a lead he never lost. He won by a minute and a half.

What a spectacle the Grand Prix was. I made up my mind to drive my Aston round the circuit. Best do it at night I thought, very late, even though it was bound to make a bit of noise. Accordingly in the early hours I took it out of its garage and started driving round. One or two patrolling policemen seemed to be waving at me cheerfully enough so I did not take much notice. Next time round there seemed to be more, and they were strung across the road. I decided not to stop; they had given me so little warning. I found a gap and drove past, managing not to hit any, but went straight back to the hotel and wakened Edgar: "This town is not for us," I told him. "I expect to be on a charge any moment, and it may take days to clear everything up. We are better out of it."

We loaded up, paid our bill, left Nice, and drove as fast as we could to Calais. We drove all night until we were so tired we had to stop. We went into a field, lay down on the grass – it was summer, the weather was lovely – and fell fast asleep disturbed only by visions of long blue lines of white-gloved gendarmes. The passport control, the police, and even the customs officials made no mention of the matter when we reached Calais, and we crossed safely to Dover. I often wonder how long the Nice Police spent looking for me.

There were limits to what I could do with the Brooklands Riley 9. It now seemed a sort of novice's racing car, and since the Aston Martin was to be specifically for events such as the Alpine, I needed a practical road car. I part-exchanged the Riley for a second-hand Ford V8 coupe. A useful workhorse, I paid £60 for it, the registration was ALT 600 and it was one of the early V8 two-seater dropheads. I did almost 40,000 miles of cheap, reliable, trouble-free motoring with it. The front end wandered a bit if you went into a corner too fast, but that was its only real fault, and I motored it to race meetings all over Europe. The only big setback it suffered was when the back axle failed, but thanks to the service network Ford had in every reasonably sized town, it was replaced in three hours for less than 25/- (£1.25).

The V8 was left in the open at night; yet the paintwork remained as good as new and it even acquitted itself well when, on the

Below: *Reggie (left) with Roy Percival's RAC Rally Ford V8-40 in RAC Rally 26-30 March 1935 based at Eastbourne, in which they won a First Class Award. One of the most charismatic of the pre-war series of Ford V8s, it offered more speed and power than anything at the price. Assembled in Ireland with the 3.6-litre American engine, rather than the smaller one introduced later for the British market.*

spur of the moment, I entered it for a reliability trial. I also drove a saloon Ford V8 BGW 239 in the RAC Rally with Roy Percival, and like my coupe it ran completely trouble-free, earning top marks for speed, reliability and comfort. For the price a Ford V8 was a marvellous all-purpose car. Dick Seaman had one too and swore by it, although he had it modified by LMB Suspensions, Leslie Ballamy's firm. His was also equipped with a split front axle and a two-speed Columbia rear axle.

After the Alpine and inspired by the Nice Grand Prix I wanted to enter the Aston Martin for a road race. But the following month, on 9 September 1933, came the Motor Cycling Club (MCC) Brooklands Meeting. This was the track's heyday, with 335 entries, a day packed from 11am to 7.30pm with 17 races (13 of which were for cars), huge fields, high speeds, and *The Motor* called it the most successful club meeting ever at Brooklands. The weather was perfect and although the attendance was not large the right crowd was there and "the whole atmosphere was one of enthusiasm." Those present were real "fans" of what the magazine happily called "the game".

At Brooklands I ran as A Vincent in the second one-hour trial, in which there were three classes, unlimited, 1600cc, 1100cc, and 850cc. The unlimited cars had to do 25 laps to qualify for a premier award, the 1600s 24 laps, 1100s 22 laps, and the 850s 21 or 18 laps for a silver, and 16 for a bronze. Accordingly almost everybody got a prize although it did mean that the big 4½-litre Bentleys were passing the J2 MGs of Maurice Toulmin and ATK Debenham every lap and a half or so. My passenger was Aston Martin racing mechanic Peter Caiger.

I took the Aston Martin to the works at Feltham on Monday to have the gear ratios raised, then went down to practice on Friday, and did a best lap of 79.04mph (126.88kph). On Saturday we changed plugs. The two lap handicaps were

popular, with 60 starters and I went out in my event at 1.10, finishing third, reaching 5300 revs down Railway Straight, which was nearly 100mph. I was only beaten by MW May's 2-litre Alvis and RC Murton-Neale's 3-litre Bentley, which gave me only six seconds.

In the One Hour Trial I had three-quarters of a lap lead on the other Aston (CH Wood) but the clutch gave up after 30 minutes running and I had to cruise at 4000rpm. Still, finishing fifth in the class was satisfactory. Aston Martins were first, second, third and fifth so Bertelli was very pleased with everything. The average speed for the hour was 72.02mph (115.61kph), the car ran well and at times must have lapped at over 80mph (128.42kph), although GE Taylor's Wolseley Hornet managed 26 laps averaging 72.81mph (116.88kph). Wood managed 27 laps at 75.34mph (120.94kph), as did CH Wagstaff in a Lea-Francis.

Unusually, even for the relaxed atmosphere of Brooklands, there was an extra competitor in heat one. Just before the handicapper flagged off the last pair of cars, a Wolseley drove down the finishing straight to the fork. Nobody expected the driver to carry on out to the track, but before the astonished officials could do anything about it, the car proceeded to do an entire lap. By the time it had completed a circuit in the middle of

Top: *Classic Trials hill, the Nailsworth Ladder near Stroud, in the NW London MC London to Exeter Trial 1933; Reggie clips the verge in the Aston Martin.*

the track, the officials were out in force and managed to turn it back on to the finishing straight, where a barrier arrested its progress. It was, it seems, a spectator who caught the enthusiastic Brooklands mood.

---

16 Sept 1933. *Wigan Infirmary £100 Trial.* Two laps of a 50-mile course with secret checks on average speed. Passenger my cousin Delia Stephens. Award: Nil.

Only got home at 5.30am so was not up in time for the beauty contest (parade of the cars) at 10.30am. I only got up at 10 giving me time to get car ready. Arrived Wigan half an hour before the start. All OK. Delia excellent. Climbed all hills on time but lost on secret checks after tying for first place. On one of the hills, Howitt, we passed a Ford on one corner to cheers from the crowd. Very pleased on both laps. Went back to presentation at 10pm after being home for food and a bath. They have asked me to help in organisation next year.

23 Sept 1933. *Brighton Speed Trials.* (Ran as A. Vincent) 1500cc sports Mechanic TJGJ. Award: Nil (Time 37.4s 48.13mph 4th in class).

Went to TJGJ's on Friday night. Went down to Brighton on Saturday morning. Rained all day. Soaked. Aston Martin went quite well. One run. Morris-Goodall said that I was the fastest unblown 1500cc but I think he must have been wrong. Watched the entire programme, then left having to carry screens etc. Could hardly see in the rain; my goggles were no good and neither was my screen. Got up to 5000rpm in first, second, and third and just got into top on the line. Went off together with Commander RT Grogan's supercharged Nash. He had ten yards lead then he left me. He won four or five events. HJ Aldington

---

could not get his Nash to start for some time.

30 Sept 1933. *Shelsley Walsh Hill Climb.* (Ran as A. Vincent) 1500cc sports; Mechanic Phipps; Award: Nil; Time: 57.4sec. Went up to practise on Thursday with Ella. Didn't remove wings or anything. Left Oxford at 8.30 in Aston Martin with Phipps in his MG. Arrived Shelsley at 11am. Met White, another Aston Martin owner, and drove his car in from the car park to borrow his racing wheels as they were smaller. The first run OK except for a false start. White's wheels were too small so changed back to my own. Got a second run through, arranging to return to the bottom of the hill immediately with Mays. It was quite good but third was too high. I was getting 5500 revs in second. Not much skidding on the corners. On the air afterwards with the BBC, which said: "A Vincent made a gentlemanly getaway and proceeded up the hill in a dignified manner." Faint praise I thought. Back in Oxford by 7pm. Phipps very helpful. Great meeting, Mays broke the record, then Whitney Straight broke it twice.

21 Oct 1933. *Aston Clinton hill climb.* (A. Vincent) 1500cc Sports and Unlimited Handicap (Quarter mile course). Mechanic: Phipps; Award: Nil; times: 27.56 secs, 23.36 secs, 23.6 secs.

Small meeting, very pleasant, beaten by Goodall's Aston Martin, which he had just sold. Benjafield's Railton Terraplane was the fastest car there. Hectic ride home. MG Garages gave me dud plugs.

18 Nov 1933. *Inter-Varsity Trial.* Passenger: Phipps. Award: first Class (Bonus of 5 marks for not using competition tyres). Arrived at start latish. Changed plugs, affixed numbers and dashed off just on time. (Kenneth had carburation trouble and so were delayed leaving

Macs Garage. He had been staying the night with me). OK after tightening shockers. Easy run to lunch check where we were early. Climbed Crowell with bouncing. Delayed at foot. Kimble has been cut out this year. Thank God! New hill called Cab Calloway failed almost everyone. Very muddy and steep. No run. Skidded off road at first bend. Finished a little tired and returned to Oxford where sat and drank beer. (KDE, Phipps, I and passenger to KDE)

Met Dugdale of Autocar and had a long talk although I didn't know him. Aston ran marvellously, better than I'd hoped. Gear ratio just right. A marvellous trial.

John Dugdale was two years younger than Reggie and became a close friend. When they met he had just joined *The Autocar* as assistant to SCH Davis. In 1935 Dugdale bought a new N-type MG Magnette, which he raced on British tracks in the 1930s, then went to Germany as witness to Goldie Gardner's successful MG record attempts with EX 135 in 1938 and 1939. Dugdale won the MC as a captain in the RASC then moved to the United States in 1949 where he represented firstly Rootes and later Jaguar until he retired in 1980. An acclaimed author and journalist, John Dugdale died in May 2000.

The Motor credited Reggie Tongue with only a second class award in the Inter-Varsity Trial, which upset him because he amends its report that claims in "Cambridge's easy victory over the dark blues," only four first class awards. An annual event over a 60-mile course, through the chalky Chilterns, it had nine observed sections with names like Ucumunstuck, and Highruse, although one, Wooley and Wilde, was deleted after what was called police interference. Forty entries included the customary Frazer-Nashes, MGs, and Rileys but there was also an ancient Amilcar reputedly once owned by Parry Thomas, a team of Trojans rescued from a coal mine, and a Morris Minor chassis with bucket seats only. The collection of doubtful vehicles bore witness more to enthusiasm than science. Lunch was taken at the Lambert Arms after which *The Motor* commented on Reggie's good performance on the difficult Crowell.

Among the competitors was Sir Alasdair W MacRobert, a Cambridge friend of Reggie's and one of the ill-fated brothers (the others, Roderic and Iain, he also knew well) who lost their lives flying. Their mother Lady Rachel MacRobert famously sponsored an aircraft for the RAF, known as MacRobert's Reply in their memory, a gesture Reggie welcomed in his 1941 diary. Having known them all, he wrote: "I know that it is just what they would have wanted." Alasdair MacRobert was driving a Crossley in the Inter-Varsity Trial and was reported as making a fine recovery on Crowell after a broadside half way up, only to fail through wheelspin near the top. Kenneth Evans (Oxford) MG nearly got up Cab Calloway, which proved almost unclimbable, only the Cambridge secretary WBM Fraser reached the top with his Alvis.

28 Nov 1933. *Went to first BRDC dinner and film show as Hon. A D Chetwynd's guest) Excellent Show.*

9 Dec 1933. *North West London Motor Club. Passenger Phipps. Award second Class. Team Placing: second to Ford team in class B (team: KD Evans, Miss D Evans (MG Midgets), and RE Tongue) This was the first time that I had competed in the Gloucester. Hills were short but snappy. Quite an enjoyable trial. Arrived at Staines. Put on special small wheels with competition tyres (18in instead of 22in) after a hectic time rushing round London trying to buy Champion R.3 spark plugs.*

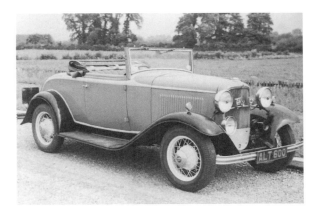

Top and left: *ALT 600 Reggie's V8-18, Canadian-built and the first Ford V8 sold in Britain. Rated at 30HP for British taxation purposes, it was expensive to run.*
For a car that cost £295 new (2-door saloon was £230 so he was being extravagant) with leather upholstery £7 10s extra, the annual road tax at £1 per horsepower was £30, or 10% of the purchase rice. Modern equivalent would have been £1200 a year for a new Ford Focus.
At 16mpg (17.6l/100km) the V8 also used quite a lot of fuel, but a sporting driver could use it on the Inter Varsity Trial in November 1935 without worrying about scratches from the hedgerows.

Obtained at Lex Garage, Piccadilly. Just on starting line when a lady pointed out that the rear tyre was nearly flat. Ran out of control slowly. Blew it up; thought a valve was the trouble; changed the valve; dashed off. Sailed up Maidens Grove in dark. Went through night (well-organised stops for coffee) OK. Old Stanway stop and restart difficult. Slow as we were in ruts (unseen in the dark). Also one tyre was at 50lbs/sq in pressure, which didn't help matters. May have lost marks through this stop and restart, and so forfeited premier award, although OK everywhere else.

Breakfast at Cheltenham. Left OK. Pumped up tyre now and again as we did in the night. Changed plugs. While at lunch check man came in and told us that our tyre was now absolutely flat. Pushed the car out of the control quarter-mile. Took off Sidcote suit, put valve into tyres. Changed both wheels with one jack and blew up tyres. Time 15min. Soon caught up field but things looked pretty bad as larger ratio with these big wheels and no tread at all unsuitable. Slid a bit on Iles Lane due to ice but going fairly fast so slid upwards. Nailsworth Ladder easy meat even without tread on tyres. AM is a marvellous car. Very fast on some hills. Climbed them all.

Had lunch with Kenneth and Co. Returned to Oxford and so to town. Had a puncture in Oxford. (Valve came right off the tube).

Motor Sport said that 14 competitors retaining 98 per cent of their marks obtained silver cups, 32 got silver medals for retaining 90 per cent of their marks, and there were 66 bronze medals for retaining 75 per cent of their marks. Accordingly only 23 starters came away with nothing at all. Seventeen cars retired, so only six finishers went home disappointed. Kenneth Evans was among the silver cups, Doreen Evans won the ladies award and Reggie was offended that the report said: 'RE Tongue (Aston Martin) got into rather a mess on one hill although he does admit to hitting the bank mildly at speed without stopping.' Following the time check at Bull's Cross, there was what it called an 'evil acceleration test' on Bismore in which cars had to be restarted on a 1 in 6 gradient, and accelerate for 50 yards in under 12 seconds. The previous year it was 15 seconds and the extra 3 seconds proved the last straw for all but 43 competitors. *Motor Sport* picked out good performances by both Evanses and by Reggie.

Phipps was marvellous throughout the trial The sliding cars on one hill pushed the loose stones aside putting the following cars at a disadvantage, so a party of local small boys, determined to see fair play, carefully put them back again after each car passed.

30 Dec 1933. MCC *London to Exeter*
(Stiffest Exeter yet, *The Motor* said, only 17 out of 250 competitors were able to claim a premier award, Simms Hill failed 95 per cent, Fingle Bridge took a heavy toll, and the weather was 'variegated').
Passenger: TJGJ Award: Nil (retired)
Team: RE Tongue; Lord Avebury; J Hamilton-Fleming
Left Virginia Water at 2.54 with dirty car as Lex Garages had forgotten to wash it, although I took it there with special instructions. Troubles began early. Dynamo

wouldn't charge. Lucas man made it OK before start. Night section OK. Foggy, icy roads. New idea about secret checks and not being more than 15 minutes early pending disqualification for dangerous driving was foolish, as people dawdled and then went like hell to catch up. Made night run a funeral procession.

Failed Fingle after good beginning due to baulk even though as *The Motor* said both RE Tongue and RE Wright (Frazer Nash) made excellent restarts. Would have climbed easily otherwise. Gorgeous day. Petered out higher up Fingle after restarting due to one petrol pump nearly getting knocked off when being pushed about by people on hill while restarting. Petrol shorted wire so blew the fuse. Repaired it and dashed on. Caught up. Failed Simms. Everyone was failing. Six had got up when we arrived (no 174) KDE MacLachlan, Elwes and Co all failed. Steam tractor with hawser pulled people up.

Climbed Inverhay and Harcombe OK. Then in rain storm magneto gave out. Walked 1½ miles to phone and 1½ miles back. Towed 10 miles to Yeovil. Left car there. TJGJ came back on the 6.50 train and was in London at 10pm. I went to Burtons, bought dry grey flannels, and socks from Marks and Spencers. Arrived Paddington dry but no coat and bundle of wet clothes at 2.45am on Sunday morning. A great trial. Magneto passed out due to condenser bursting.

Had a bad skid on icy corner downhill, just after leaving Exeter. Hit bank. Nearly everyone did. Told AM man to warn people or there would be a bad crash.

My entry for Le Mans came about through the Hon Adam Chetwynd who was at Oxford with me. Although no longer a student, he lived at Abingdon-on-Thames and came into the town a lot. Chetwynd was mad keen on cars; he and his wife both raced MGs and Lea-Francises at Brooklands. His wife drove at Le Mans in 1931 with HH Sisted, in the MG Midget she also used in the Brooklands Double Twelve. It was modified and ran unsupercharged, with an enlarged fuel tank, but retired on the first night.

One morning, over coffee in Ellison's Café, Chetwynd told me he had an entry for Le Mans and was going to acquire the Aston Martin Mark II LM10 that had qualified for the Le Mans Rudge

Biennial Cup in 1933. The Rudge Cup was an award that assessed a car's performance over two years, and dated back to the race's foundation in 1923 when it was the premier honour, the Triennial Cup. Its complicated scoring had made Le Mans a difficult race to follow so to simplify things it was made a Biennial Cup. Nevertheless for many years, so far as the Automobile Club de l'Ouest (ACO) was concerned, it remained the race's first prize.

A car qualified in year one by exceeding the minimum distance laid down for the class, its success depended on by how much. If it exceeded its minimum by more than the other qualifiers in year two, it won the Rudge-Whitworth Cup. To most people however, despite what the ACO and

Emille Coquille of Rudge-Whitworth, one of the race's founders thought, what counted was the general classification, the real finishing order on the day. Real winners could not be decided on calculations of mathematical formulae.

I surmised Aston Martin might give a Biennial Cup car some backing so I was interested. Chetwynd had the entry and the prospect of qualification but he could no longer afford to take it up. Would I like to buy it? I had not got a car suitable for that sort of thing, my Aston Martin was more of a road car than a racing car, and Chetwynd wanted twenty quid for the entry. I did not know what I would do with it, but I handed over the money, and then began to think about a car. I had done the Alpine Trial in my Aston so I already knew the people at the factory. The Bertellis – AC (Augustus) and Enrico (Harry) were Italian and delightful, and when I told AC Bertelli what I had done, he immediately agreed that I should have LM10. I was delighted, sold the Alpine Aston road car and bought the factory LM10 racing car. So having paid for the entry and obtained the car I was set up for Le Mans.

Aston Martin LM10 was the most reliable racing car I ever owned. It emerged with credit in every race in which it was entered, and in due course became well known in Vintage and Classic racing. It was advertised in the 1980s for about the same price I paid for it in 1934.

Previous page: *June 1934 en route to Le Mans with Aston Martin LM10 and co-driver Cambridge student Maurice Falkner, a month off his 22nd birthday Reggie wonders what he has taken on.*

Far right, top: *LM10 is unloaded from the night ferry in France.*

Far right, below: *In France a stop 176km (109.4miles) from Le Mans. The works team cars line up with TS Fothringham alongside LM14 to be driven by Bertelli and Penn-Hughes.*

There was a certain naiveté about Reggie Tongue's early years in motor racing, particularly in the choice of the Le Mans 24 Hours Grand Prix d'Endurance, as his first big event. He was still only 22 and began his ERA career, not far off full-blown grand prix racing, only two years later. He showed a lot of self-confidence, but scant patience with a step-by-step approach, which might have been wiser. He loved racing, and although winning was pleasant taking part was more important. An amateur driver who paid for his racing from private means, he still found common cause with the smart Brooklands set, who though they admired winners, retained the conviction (quaint by the philosophies of the 21st century) that taking part was just as worthy.

Aston Martin's history was punctuated by financial crises and changes of ownership, yet it still gained the reputation as one of Britain's premier sports cars. The prototype was made in 1914 by Lionel Martin and Robert Bamford, the name coined from a hill-climb course popular before the first world war, at Aston Clinton near Aylesbury, Bucks. The first car had an undistinguished 1.4-litre side valve Coventry-Simplex engine in a chassis copied from an Italian design. Production began in 1922 of a plainly engineered 1.5-litre car selling for £850, and by the mid 1920s, the firm was making around 20 cars a year. With a racing programme inaugurated in 1924 came overhead cam engines and lightweight chassis. There was an optimistic showing of Aston Martins at the Olympia Motor Show in 1925, but within weeks the company was wound up.

Its rescuer was a designer AC Bertelli, who restarted production at Feltham in 1927, produced racing versions in 1928/29 but successes on the track were not matched by sales. Following another financial crisis in 1931-3, Sir Arthur Sutherland the shipowner took over, and in 1933 installed his youngest son Gordon Sutherland as joint managing director with AC Bertelli. They sustained the firm's dedication to motor racing even though the cost of it had nearly done for the previous management. Sutherland inaugurated an era of notable sports cars such as the 80hp Ulster of 1935, and the Speed Model, which were as outstanding for their performance as they were for their appearance. Aston Martin represented the archetypal sports car; with cycle-type wings pointed tail, and spartan open two-seater bodywork.

The 24 Hours race at Le Mans was the pinnacle of sports car racing. The Biennial Cup was next in importance in publicity terms to outright victory. AC Bertelli and LP Driscoll had won it in 1932 and Bertelli and SCH Davis qualified again in 1933, finishing seventh in a lighter version of the second LM (for Le Mans) series of works-prepared cars behind Driscoll and SC Penn-Hughes, who were fifth. The cars were chassis numbers LM 9 (Driscoll and Penn-Hughes) and LM10 (Bertelli and Davis). Reggie for practical reasons still had to keep the family trustees in mind.

Overleaf: *Le Mans by night. The heavy, dank, Sarthe night, the lights shining like beacons over spectators and the Tribune de la Presse opposite the pits, the oil-stained track, the refuelling hoses and anxious tired crews working on a solitary car as the drama of the 24 Hours race unfolds.*

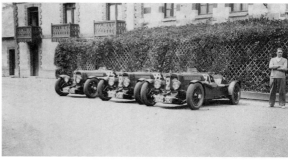

I entered for Le Mans under the name of A Vincent, because I was still afraid of upsetting not only the family, but also the trustees looking after the family money on my behalf. I had been planning an overland car trip to Timbuctoo in the Sahara, but that idea so upset my aunt that I felt that I could not go through with it. Her own son had recently died, and since it would have put her under an intolerable strain, I decided against it.

For Le Mans I threw in my lot with the factory even though I was a private entry. The pit manager was Sammy Davis, whom I had known since the 1932 London-Exeter, and he took charge of the two private entries as well as the team cars. It was a good arrangement in view of our inexperience, giving us a number of advantages in access to works mechanics' skills and team organisation, but as things turned out it had disadvantages as well.

My next priority was to find a second driver. Fortunately Maurice Falkner from Manchester was at Cambridge, a member of its motor club, lived near me at Knutsford in Cheshire and could

put up £100 towards the expenses. I went into serious training about eight weeks before the race. I kept regular hours, bed 10.30, Ovaltine every night, rowing and plenty of exercise, and since I had no car I bought a 490cc ohv Norton to keep my eye in. I had a minor operation on my jaw with a fortnight to go, but fortunately it was fine in time. I did begin to worry though. Supposing I made a complete fool of myself? But as the time drew near I grew more confident. By way of reassurance, Maurice and I drove to Brooklands in his Alfa-Romeo, for a shakedown drive of the Aston. Sammy Davis was in charge and extremely helpful. We were quite relieved to be tutored by someone with experience, not only with Le Mans and this Aston (he drove it in the 1933 race), but also in the elementary principles of running a team.

Sammy organised us pretty well, LM10 was the soul of reliability, most unusually (perhaps uniquely) making its third appearance in the race. The second private Aston Martin entry was a standard Le Mans two/four-seater of JC Noel and A Wheeler, amateurs like we were, but quickly learning the ropes.

The cars were all tested at Brooklands by the works, another benefit of our association with the official team. The works cars were developments of the earlier series, of which LM10 was one, bearing chassis numbers LM11, LM12, and LM14. LM13 was omitted for superstitious reasons. Each of the new cars was slightly different. LM14 to be driven by Bertelli and Penn-Hughes had a high compression cylinder head and could do 110mph (177kph). LM11 driven by TS Fothringham and John Appleton had a less highly stressed engine, and LM12 was the strongest with a low axle ratio in view of the extra weight. We assembled in the works yard at Feltham, loading

our spares and baggage on a long-chassis tender, specially prepared for the event. It was piled high with kit for a forty-strong team confident of success.

TIMES . JULY 13ᵗ 1934

UNIVERSITY FLYING

OXFORD AIR SQUADRON IN CAMP

FROM OUR AERONAUTICAL CORRESPONDENT

EASTCHURCH, JULY 12

After 10 years of work there may be less excitement, but there is certainly no less keenness, in a camp of the Oxford University Air Squadron. The second attachment of 25 members is now undergoing its fortnight of intensive training here. The work of the third party will begin in nine days, and, when the camp ends, all the members will have flown solo and some will have learned to find their way about the country. Yesterday one man made his first solo flight; another set off alone for Leuchars.

Five years ago the old hands of the squadron would more probably have been learning to perform aerobatics in a service type of aeroplane, possibly an Atlas. To-day the senior member is required to fly a training aeroplane from one point to another, sometimes separated by 500 miles of country, and to bring back his Avro Tutor in good order at the appointed time.

The alternative course open to the young man who wants power and speed has already been followed by many members. Nine of the present members have been recommended for permanent commissions in the R.A.F., and five old members of the squadron are now pilot officers in No. 601 (County of London) Squadron of the Auxiliary Air Force. One of these is Sir Archibald Hope, who won the Siddeley trophy as the best pilot while he was with the Oxford Squadron.

FLYING AT 6 A.M.

The squadron remains, as it has always been, representative of all schools and of most parts of the Empire. There are 10 Rhodes Scholars, prominent representatives from the Rugby, swimming, lacrosse, and ski teams, and from the drag and the racing motorists. The colleges which supply the greatest numbers of members are Christ Church, New College, and Magdalen, but almost all colleges send their quotas, and the squadron acquires the true character of a university institution. Wing Commander C. N. Lowe, well known as an international Rugby half, as the squadron's chief instructor, has concentrated on packing as much useful instruction and practice as possible into the 3,000 hours of flying done in the course of the year.

In this camp, flying begins at 6 a.m. and ends for the day at 1 p.m. The 6 o'clock start is the measure of the keenness of men whose term-time roll-call is some two hours later and whose vacation habits though unspecified may perhaps **not** run along the same lines.

Aston Martins had traditionally done well at Le Mans so the firm was unprepared for its worst performance ever. The Brooklands trials were satisfactory, and the following Tuesday we went to the works, collected the car and set off for Newhaven. We oiled up a plug on the way but arrived together, ten Aston Martins in line ahead, an impressive sight. We crossed by the night boat, Morris-Goodall, Elwes, Falkner and I sharing a cabin next to Sammy and AC Bertelli. We left Dieppe in convoy and before we had got very far Earl Howe shot by on the Mercedes with his

Far left: As Alfa Romeo heads for its last win in the 24 Hour classic followed by four Rileys and an MG, Reggie Tongue's Aston Martin LM10 leads the Lagonda Rapier of Brackenbury and de Clifford that finished 16th through the Esses.

Left: There was not much time to spare between motor races for flying but Reggie found it. The OUAS camp at Eastchurch was somehow squeezed in between engagements.

Right: Racing under a nom de guerre was not unusual. Reggie's "A Vincent" was not to last however, a matter of some relief to writers like SCH Davis who knew the subterfuge and was grateful when allowed to call him by his real name.

blower going hard. He dashed on ahead to order a lunch for the whole equipe.

The only untoward event in practice was the discovery that LM12 (Morris-Goodall and Elwes) with the least powerful engine, lower axle ratio and encumbered with more weight, was proving faster than the high-compression LM14 (Bertelli and Penn-Hughes). The lighter cars were not gaining the full benefit of the higher axle ratio so the mechanics set to work to change axles. I gained in confidence, feeling I would have no difficulty in going as fast as the car would allow. AC Bertelli took me round the circuit in LM10 giving me the benefit of his experience. He showed me the best lines through corners, the best gearshift points, best braking areas and although still rated as a newcomer I must have been quite adept because I was soon taking White House Corner (scene of the great Bentley team crash of 1927 of which my father had spoken so often) at 100mph (160.9kph). It was difficult to find my braking point for the pits, and once arrived sliding with the wheels almost locked, although more or less under control. I thought the pit staff was jumping behind the counter in mock alarm, only to discover that their agitation was quite genuine. I also had a bad skid at Indianapolis, the sharp left and right before White House, through trying to take it too fast, but by the time the race was underway I had enough experience to get it about right.

Another blow fell before the race started. We stayed in the Hotel des Ifs in the middle of the town, but after each practice session adjourned to the Hippodrome café on the Mulsanne Straight, for a glass of champagne. There I received a telegram from my uncle saying that my cousin Delia had fallen off her horse and broken her collarbone. She was all right but he felt I ought to know. I was now apprehensive. Supposing I had an accident, the first intimation anybody would have of it would be when a morning paper reported a British driver crashed at Le Mans. I telegrammed to confess my duplicity, telling my uncle that I was not just a mechanic or pit helper as I had implied, but that I was actually driving under the name of Vincent. By return I received a superb response: "All here wish you the very best – thought as much from the word go. Knew you wouldn't be content with just being a watcher".

Once the race was under way I was puzzled to find Charles Faroux, Clerk of the Course and deeply respected, in the middle of the road waving his flag at me every time I came past the pits. I tried him with my lights on and then I tried him with them off. In the end he seemed to be reconciled to whatever it was and I was not stopped.

The works team's troubles began soon after the famous Le Mans start, in which the drivers sprinted across the road, jumped into the car and started the engine. When Le Mans began this was supposed to be a demonstration of easy starting; happily by 1934 the organisers had stopped insisting on hoods being erected as well. Coming to Arnage in the opening laps, Bertelli's gearbox seized and he spun into a sandbank. It took him half an hour to remove the gearbox cover and shift the selector forks, enabling him to return to the pits. The other cars were held back by brake trouble, but by the evening things had settled down. Bertelli and Penn-Hughes were back in the running, and the works cars were sixth, seventh, and ninth.

Disaster struck just after midnight. Bertelli's engine seized due to its over-keen weight-saving measures, Appleton spent a good deal of time digging his car out of the sandbank after going off on the main straight, and just after 10 on Sunday morning Morris-Goodall went out, with a rod through the side of the crankcase. There was some consternation because just as Morris-Goodall's car failed, I was delayed in LM10 by a

puncture, and Appleton's engine seized. Three team cars dropping out on the same lap brought back shades of the 1927 Bentley White House accident, until I was able to reassure Sammy Davis when I limped round, that on this occasion everybody was safe.

All the factory cars were out however and thus could not qualify for the following year's Rudge Cup. This was especially upsetting in view of the performance of the Morris-Goodall/Elwes car on Sunday morning. It had lain second overall behind the eventual winner, Chinetti and Etancelin (2.3-litre Alfa Romeo) from 2am till 10am even though a long way, some ten laps or about an hour behind. Fothringham and Appleton had reached third place at 1am before dropping to 14th by 3am. They had climbed back to tenth before disaster overtook them once more. Although Appleton remained in the race until 10am, the AC de l'Ouest expunged his car from the records from its 81st lap just after 2am when, the officials claimed, it should have been stopped for a breach of race regulations by the driver.

Whatever happened now, Aston Martin wanted to keep us running, so imposed a limit of 4000rpm to preserve the engine. The disadvantages of being a semi-official non-works team were now apparent. I felt we drove well but being slowed by so much was irksome. We finished tenth but we could have finished third or fourth. The car had been fifth in 1932 and seventh in 1933 and I do not think it would have broken. It had none of the modifications and lightening that had made the works cars so fragile.

After the disappointment of not being allowed to do better at Le Mans, there was nothing for it but to compete in another long-distance race. The 10-hour Grand Prix of Francorchamps on 8 August was a tempting target, so I had the car checked over and prepared by the works. Once again it went well, finishing second in the 2-litre class by a little under a lap.

I had been pleased with the car at Le Mans,

and now I wanted to drive it without the burden of team orders, to see if I could do well on my own. I had to go to the Oxford Air Squadron camp at the Air Armament School RAF Eastchurch, so left the matter of finding a spare driver with Aston Martin. I tried Fothringham first but he was soldiering. Eventually Jim Elwes decided he could come. He went over with the car on the Wednesday before the race with a mechanic. I went down to Dover in a friend's 4½-litre Bentley and saw them off. Next day Thursday I flew to Hawkinge near Folkestone, then by road to Dover and caught the Ostend boat. I reached

Below: Le Mans, the right hander after the pits leading to Tertre Rouge. LM10 passes Mme Itier's 844cc MG, which finished 17th behind the Lagonda.

Venners at midnight and took a taxi to Francorchamps where we were staying, arriving after 1am on Friday following a most hectic ride over hill and dale.

Jim Elwes informed me that Customs would not release our spares unless we produced a list of them in their language. Who knew what a valve spring was in Belgian? It was with difficulty that we found one of only about six men in all Belgium who did. It took several hours to obtain the translations and brought the spares in a lorry we had hired to Francorchamps. Such bureaucracy.

Jim called into my room at 6am on Friday to tell me everything was in order, and then went off with Rupert the mechanic in the lorry, leaving me to get a little sleep. I was up and waiting when they got back and went out to official practice on Friday afternoon. Jim had already practised and knew the course. I had been round slowly

beforehand and knew it fairly well.

The engine was misfiring through the mixture being too rich on one cylinder. We had the magneto overhauled twice by Scintilla, installed new leads and eventually got the mixture right with the help of M Rosli of Champion. After more experimenting we were ready for the race at 7am on the Sunday.

The 2-litre class was going to lie between us and the Bugatti of S du Roy and De Blicqy-de-Berc. At half-distance we led by 518km (321.87miles) against the Bugatti's 496km (308.2miles). Rupert and a helper from a local garage were in the pits together with the driver off duty. I got away to a good start and had an uneventful first spell, handing over to Jim after about 2½ hours, after a quick pit stop. A car went off the road in front of him at 100 mph and several more crashed including Raymond Sommer's brother. It was a tricky course, up hill and down, with little real straight but long 100mph bends.

Towards the end things got exciting and crowds came round our pit. I could not keep still as it was my first lone venture and we were winning the class. The Bugatti was faster than we were but was delayed many times in the pits. At the finish we were declared winners and given champagne and flowers, but then we were sent for and told that after all the Bugatti had won the class, having covered 1,042.77km (647.96miles) against our 1,033.48km (642.18miles). This was a pity, nevertheless we had a great race, and it was satisfactory to finish sixth overall. Doubt over the finishing order continued and *La Meuse* of 8 July credited the Aston Martin with 70 laps and the Bugatti with only 69. It looked like a stitch-up; every report including the lengthy one in the *Gazette de Liege* for 9 July put the Aston Martin (they called it an Asson Martin) in the lead throughout, at two hours, three hours (*Aston Martin a pris le commandement de place de la Bugatti*) mid-way, seven hours, and nine hours but the

Bugatti mysteriously took the lead in the end, perhaps after the chequered flag had fallen.

We went to the prize-giving in Spa in the evening where everyone tried to console us. Perhaps had we been more experienced and more confident we might have officially disputed the result, but there it was, we thought the umpire's word was final. Next morning we left early and after lots of weighing and counting, got the spares passed safely out through Belgian Customs, and on to the train. We put Rupert on the train to accompany them and Jim and I came by road. We missed the first boat but caught the midnight one from Ostend.

I was thoroughly enjoying sports car racing. The cars had to be road-equipped two-seaters with mudguards, starter motors, lights and everything else. However I decided that the next race should be at Phoenix Park, in the Irish Motor Racing Club's Junior event, where the rules on road equipment were more relaxed. We took the mudguards off to lighten the car, and it was in fine fettle when we went off to Phoenix Park, a pleasant stretch of parkland with a 4½-mile (7.25km) road circuit in the middle of Dublin. In Ireland I stayed with another Oxford contemporary Walter Peel, growing fond of his sister Cicely, and garaging the car in the old coach house where they kept the traps. We drove to early morning practice on the public roads, with no silencer to speak of, no number plates and I don't think even a horn. The Irish seemed prepared to put up with that and we finished third overall.

I used other Aston Martins besides my own LM10, including a rare long chassis model AMG 490, which was much smoother and had a lot of room even for a four-seater. I borrowed the grey four-seater for the London to Lands End Trial of March 1934, with Phipps as co-driver, winning a silver medal. It was something of a responsibility being lent a car, but I was delighted that a manufacturer should consider me so capable. It was cold when we left Virginia Water and there was frost during the long night drive to the West Country. The organisers had set up secret checks, which were a great nuisance, as we were always more than a quarter of an hour ahead of schedule just with ordinary driving.

Shortly before breakfast a wing nearly fell off. This was due to damage to the wing stays sustained in an accident that Masters, the company secretary at Aston Martin, had had a few days previously when he hit a pedestrian. The repair welding had not been well done and we had to tie it up with copper wire, which kept stretching, so we had to buy a great reel of telegraph wire in Taunton.

We went well on the early hills, Grabhurst Station and Lynton, and we were in good form up to Gooseham, with Phipps sitting on the hood overhanging the tail to give the rear wheels more grip. Strictly speaking he was improperly seated, and as soon as I saw where he was, I turned round in my seat to get him off. That was my mistake. The moment's loss of concentration caused me to hit the bank, and although I carried on without stopping, the axle was bent and the tyre flat. One wheel had spokes missing and a piece of rock was lodged amongst the remaining spokes. A lot of cars failed here. We stopped on a level non-stop section at the top, where so many cars with numbers were parked, that I thought that I had missed the 'Non Stop Section Ends' sign. We reported to a marshal, changed the wheel, and were given some beer by kind friends.

Below: *July 1934. Thwarted by officialdom, Reggie is unable to conceal his disappointment at finishing in second place to a Bugatti in the exhausting Belgian 10 Hours race at Spa. Mechanic Rupert stands on the left, co-driver Jim Elwes seems more content after a stirring drive.*

I quite fell in love with the long chassis tourer. It had a sweet engine, lots of power and felt quick. Unfortunately we failed on Hustyn although got away again under our own power. Within a few miles the mudguard developed a serious and pathetic droop. We used the wire to bind up the wing, and threw the rest into the passenger's footwell. On the way home on Sunday we left St Ives with the Evanses, except for Kenneth who had again blown up the MG. We met Jack Temple MG's competition manager, and near Camberley, Mortimer Morris-Goodall. We stopped for a drink and on starting up smelt burning. Phipps said that it was wire under the propshaft, which I thought was an odd place to have wire. Upon investigation we found that the wire we had bought for doing up the wings had unravelled in the passenger's footwell and wound itself round the propshaft. We unwound it by pushing the car backwards and forwards but it took us about an hour to cut it free completely.

Right top and below: *Always a competitor for MG, the Singer Nine had an overhead camshaft engine, twin carburettors, and hydraulic brakes. Reggie's Nine Le Mans had a high-lift camshaft, and provision for two spare wheels behind the slab petrol tank at the back, a sure sign of a sports car. An extra spare wheel was an advantage on trials where the extra weight was an advantage. It cost £215 and the engine revved freely up to 6,000rpm. Speed Special 2-seaters could do 75mph (120.4kph).*

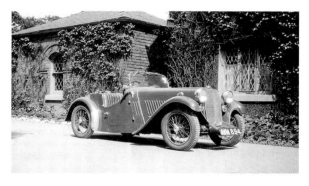

The Alpine Trial 1934

The Alpine started in Nice on 7 August and finished in Munich on 12 August, five days through six countries, covering some 1810miles (2913km). The first day's route was 302 miles to Aix les Bains, the second Aix to Interlaken, 261miles (420.027km), the third Interlaken to St Moritz 230miles (370km), the fourth St Moritz to Venice 345miles (555km), then Venice to Zagreb 290miles (467km), and finally Zagreb to Munich 383miles (616km). Timed sections included most of the classic Alpine passes, such as the Col du Galibier on the first day and the Stelvio on the second which had to be covered at prescribed average speeds ranging from 40kph (24.9mph) for the 3-litre class, to 35kph

Right: *All downhill at Donington. The Craner Curves of the pre-war track, opened in 1933, down to The Hairpin and the impossibly narrow-looking Starkey's bridge remained recognisable when the modern circuit was built in the 1970s. The woods gave way to spectator areas. In October 1934 a Bugatti leads two Frazer-Nashes and an MG. Reggie's Aston Martin stripped of wings and lights for racing is lying fifth.*

(21.8mph) for the Group 5 cars of 1100cc that included the Singer. The target for supercharged cars was raised by 10 per cent. There were speed tests on 10 kilometres of level road that had to be covered at between 110kph (68.5mph) for the big cars and 85kph (52.9mph) for the 1100s. Each car started with 1000 marks; exceeding the allowances resulted in marks being deleted.

Prizes were allocated to teams, a three-car entry gaining an International Alpine Cup, with the drivers receiving replicas. Individual drivers gained a Glacier Cup or plaque. Among the other classic Alpine passes used were the Col de la Cayolle, Col de Vars, Col d'Izoard, Col de la Croix de Fer, both the Little and the Grand St Bernard, Col

du Pillon, Grimsel, Furka, Oberalp, and Splügen,. The roads varied from well-engineered highway to unsurfaced dirt, with a hot dusty trail from Fiume on the Adriatic. This was Rijeka, an Austro-Hungarian port disputed since 1919 by Italy and Yugoslavia, and only settled in 1947 when the Treaty of Paris finally decided it was Yugoslav. The route went to Zagreb by way of Karlovac, a twisty hilly road later replaced by a motorway.

British cars had traditionally given a good account of themselves. For 1934 a regulation was introduced aimed at keeping cars closer to standard specification. This specified that to be eligible, at least 100 identical examples must have been made. It was a condition that worked against small producers, in an era

71

when 100 cars of one type could be quite a lot — for Aston Martin for instance. It precluded some cars sold in limited numbers at the expensive end of the catalogue.

A let-out clause lay in the requirement for the minimum number applying only to the chassis. The bodywork could be pretty well anything, provided it was no lighter than the corresponding standard model, and it was unnecessary to fit the rear seats in a four-seater body. There was a good deal of relief at a late change allowing fuel and oil tanks to be made bigger, and a fan could be fitted, provided the radiator was left alone. Extra instruments, such as rev counters and water thermometers were permitted.

I went to see FS Barnes some time before entries closed for the 1934 Alpine Trial to see if there was any chance of a drive in a works-supported Singer. There was not, but if I bought one Singer would prepare it for me, and render whatever assistance they could on the event.

The 1934 regulations stipulated standard cars, so it was my intention to use it for the Alpine, then run it on the road and in the occasional trial during the winter.

I collected my new Singer Le Mans a week or so before leaving for the Alpine and ran it in carefully. It went back to the works for preparation, fitting a duo thermometer and spot lamp, and I met the Singer contingent in Coventry the day we were due to go to Dover. I picked up a non-driving passenger, whom Autocheques had asked me to take, in London. I had never seen him before, and after driving him round the Alps for a week, dropped him off back in London and never saw him again.

I arrived in Dover in the evening, changed the oil, and caught the boat the following morning. The Talbots made a fine sight coming past just after leaving Calais, and we reached Rheims the

first night, and next day went on to Grenoble. I arrived here first and met some of the Triumph people for a dark nut brown beer. How excellent! I got separated from the convoy due to the windscreen coming off, then through being stopped by a gendarme for speeding. Next day we went and tried the Galibier, at 2556metres (8386ft) the highest of the rough, stone-strewn, and usually dusty Alpine passes in the French sector between Nice and Geneva. We did not manage down to our target time, and then the rain came — apart from preparation time at Nice it rained every day. We ran down to Briançon, had a meal and some brandy, and decided to stay the night. I was in a team with FS Barnes, Kay Petre, and Jack Connell. Mrs Petre and Jackie Astbury went off and found rooms for about 20 people. In the evening we tackled the Galibier again, with more success.

We took the opportunity to do some fine-tuning to the cars, gaining experience of the conditions, to achieve our required average speed. Then came a marvellous run in the dark back to Briançon, and food and bed with more brandy at a 50% reduction to those competing in the Coupe des Alpes. The Ford team was staying there too. Next day in heavy rain we went along the course in the opposite direction, through Guillestre in the heart of the Hautes Alpes, down the sinuous Provençal roads to the sea at Nice, the weather ruining whatever coastal views there might have been from the southern slopes of the Alpes Maritimes.

The following day was spent in preparation and scrutineering, with about 60 seals put on the car, and this year radiators had to be sealed for each day's run. This did not worry us although they required a deep draught each night of about 1.5 gallons (6.8 litres) to top-up.

At last the start came. We carried few spares, coil, distributor, petrol pump and some gaskets, none of which was used. We never even needed to change the plugs. The first day's run to Aix-les-Bains was uneventful although still wet. Towards the end the engine boiled a little as a result of running short of petrol and having to fill up with a commercial grade causing overheating.

We were at the tail end of the trial so saw little of the other competitors, but on the second day came across Mrs Petre with carburettor trouble. She got going again quite quickly and all seemed well. The Galibier had to be bypassed, due to floods washing away bridges on the far side, which was frustrating after all our hard work three days before. Accordingly the zig-zag Stelvio was the first tough test, and it was here that we ran into difficulty. For some reason that we were unable to understand, the engine lost power and we failed to meet our time. FS Barnes blamed fuel starvation, or temporary ignition problems, which he attributed to my mechanic's inexperience. The other Singers were OK although once again we passed Kay Petre changing a wheel, having hit the wall on one of the corners. We stopped to help and found her car drivable although the steering was bent and loose. We tightened the steering up and put right several other things, as the buffetting was causing everything to come loose, but we eventually had to leave her stranded. Her luck finally ran out with a burnt out dynamo and a stuck valve, the accident had set back the front axle, so she retired at Venice.

We pushed on over the next two days, with one of the night stops at the St Moritz Palace Hotel, where Martin the proprietor was hospitable as always. Very late on the fourth day we did a speed test in the dark, reaching Venice where we drained our oil. We had time to be impressed by Venice despite being tired, and saw St Mark's

Top right: *Petite Kay Petre on the left with Jackie Astbury and the troublesome Singer on the Alpine Trial.*

Square. The hotel was a long journey by canal, and next day we had to be up early, for a dash over good roads to Trieste and Fiume. We had time for breakfast at the frontier but in Yugoslavia drove through continuous dust clouds all the way to Zagreb. It got into the carburettors and everything else, even our suitcases. We left Zagreb on the Sunday, and departed the country through miles of cheering people lining the roads.

One hill, the Turracher Höhe in Austria, was like an English trials hill – very steep and muddy, and several cars had to remove their luggage and reverse up. We just made it, picking our way with care. We then drove on to Munich still in steady rain, where the town roads were closed off for us, enabling us to rush through at speed with uniformed Nazis controlling the other traffic.

There was one tense moment when everyone was late for a check. An underestimate of 18km (11.2miles) was discovered on the route card however, so we were allowed an extra half an hour.

Several luncheons and city tours took place in Munich, where we were guests of the German club. English wreaths were laid on the local unknown warrior's grave, which struck me as ironic, and led me to think how vigorously peace ought to be pursued. Meeting all nationalities on an event like this made the very idea of war seem absurd. How terrible it seemed, to strike up such friendships with people from all over Europe, then face the possibility that some day we could be fighting one another.

We left Munich at 5am on Tuesday. Owing to the German currency restrictions I had to pay in

registered Reichsmarks, as I was unable to bring them out of the country, and I left my passport in the bank at Stuttgart. I only discovered this at Baden Baden, and had to go all the way back in the rain to get it, so we did not reach Reims until 10pm. We ate at the Lion d'Or, after driving 960kms (597miles) with only half an hour off for food, and were home next day after a night's stay in Calais.

I had stopped using my *nom de guerre* A Vincent for rallies, so *The Autocar's* report said, "Tongue, who can now be called by his proper name, had three punctures." We won a Glacier silver-gilt plaque with 973 marks against Connell's 100-mark clean sheet for a Glacier Cup.

The Le Mans two-seater Singer Nine AVM 894 that I used for the Alpine had nowhere near enough power. We failed to reach the minimum time on several passes so many marks were lost. It managed through the event without any mechanical failure, but it was easy to over-rev, which we knew would break the crankshaft. The steering was not very good and altogether I was disappointed with it. I kept it only a few months, for one or two minor events, winning a first-class award in the Inter-Varsity trial.

I went by train to the Donington Park meeting on 18 August with Kay Petre. The Singer was in dock so the mechanic Mac brought up

Above: *Donington, Coppice Corner, July 1934, fresh from his successes at Le Mans and Spa, Reggie in white helmet driving Aston Martin No16 comes up inside Powys-Lybbe's Alvis.*

Right: *Wet Shelsley Walsh. Some 10miles (16km) west of Worcester the 1000-yard (914.4m) hillclimb was first used in 1905, and by the 1930s was a well-established motor sporting fixture. Reggie hopes the rain will blow past the mica visor on his helmet as he prepares for the off. See account page 76.*

the Aston Martin. Everything was fine, the car was stripped and going really quickly, then maddeningly I caught the rear wheel centre-lock spinner on the gatepost going out of the paddock. The impact cracked the plate holding the back axle casing to the spring pushing the axle back. I was furious with myself for my carelessness.

Cyril Paul dragged me back into the paddock on a jack, a new bolt was provided by Raymond Mays' travelling van, but after asking Temple of MG, Charles Brackenbury, and some others whether it would be wise to run I decided to scratch. It was as much to Mac's disappointment as mine. He took the car back to Aston Martin, and Colin Richardson of Riley towed me with his racing Riley as far as Coventry, where we stayed the night.

For the Phoenix Park race on 15 September I left London with Mac in the Aston Martin, and James Jefferiss came up by train with the spares. We called at Fort Dunlop for new tyres on way the way to Heysham, crossing the Irish Sea on Tuesday night. It was a smooth voyage, and Walter Peel, a member of the Oxford University Motor Driver's Club (OUMDC) duly met us. Our friend Brennan had put us in touch, and even though I did not know him, the club connection was enough to ensure his hospitality while I was in Dublin. James and Mac meanwhile were put up at a good hotel.

We soon had a pit and all the tools organised, but encountered trouble with a bent wheel, which was found to be touching the tie bar. This was only discovered after difficulty getting the wheel on and off the splines, and there was no indication how it got bent. There was an inspection of the cars on Wednesday afternoon, and in deference to Irish nationalism, we covered up the Union Jack plaques on the sides of the bonnet. This caused great amusement, and on Stanley Woods'

assurance that the English were not as unpopular as all that, we uncovered them again. It was straightforward at scrutineering. The brakes were the main item of concern and they turned out to be 90% efficient.

Practice was early on Wednesday morning and it was still dark when we arrived at the park passing through several guard points. I found the course very fast. In order to maintain the fairly generous handicap the race organisers had given us, I did each bit flat out on separate laps. Accordingly my best practice lap was 3 minutes 35 seconds, but I managed 3 minutes 15 seconds in the race by joining up all the flat-out bits. Returning after practice, the Garda ticked us off for having no number plates, no wings, silencer, or even road licence. We only went free after a long argument but we were ready to race with time to spare.

I gave Mac the day off then went to watch the Junior Race. It was stopped a lap too early, so when the flag came out after the Senior Race, I did extra laps just to make sure. The Aston Martin went well at first. It was very fast and reached 5600rpm on 18in wheels and 4.2:1 axle. Unfortunately a valve stretched so it was running on only three cylinders for much of the race. It was fine below 4500rpm, with enough acceleration to keep up, but lap times started to suffer. I nearly came unstuck when a car skidded in front of me as I was passing it on 20mph bend, finishing third behind a Ford V8 and an MG Magna 1100cc. The handicap demanded that I make up a whole lap on the MG, which was well beyond me.

---

29 Sept 1934. *SHELSLEY WALSH*. *(Phillips helping as second mechanic).*

I came down from Manchester and met Mac for practice at Shelsley Walsh. It was a boiling hot day and we had preignition. Eventually curing it by adding more benzol. The problem was traced to the plugs, so after three practice runs we seemed to be running well, although we did not know our times. I went off to Worcester to stay with the Evanses and Major Gardner.

Mac went off alone with the Aston Martin, with instructions to be back at the hill by 10.30 the following morning. Chris Staniland and Von der Becke were at the hotel at Tenbury Wells with Jackie Astbury, and on the Saturday I brought Doreen Evans in the Singer.

Saturday's heatwave gave way to heavy rain on Sunday but we got two climbs, 57sec on the 1st and 57.4 on the 2nd. This one would have been much faster if my foot had not slipped off the accelerator after the second bend. The Aston was not really suitable for Shelsley. It was too heavy although very good fun. Hacker crashed just before Mays's first run, so I was delayed 15 minutes while they cleared the course. It was very trying as it was raining and I had hard plugs in, and didn't want to restart the engine again then have to stop it in case they oiled up. Fortunately the engine did not get very cold waiting. First and second gears were satisfactory, but third was too high; 2000rpm short to be exact, using the 6:1 axle ratio. Raymond Mays was faster than Whitney Straight.

Mac took the car back to London and I had dinner with the Evanses at the Star where I met Cecil Kimber, managing director of MG, and was surprised to find he knew that I drove Aston Martins, was third in Phoenix Park and also an Oxford undergraduate - what a compliment. He did not seem to recollect the 1932 Isis article on the J2 on this occasion.

The Cork Examiner enhanced my standing in motor racing. "There are two Aston Martins. One of these has been driven at Le Mans, in the famous Grand Prix d'Endurance, and its driver in Dublin RE Tongue is known as a competitor in the Belgian Grand Prix on ten hours, and The Coupe des Alpes as well as Le Mans." We had a large party at the prize-giving dance, winning two prizes, one for finishing first in the two-litre class, so I made a speech and drank champagne from the cup.

It felt quite professional to receive a telegram in Ireland, asking whether any petrol and oil contracts I held would prevent me driving the Appleton Special (Maserati chassis, Riley engine), in the Brooklands 500 mile race on September 22nd. There was a good entry for Class G; the Rileys of Ashby, Dobbs, Paul, and Fairfield, Cuthbert's blown Riley 9 Cuthbert Special, and ten MG Magnettes. They were all blown, including Horton's fast offset single-seater, and those of Captain George Eyston and 1933 winner Eddie Hall as well as the Appleton. In the event Henry

Edwards of the organising club felt I had not had enough track experience so Goodall was asked to drive instead. I went to Brooklands to watch practice and found the car had blown up. Cracked con-rods were diagnosed, and since it was too late to get new ones, it was scratched. As compensation for not driving I had an amusing tea and talk with Thomas Fothringham at the Aero Club. I was tempted to buy his 2.3 Bugatti, but realised that it was too big a step up from the Aston Martin.

Top: Freddie Dixon in white helmet with one of his famous offset single seater Rileys at Donington Park paddock, October 1934. Dixon was an accomplished engine tuner, a successful driver, and earned great respect in motor racing for blunt words but remarkable achievements.

There were three races at the Donington Open Meeting on 6 October 1934, one 25-lap Handicap, one a 50-lap scratch race for larger cars, and the Nuffield Cup – over 100 miles on handicap for cars under 1500cc. There was a good entry for the Nuffield Trophy including Lord Howe (Delage), Raymond Mays and Humphrey Cook (new ERAs), Freddie Dixon and Percy McLure (Rileys), and Seaman, Martin, Jackson, and Dodson (MG Magnettes), and Aldington (Frazer-Nash). Staniland was in the white Riley belonging to Raymond Mays that had effectively been the ERA prototype. Mays won the £200 first prize in heavy rain, from Dick Seaman (MG Magnette) and Kenneth Evans (supercharged MG Midget) to give the ERA its first victory. Humphrey Cook in an 1100cc ERA finished well confounding critics who prophesied the new design would not last a course heavy on engines and brakes.

Whitney Straight was never pressed in his 3-litre Maserati throughout the 50-mile scratch race and was able to ease up in the later stages. He was lapping at a new record speed for Donington of over 70mph in practice but his best lap in the race was 2 minutes 14.6 seconds, 68.7mph (110.3kph). Among Reggie Tongue's 13 competitors were Appleton in the twin rear tyred Appleton Special, looking extremely unsteady according to *The Motor*, Geoffrey Dunfee and Allen in MG Midgets, and various Frazer-Nashes, Rileys, a supercharged Morris and Powys Lybbe in his Alvis.

Reggie grumbled to his diary about the amount of unproductive waiting on race day and gave an account of the handicap race. The Brooklands handicapper, AV Ebblewhite was brought in to take charge of the handicapping arrangements, which were a feature of British motor racing throughout the 1920s and 1930s. Competitors were sparse; there were relatively few proper racing cars, their performance varied enormously and while class wins were all very well, successes could be hollow when there were only one or two cars in contention. To give everybody some chance of an outright win, handicapping began in the early days of Brooklands, another legacy of its horse-racing heritage. Cars were set off together in groups based not only on practice times, but also on Ebblewhite's years of experience of form at the track. If his handicapping was well judged, the fastest cars should have been catching the slowest just as they reached the finishing line. First off were the so-called "Limit" cars.

Right: *Reggie's quest for something faster led to the MG Magnette of Dick Seaman and Whitney Straight, standing left and right behind the car in the paddock at Donington.*

The Brooklands clubhouse was a great place for getting to know the colourful personalities of motor racing. On this occasion I met Chris Staniland, Major Gardner, AO Saunders-Davies, and Alec Cuthbert for the first time. I spent the race in John Appleton's pit, next to Dixon's and it rained, leading to a number of bad skids and accidents. Pat Fairfield's Riley spun wildly at The Fork, hit the fence beside the scoreboard, and although Pat seemed to recover it, skidded again on the Railway Straight and went backwards through the iron fence. Freddie Dixon spun at The Fork as well, although he went on to win, and John Cobb withdrew the Railton due to the weather. Percy Maclure and Von der Becke were second in the Riley and Major Gardner third with Benjy. I went to Gibsons as Major Gardner's guest after the race on Saturday.

I came to Donington after spending a few days with my grandparents and met Mac with the Aston on Friday lunchtime. Everything was OK in practice except that it rained most of the time, and we had our old oiling trouble. After five fast laps the oil in the tank got into the sump by way of the vent pipe due to hard braking. We cured this by draining about a gallon out of the tank. I nearly came unstuck in the rain on one corner, and then a bonnet flew off a Bugatti just when Mays (ERA) and I were about to pass it. Fortunately nothing happened and the bonnet landed in a field.

I stayed at Donington Hall, and went into Derby in the Singer, dining with the Evans family. Kenneth came third in the Nuffield Trophy next day. Donington Hall was built in the 17th century and had been a prisoner of war camp in the First World War. They still had the tunnel the Germans had dug to try and escape. It was a barrack of a place run by a woman housekeeper on behalf of the owner of the estate. JG Shields. The Hall had nominally 80 bedrooms and when Fred Craner and his Derby and District Motor Club developed the 2.19 mile (3.52km) circuit in 1933 it became the clubhouse. We slept in a sort of dormitory with beds down both sides. Still we got a good breakfast and dinner and were well looked after.

One of the guests was former motorcyclist Freddie Dixon, a popular Yorkshireman, Brooklands regular, and expert with Rileys. Some of Freddie's conjectures on engineering did not stand the test of time, but one on which there was no doubt was his obsession with reducing friction. Everything in his car was polished and every bearing made as frictionless as could be. The result was that his cars went extremely well. Freddie could be abrasive but he was tough, and had it not been for his predilection for drink, he would have enjoyed a longer and perhaps more distinguished career. As it was he did pioneering work with Tony Rolt on four wheel drive and four wheel steering, and they planned a record car with a swash-plate engine.

Freddie went down to the Donington Hall kitchen in the dead of night to try and rustle up some food. Perhaps dinner had not been lavish. Unfortunately the chef was still up, and mistaking Freddie for a burglar, picked up a meat cleaver and challenged him. Freddie was as plucky on the track as anyone, but confronted by an irate chef with a large knife, made off. It was a noisy altercation, Freddie running through the dormitory screaming, but the incident passed off without injury.

I made a tour before the start of the handicap race and as we went off it began to rain. The Limit cars were Geoffrey Dunfee's Midget, the Appleton, Cuth Harrison's 1080cc Ford, Parrish's Austin, CA Richardson's Riley, and Fred Allen's Midget. When the Get Ready was called frenzied efforts were still being made to start the Appleton – Dunfee and Harrison had kept their cars running although the Ford was boiling. Ebblewhite dropped the flag for an untidy start.

My Aston was among the eight cars in the second group starting 40 seconds after the Limit men. Peter Skinner's little red Morris Minor, timed at 100mph at Brooklands, made the best start. The first excitement came when Harrison, in his white Ford leading the Limit cars went out of control on the downhill stretch towards the hairpin. He was in a desperate plight by the time he got to the bottom and duly went off. Clayton's Amilcar and Greaves's Aston Martin spun in front of me at Starkeys. I narrowly missed them and eventually worked up to fourth, losing third place by 1sec after being next to last away. On the second lap a more serious incident took place. C D Parrish (Austin) and Dunfee (MG Midget) had been duelling happily, when Parrish skidded on a bump at Coppice, and Dunfee could not avoid touching wheels with him. The Austin overturned and the MG went backwards through a fence at speed, finishing up 200 yards away. Parish probably owed his life to his crash helmet. It had several dents in it, and although he was taken to hospital with cuts and bruises, his injuries were not severe. Peter Skinner with his Shelsley Morris Minor Special set fastest lap, gaining on Richardson's Riley that had overhauled the Appleton only to run out of petrol. Nobody could catch Richardson who started 40sec ahead.

Thus the active season ended. The Aston Martin went back to town with Mac. I went to Derby and dined with the Evanses, Major Gardner, and TASO Matheson. But the social season was barely starting. I attended the final Brooklands meeting on 13 October as a spectator, saw Mrs Petre break the lap record in practice, and Doreen Evans win the women's' mountain race. On the 19th I was awarded the OUMDC Shield, for best performance by an Oxford member during season, and the following day began trying to sell the Aston Martin through Winter Garden Garages at Olympia.

It had been a marvellous car all season. At Donington I was using 5500 rpm in the indirect gears and 5300rpm in top. These were very demanding speeds, at which the engine was highly stressed, yet it never displayed any temperament. Its survival was a tribute to good design and careful assembly, with great attention paid to balancing all the components.

Top: Two cars take to the grass while Reggie speeds past at Donington.

After the experience in Ireland however I felt that the Aston Martin was not quite fast enough for what I wanted, and in October I got Dennis Evans of Bellevue to enquire about the Whitney Straight MG Magnette that Dick Seaman had been driving all season. He reported back that it was available and by 1 November I had bought it for £400. I went to Brooklands on 10 November with Phipps and Neill, and met WE "Wilkie" Wilkinson the Bellevue head mechanic with the car. The track was closed and it was raining hard, but I was able to try the car out on the aerodrome road. It was excellent and felt fast. It did not steer at all badly even though MG persisted with the awful Marles-Weller worm and peg steering and only 1934 K3s had proper Bishop Cam worm and wheel. The body felt a bit loose which made the steering column waggle about but this seemed easily curable.

I kept advertising it. It was featured in *The Autocar* two weeks running: "ASTON MARTIN raced Le Mans 10 hour Spa, Phoenix Park, Donington, etc, excellent history, latest type, chassis No LM10; £450 RE Tongue, 6 Ship Street, Oxford." The only result was a letter from a man called Oats trying to sell me a supercharged Aston Martin.

The Inter Varsity trial in November, with Phipps as passenger in the Singer, fulfilled an ambition when we won a premier award for the third year running. It was debatable whether to use ordinary tyres or, as we eventually decided, competition tyres. With only ten days to go the car was still going badly until Wilkie discovered the timing was out and reset the valve clearances. We practised the special tests before the trial on Friday, failing Crowell on the first attempt. It turned out better to keep the foot down at 6000rpm in first, even when wheelspin came on, and managed up after a restart. With new plugs and Benzol/petrol 50/50 it was plain sailing on the day. We sprinted up Crowell in spite of being baulked by Kenneth Evans, and finished back in Oxford, with Charles Penn-Hughes and James Jefferiss who were staying with me.

I introduced Penn at the OUMDC dinner where he gave a first-rate display of films he had taken. It was also an excellent dinner and I gave a breakfast party for twelve on the Sunday morning. I grasped the opportunity to drive his Mille Miglia Alfa Romeo 2.3-litre on Sunday. It was unforgettable. I did not realise I was doing 100mph until he pointed it out. He took it up to about 120mph, well off the clock. It was a beautiful car, superbly maintained, and gave me more pleasure in a shorter time than any car I have ever driven. A friend who raced a BMW marvelled at its flawlessness, but acknowledged that fast motoring in it over long distances became too easy, even boring. It was a philosophy of driving with which I found myself in agreement. So long as cars like the Alfa Romeo did not have a completely effortless performance, driving them never lacked interest. Poor Penn was later killed in a flying accident in 1939.

I began to think of competing in a race to Capetown. Captain Duff had the idea that it could be a great overland adventure and aired it at the CUAC dinner in December. I was invited to speak about Le Mans and the other races in the season to an audience that included Raymond Mays, Humphrey Cook, Graham Walker, and Oliver Bertram. The year ran out with the London to Exeter on 28/20December, when I went to the start with JF Claxton, and followed the Evanses as a non-competitor. We left half an hour after them but overtook six three-wheelers before Shaftesbury. We saw the bikes up Fingle where we met Phipps, Neill Melrose and John Dugdale then went to Simms where FS Barnes and Lionel Martin were watching.

International Press-Cutting Bureau, 110, Fleet Street, London, E.C.4.

Extract from
Sporting Life
LONDON
— 2 NOV 1935

INTER-'VARSITY TRIAL

Seventy Entries For To-day's Event

The Inter-'Varsity Trial, which takes place to-day, has attracted an entry of seventy.

The event starts and finishes at the Royal Huts Hotel, Hindhead, and the observed hills include Begley Farm, Gosford Hill ("exhilaration test"), Blind Lane, Abster's Hollow, Scotland Hill (timed section), Oakshott Hill, Unterturkheim, and Steep Hill I. and II.

The event starts at 11 a.m. Entries are as follow:—

MOTOR CYCLES.

W Clarke (499 Vincent H.R.D.), O.U.M.D.C. (v); N Leadley Brown (493 Sunbeam), C.U.A.C. (R); R C Tattersall (348 A.J.S.), C.U.A.C. (R); C A Burfield (348 Velocette), C.U.A.C. (V); B T Hardy (498 Raleigh), C.U.A.C. (V); B G Rawlins (249 B.S.A.), C.U.A.C. (R); L F Fox (490 Panther), C.U.A.C. (R).

CARS.

R E Tongue (3,622 Ford), O.U.M.D.C. (v); W M Peel (1,496 Frazer Nash), O.U.M.D.C. (r); N G Watson (1,496 Frazer Nash), C.U.A.C. (R); P N Whitehead (3,622 Ford), C.U.A.C. (R); A C Fairtlough (1,991 A.C.), C.U.A.C. (V); J D im Thurn (1,944 A.M. Special), C.U.A.C. (V); G F Stooks (847 M.G.), O.U.M.D.C. (v); K D Evans (1,287 M.G.), O.U.M.D.C. (v); I O F Peters (1,496 Frazer Nash), C.U.A.C. (R); Hon J C C Cavendish (3,622 Ford), C.U.A.C. (R).

H G Conway (1,991 A.C.), C.U.A.C. (V); A B Waters (2,054 Avon Standard), C.U.A.C. (V); A R Phipps (1,495 Aston Martin), O.U.M.D.C. (r); J B Webb (1,287 M.G.), O.U.M.D.C. (r); A A Millard (1,496 Frazer Nash), C.U.A.C. (R); J P Eber (847 Vale), C.U.A.C. (R); I F Connell (1,991 Triumph), C.U.A.C. (V); J K Maw (1,287 M.G.), C.U.A.C. (V); P D Odlum (1,287 M.G.), O.U.M.D.C. (r).

G B C Sumner (2,994 Austro-Daimler), O.U.M.D.C. (v); L P Jaques (1,200 Triumph), C.U.A.C. (R); A R Porter (2,966 Bentley), C.U.A.C. (R); K M Petter (1,087 M.G.), C.U.A.C. (V); D D Clapham (1,496 Alvis), C.U.A.C. (V); J E B Simeon (1,075 B.S.A.), O.U.M.D.C. (v); J G C Ruston (1,642 Wolseley), O.U.M.D.C. (v); D C Stenning (1,104 Lagonda), C.U.A.C. (R).

R M Proctor (1,170 Ford), C.U.A.C. (R); R de Yarburgh-Bateson (1,991 A.C.), C.U.A.C. (V); M W B May (1,702 Alvis), C.U.A.C. (V); G Treverton (1,496 Frazer Nash), O.U.M.D.C. (r); P McEntee (3,622 Ford), O.U.M.D.C. (v); K Buckley (2,996 Bentley), C.U.A.C (R).

R A MacRobert (1,104 Lagonda), C.U.A.C. (R); P Mursell (933 Ford). C.U.A.C. (V); T A Frazer (1,496 Frazer Nash), C.U.A.C. (V); M G Ashby (1,495 Aston Martin), O.U.M.D.C. (r); Hon A D Chetwynd (3,622 Ford), O.U.M.D.C. (v); B Heath (1,185 Hillman Minx), C.U.A.C. (R); E Brettell (747 Austin), C.U.A.C. (R); E W Bass (1,196 Lancia Augusta), C.U.A.C. (V).

R V C Bolster (1¾-litre Morris Cowley), C.U.A.C. (V); Lord Avebury (1,493 Singer), O.U.M.D.C. (r); J R B Hartnoll (1,496 Frazer Nash), O.U.M.D.C. (r); H P Dixon (1,500 Delage), C.U.A.C. (R); P A G Dixey (1,991 Lagonda), C.U.A.C. (R); D H Murray (1,496 Frazer Nash), C.U.A.C. (V); M A A Allfrey (3,622 Ford), C.U.A.C. (V); — Berresford (847 M.G.), O.U.M.D.C.

P Hall (1,385 Wolseley), O.U.M.D.C. (r); O M Williams (2-litre Rover), C.U.A.C. (R); T Zissu (3,622 Ford), C.U.A.C. (R); E J Kehoe (3,622 Ford), C.U.A.C. (V); J C Smith (1,125 Austin), C.U.A.C. (V); R Breare (847 M.G.), O.U.M.D.C.; R Powell (1,100 Wolseley), O.U.M.D.C. (r).

G C Chalkley (2,996 Bentley), C.U.A.C. (R); A M Leitch (2,230 Ford), C.U.A.C. (V); J Sharpley (1,496 Frazer Nash), O.U.M.D.C (r); R Hanson (2-litre Bugatti), O.U.M.D.C (r); R Byrie (4,398 Bentley), O.U.M.D.C. (r); J Tait (3,622 Ford), O.U.M.D.C. (r); J R Aldworth (1,496 Alvis), O.U.M.D.C. (r).

Abbreviations: V, veteran; R, resident members.

5 1935

I was engaged by the Evanses to organise a team of mechanics for a race in Italy. I was still only 23 and slow to realise when mechanics were disgruntled. They did not like Italian food, and I had to try and keep control, because they were threatening revolt. I felt I must make a stand even though they were mostly older than I was. I overheard one: "Any more of this bloody nonsense from Tongue, and we'll go back to England, and leave him with the bloody vans and the cars and let him sort it out." This would have been a disaster. We still had a race in hand after Italy so I thought I had better try and placate them.

Fortunately I knew a restaurateur on the Swiss border so I rang him up: "We're coming through on Sunday and I want you to prepare a British Sunday lunch. I would like tomato soup, roast beef and Yorkshire pudding, two veg, apple pie, custard, and plenty of beer. We'll arrive at half past twelve." He had it ready, the crew had a great big good solid feed instead of the spaghetti with which they were pretty bored, and they loved it. I overheard them saying: "He's not such a bad chap, I think we ought to give him a bit of support." It was amazing. They say the way to a man's heart is through his stomach and it applied just as well to tough motor racing mechanics.

It was an object lesson in running a racing team when, at the beginning of 1935, I took the K3 MG Magnette to be prepared for racing. Kenneth Evans was at Oxford with me, and he with his

brother Denis and sister Doreen ran the garage in Bellevue Road, Wandsworth Common although Kenneth never actually went into the garage business, he ran the family firm of chartered surveyors. Bellevue had the MG agency and its teams of J2, Montlhéry models, Magnettes and Q-types were very successful. Doreen was the youngest but raced on equal terms with everybody, progressing from J2 to L-type and R-type, then drove at Le Mans in a P-type as one of George Eyston's famous Dancing Daughters team. All the Evans cars were painted pale green with a thin green coachline on each side, and after 1937 were raced by Bellevue Garage (Racing) Ltd established on the other side of the road, of which Wilkie Wilkinson was a director.

I was instrumental in Doreen marrying Senator Phipps' son Alan in July 1936. He raced an MG once or twice in England, and I had asked Doreen to come down to Oxford for the weekend, but she only agreed provided I introduced her to some nice Americans. I never saw anything like it. Alan came into my digs in Ship Street, they took one look at one another and that was it. It was the most remarkable example of love at first sight I have ever seen, and they had many years of happy married life, until she died in California in 1982 shortly before her 66th birthday. Denis also went to live in America and Kenneth became chief flag marshal of the BRDC.

Although both Dick and Whitney had enjoyed a good deal of success with the K3, by the time I got the car the best seemed to have been taken

out of it. I got a lot of useful experience with it and it was very fast, but it was not going to take me forward, and it certainly was not sufficiently reliable for my purposes. I always thought that Dick and Whitney had access to better tuning ability than was available to me. Wilkie Wilkinson who tuned it, and whose reputation flourished in the 1950s with Ecurie Ecosse and two Le Mans victories, was an able enough technician but somehow success with the Magnette eluded him. It did not perform as well as I expected.

Previous page: *Brooklands, April, 1935. Mike Couper in his immaculately-prepared Fox and Nicholl Talbot leads Reggie in his newly acquired MG in the Senior Long Handicap race. JC Davis won at 113.03mph (181.45kph) in his 1.5-litre Delage from Hamilton's Alfa Romeo with Reggie third.*

The K3's influence on motor racing dominated by Continental European manufacturers was significant. The Midget was well established in Britain, MG had made its mark in Class H record-breaking, but anything in top-flight international racing seemed beyond the scope of British manufacturers and MG looked as though it would be outclassed in the Mille Miglia or at Le Mans.

Lord Howe was an experienced racing driver in Bugattis and Alfa Romeos, but he desperately wanted success in a British car. He encouraged Sir William Morris to authorise MG's participation in the Mille Miglia, taking a K3 on an exploratory run over the course in 1933, accompanied by the great Anglophile Count Johnny Lurani. The drivers were to include Sir Henry "Tim" Birkin whose tragic death occurred not long afterwards. The K3s suffered from plug trouble and punctures but won the team prize, the important Gran Premio Brescia, never before gained by a foreign team.

MG K3 chassis number K3011 was bought by American Whitney Willard Straight, who created something of a stir by sitting a university examination one morning and flying himself to Brooklands in his De Havilland Moth in the afternoon. He gave up his studies to form Whitney Straight Ltd buying two 2.9-litre Maseratis and two Magnettes. His head mechanic was Giulio Ramponi, and his protégé Dick Seaman, who drove one of the MGs and modelled his career on the business lines Straight advocated. Whitney Straight had an outstanding wartime career in the RAF and became managing director of BOAC.

Further accomplishments followed at Brooklands, and Straight scored a notable victory in the Coppa Acerbo at Pescara, beating strong Maserati opposition by a fifth of a second. Nuvolari drove a K3 to victory in the Ulster Tourist Trophy. Further successes at Brooklands followed and a K3 took the Class G outer circuit speed record. In the 1934 Le Mans a K3 was in second place when it was forced off the road, but in 1935 it won the 2.0-litre class. A K3 won the 1100cc championship of Italy and the brilliant pair of Richard Seaman and Hugh Hamilton scored some notable successes.

The Seaman-Tongue Magnette differed from the standard K3, which had a heavier slab-tanked body, like the Mille Miglia cars. Their K3011 had a tapered tail with a large fuel tank and two quick-action filler caps, one to let the petrol in, the other to let the air out. Its 6-cylinder overhead camshaft engine was 57mm x 71mm, 1087cc, and with its supercharger driven off the front of the crankshaft, it gave 120bhp (89.5kW). Top speed was 110mph (177kph), when new it cost £795, and it had enjoyed a good deal of success although Straight never seems to have liked it much. In the 1970s he admitted to *Classic Car* that K3011 had given Thomson & Taylor considerable pains mainly due to unspecified troubles with the cylinder head. An early 1933 model, Straight believed it was inferior to the works cars in quality and performance. Perhaps he was relieved when it was off his hands and Reggie's verdict that

Far left: *Doreen Evans and her brother Kenneth accompany their monoposto MG Q-type out of the Brooklands paddock pushed (centre) by Bellevue chief mechanic WE Wilkie Wilkinson.*

Left, above: *Brooklands first meeting 1935. Doreen Evans with her mother in the pits.*

Left, below: *The Magnette at Donington.*

the best had been taken out of it was conceivably an understatement.

A good deal of the commercial rationale for Reggie's motor racing career took place through the connections he made with Seaman, Whitney Straight, and the K3. Straight had a successful season racing his Maserati and K3 on the Continent, and it was from him that Seaman, and subsequently Reggie, learned that there was money to be made there. Straight took the view that racing in Britain was essentially for wealthy amateurs, with nothing in the way of starting money, and very little prize money. He found it was different on the Continent where motor racing was a professional business. Seaman bought the car secretly for the 1934 season. He did not want his parents to know, so it was made to look as though he was driving for Whitney Straight Ltd, which continued to enter it for European races. The arrangement was that it would be supplied with fuel, oil, tyres and plugs, with the starting money and prize money shared between Seaman and Whitney Straight.

Well proportioned, the K3 was low-built and purposeful, the archetypal sports racing two-seater, with a single aero screen and a supercharger slung between the front dumb-irons. The single SU carburettor poked up through the supercharger cowling. Whitney Straight commissioned bodywork from Thomson and Taylor who maintained the car throughout 1933 and 1934. After it won the 1933 Coppa Acerbo Junior, disbelieving Italian rivals demanded that the engine be dismantled to check the dimensions. Dick Seaman began his career with K3011

winning his class and setting a new sports car record at Mont Ventoux but the only major race he won with it was the Berne Grand Prix. His other best place was second in the Nuffield Trophy but even Seaman, for all his gifted driving, was unable to coax much success from the car.

It was some time before the administration of Reggie's motor racing was anything but hand-to-mouth. He cast envious eyes on the way Seaman and Straight seemed to make a commercial success of it, although he may have being deceiving himself. Both were gifted drivers; Reggie Tongue knew he was never in their league of skill and daring, and

that they had far more substantial fortunes to invest in the best preparation and the best machinery. Reggie had an ample private income from his grandfather's Trust and was able to set his motor racing expenses against tax, but his resources were never a match to those of Straight and Seaman, which would be the equivalent of millions in 21st century money. Their wealth would be matched in the years ahead by other rivals, such as the Siamese royal house of Bira and Chula, and the works-backed

ERAs of Raymond Mays.

It was not long before Reggie got to grips with the business side of motor racing however. As a driver he was perhaps too cautious to be completely successful. Racing driving demands sometimes taking a car to the threshold of disaster, just to determine where that threshold lies. It also means crossing the threshold occasionally and crashing. Reggie rarely had accidents. He had a more measured approach, taking as few risks as possible, which had as much to do with not incurring expensive damage to his car as fear of injury. "An outstandingly safe and regular driver", as his friend AF Rivers Fletcher put it in his obituary, "… he was an amateur sportsman of the finest sort … but best-known for the long-distance races, in which he was amongst the front runners staying the distance, but not actually winning … a fine sportsman, one of the last of a breed of pre-war top drivers."

The MG R-type was the last pure racing MG, drawn up under

Above: cowled front of the narrow-bodied R-type MG single seater.

Pages 86-87: Pescara, Italy, the Coppa Acerbo. Reggie's second MG, the ex-Malcolm Campbell R-type with all-too-independent four-wheel suspension.

Left: Backbone chassis of the R-type, an inspired design never fully developed following MG's precipitate withdrawal from racing.

MG K3

1933: owned by Whitney Straight

Date	Event	Driver	Result
13 Aug	Coppa Acerbo, Pescara	W Straight	1st
16 Aug	BRDC 500 miles, Brooklands	W Straight/	
		T Rose-Richards	retired
23 Sep	Brighton Speed Trials	Miss Psyche Altham	1st 1100cc
30 Sep	Shelsley Walsh	Miss Psyche Altham	
7 Oct	Donington	W Straight	non-start
14 Oct	BARC October Brooklands	Miss Psyche Altham	3rd Ladies race
		W Straight	two 2nds, lap rec

1934: sold to Richard Seaman

Date	Event	Driver	Result
3 Mar	Brooklands	RJB Seaman	unplaced 3 races
24 Mar	Donington	RJB Seaman	retired 2 races
March	Inter-Varsity Speed Trials	RJB Seaman	1st
2 Apr	Brooklands	RJB Seaman	unplaced 2 races
23 June	British Empire Trophy	RJB Seaman	retired
22 Jly	Albi Grand Prix	RJB Seaman	retired
12 Aug	Coppa Acerbo, Pescara	RJB Seaman	3rd
26 Aug	Berne Grand Prix	RJB Seaman	1st
16 Sep	Mont Ventoux hill climb	RJB Seaman	1st in class
6 Oct	Nuffield Trophy	RJB Seaman	2nd
13 Oct	BARC October Brooklands	RJB Seaman	2nd Mountain class lap record

1935: owned by Reggie Tongue

Date	Event	Driver	Result
16 Mar	BARC Brooklands	RE Tongue	retired unplaced
23 Mar	Inter-Varsity Speed Trials Syston Park	RE Tongue	1st 1100cc racing
13 Apl	Donington	RE Tongue	unplaced
22 Apl	BARC Easter Brooklands	RE Tongue	3rd and unplaced

owned by Sam Collier

Date	Event	Driver	Result
22 Jun	County Down Trophy	S Collier	6th
14 Jly	Albi	S Collier/G Rand	retired

Hubert Charles and developed by Cec Cousins, Syd Enever, and Bill Renwick to a most adventurous design. Its factory designation was EX 147, and it had the Q-type's engine with a Zoller supercharger. The chassis frame was a novel backbone design, welded up from 16-gauge steel, light enough to be carried by one man, yet immensely strong. It took the shape of a Y with the prongs at the front joined up by a box section holding the engine, not unlike the Lotus Elan of 1968, and the differential was mounted at the rearmost end. A radical feature was independent suspension to all four wheels, by torsion bar springs, revolutionary for a firm that had been making beam axles and half-elliptic springs ever since its foundation. The R-type even had hydraulic shock absorbers.

The intention was to have a racing car capable of handling the Q-type's substantial power output of 113bhp (84.3kW) rather better than the Q-type could. The engine capacity was only 746cc, and a preselector gearbox was used as much to provide a clutch that would take up the drive smoothly enough to preserve the transmission's integrity, as achieve swift gearchanging Much was expected of these small jewel-like single-seaters with lightweight aluminium bodywork that made them look like miniature grand prix cars. Ten were built between April and June 1935 before Lord Nuffield took MG out of racing.

The announcement that works participation in racing was to cease left MG shocked and offended. The cars had not yet undergone the planned development programme, nor had they had time to show winning form. Four were entered for a race at Brooklands driven by Malcolm Campbell, Norman Black, Wal Handley, and Doreen Evans.

Only two finished, coming first and second in their class, and although running well they showed a worrying amount of roll on corners. The short drive shafts proved troublesome in their next race, but the works was confident, and probably well capable of putting this right given the necessary resources.

It was not to be. MG had been Lord Nuffield's personal property until July 1935 when he sold it to Morris Motors Ltd, Leonard Lord was put in as managing director, and Cecil Kimber effectively demoted to General Manager. One of Lord's first actions was to go to the competitions department and famously remark, "Well that lot can go for a start."

Left: *R-type awaits the starting signal at Shelsley Walsh. Behind Reggie, with hands on hips, the ever present Bellevue head mechanic Wilkie Wilkinson.*

Top right: *Reggie photographed for his album Kenneth Evans and Dr Harry Carleton, Reggie's friend from his days at Oxford, who accompanied him to races as often as he could.*

Bottom right: *In the pits at Berne the winning Mercedes-Benz W25B of Rudolf Caracciola with its supercharger air intakes visible through the front grille.*

I raced the K3 towards the end of 1934, mostly at Brooklands, although I also took it to Ireland but without much success. It was very fast due to the high supercharger boost employed but the Magnette was unreliable. After one or two Brooklands races and speed trials I decided to sell it in mid-season. By 1936 I felt I was ready for a single-seater. There were opportunities in small-capacity single-seater racing both in Britain and on the Continent, and Sir Malcolm Campbell wanted to sell his R-type, one of the survivors of MG's last works team. The Magnette was sold to Sam Collier who took it to America in 1936 where it remained until 1979. The disbandment of the works team of R-types seemed to be my gain and I decided to take it to Europe at the height of the season. The noise the little supercharged engine made was ear splitting. It was one high screech but when I got to Pescara I broke a gear in the gearbox. I thought I would have to withdraw until a man came along and said, "I hear you are unable to race on Sunday. It is no problem," he assured me, "I can make you a new one." We stripped the

I had been fastest 1100 with the K3 in the Inter-Varsity Speed Trials of 1935 and in 1936 made fastest time of the day with the R-type, setting a new record for the course that stood for several years. In long distance races however the car was inconsistent; it never gained the success its radical design deserved, and to which MG had by now grown accustomed. It deserved further development, cut short alas by Lord Nuffield's withdrawal of financial support.

Top left: *Reggie puzzles over a new-fangled parking meter in the United States.*

Below: *Dick Seaman's difficulties with his ERA R1B in 1935 led Reggie to have his serviced by Thomson and Taylor in 1936. Nevertheless he won the Coppa Acerbo (pictured here) his first win with the car at 78.99mph (126.8kph). On the right his manager Tony Birch.*

box down and he came back in a very short time with a beautifully made replacement that fitted perfectly. Unfortunately I was late for practice and there was no time to do the necessary fine-tuning. "Don't worry about that," he said. "I'll talk to the police." So with the tacit permission, if not actually the connivance of the local constabulary, I tested this car round the houses and in the streets near the Station Hotel where I was staying. Everybody came out and sat on the pavement or on chairs outside their front doors while I hurtled round Pescara. It could never have happened anywhere else, except perhaps Ireland.

The R-type represented a huge advance in British racing car design. Although well made it did not have quite enough power in relation to its weight. The carburation was difficult to get right, the supercharger was troublesome, and the suspension turned out to be too independent. Going round a corner at speed was like being in an aeroplane, the whole car banking steeply due to the torsion bars being too resilient. This was later modified and I did have one excellent success before parting with the R-type to Charlie Manders.

6 ERA 1936

Alfa Romeo, Mercedes-Benz, and Auto Union was outclassing everybody in grand prix racing, the German teams winning more or less as they pleased by virtue of lavish resources, technical superiority, and efficient organisation. Such opposition as Bugatti, Maserati, Talbot or Delahaye could muster was eclipsed, and private entrants generally came nowhere.

Sports car racing was not so beset. As Reggie demonstrated in 1934 at Le Mans in his first big race, a private team could give a good account of itself at the highest level, and there was rewarding sport to be had in some single-seater classes. Organisers were often eager to run quite major events not as grands prix, but from 1932 onwards, for voiturettes. From almost the start of motor racing there had been classes for cars of a different sort to those in the main events; in the 1930s these were the national grands prix. The term voiturette was derived from voitures légères or light cars, the 3-litre cars of pre-1914 when grand prix cars were 12- or 14-litre giants.

In the 1920s the smaller races were run for petites cylindrées or voiturettes, the prescribed engine size depending on the premier formula in vogue. Sometimes the limit was 1100cc, sometimes 1500cc, but although the cars were smaller the importance of the races was scarcely

diminished. It was not like the modern Formula 2 or Formula 3, regarded as cadet classes. It was almost as important as a proper national grand prix and there was plenty of competition both from purpose-built racing cars and stripped-down sports cars such as MGs, Aston Martins, Maseratis, Bugattis, Rileys, and Amilcars.

English Racing Automobiles (ERAs) were new purpose-built voiturettes. Ten years had gone by without a British victory in a grand prix and none seemed likely, but the astute and well-established driver Raymond Mays, financier Humphrey Cook and engineer Peter Berthon in 1933-1934 grasped the opportunity to create a team of British cars. Reid Railton designed the chassis. He had been responsible for the Railton car, and was connected with the Brooklands engineering firm Thomson and Taylor, where the chassis frame was built.

ERAs could be bought off the peg. Prices for 1100cc, 1500cc and 2000cc in 1934 were £1500, £1700, and £1850 – about the price of a new 3½-litre Bentley, and rather more than its rival, the Alta of Geoffrey Taylor, although still four times what Reggie Tongue paid for the K3 MG. The basis of the ERA was a stout chassis frame with, at first, plain semi-elliptic springs front and rear. The engine was a highly tuned version of a 6-cylinder twin high-camshaft engine based on a Riley

design, there was a Roots-type supercharger designed by Tom Murray Jamieson and the 1½-litre produced about 150bhp (111.9kW) at 6,500rpm, soon raised to 175bhp (130.5kW). For 1936 it was between 220bhp (164kW) and 230bhp (171.5kW), but there was not much of it around 3500 to 3750rpm. Later 2-litre cars with Zoller blowers were said to be good for 340bhp (253.5kW). The gearbox was a Wilson preselector.

An early ERA weighing 1624lb (736.6kg) would reach 125mph (201.1kph), depending on the final drive ratio, and although its first appearances in races were unsuccessful it quickly established a reputation for speed and reliability. ERA's plan was to enhance power output by increasing the boost of the Zoller supercharger. Historian and ERA authority Peter Hull writes about driving one: "Even by modern standards an ERA is fast, being capable of at least 125mph, some nearer 150mph, but the suspension is hard and the roadholding on the primitive side. Perhaps that is not so significant on modern circuits because paradoxically as racing car suspension has improved, so track surfaces have been getting smoother, and the circuits are made to suit the cars with great precautions not to upset them or their drivers – in both senses of the word." He found the preselector gearbox took a bit of getting used to, as two separate movements were needed to change gear instead of one complete one.

Reggie Tongue had been impressed with the ERA at Donington in October 1934, when he had been put out at receiving an invitation with his Aston Martin only for a lesser 25mile handicap and not for the main event of the day, the Nuffield Trophy. Bearing in mind his fine performances at Le Mans and Dublin, and his lap speeds in the Aston, the oversight looked curious. His worry was that

ERA might not look on him as a suitable candidate for one of its cars, although in truth it was such a hand-to-mouth outfit that it was only too pleased to take his money.

ERA took firm orders for seven 1500cc cars in the winter of 1935-1936, more staff was taken on, and the workshop extended in order to cope. The first order came in October 1935 from Prince Chula for his cousin Prince Bira. Chula was planning a busy season for Bira and decided one car would be inadequate so ordered two. The others were for Dr JA Benjafield, Arthur Dobson, Earl Howe, Dennis Scribbans, Peter Whitehead, and Reggie Tongue. Richard Seaman meanwhile had grown disillusioned with ERA Ltd, sold his 1935 R1B, and with Ramponi his mechanic embarked on modifying Lord Howe's 1927 GP Delage. He felt he had been badly let down, particularly after Mays and Berthon tried to foist a dud second-hand engine on him, and beating the works ERAs with a car already nine years old appealed to him.

P93: Reggie's first major win, at Cork with the ERA. He does a tour of the course with A Powys-Lybbe (with cap) and Austin Dobson, who finished second and third.

Top left: *ERA artistry. Dick Seaman in R1B on Corner 14 of the Grossglockner hill climb. Loose surface, straw bales, and virtually unguarded drops a challenge to drivers of upright English single seaters.*

Right: *Pescara. Dick Seaman with mechanic Jock Finlayson.*

ERA was holding out the promise of making a few cars for private individuals, and I asked to be put on the list. It would change the whole of my racing experience. It was a thoroughbred out and out racing car, and in February I went to Bourne to see Peter Berthon, to be told the one I had ordered would not be ready until the second week in April, which was disappointing. Raymond Mays and Humphrey Cook wanted me to have a sprint engine as well; I decided on the special differential to help me on getaways. When I was passing Donington the following month, Mays was trying out an ERA, so I stopped and watched and listened to the familiar noise and took in the pungent smell of Castrol R.

The advent of the ERA was important to enthusiasts, as reflected in *Motor Sport,* which in September 1935 declared the ERA successes the most remarkable feature of the whole season. It said that as a result of the sudden rise to supremacy of ERA Continental organisers were ordering new gramophone records of the British national anthem to play at the end of races. The ERA was now regarded as unbeatable. Maserati and Bugatti it said cheerfully (and as it turned out, wrongly) had been subdued.

I was looking forward to driving the ERA, especially after blowing up the R-type in March at Brooklands. Its supercharger shattered into a thousand pieces and I had to dash to London for

another one. The mechanics fitted it quickly the same afternoon, but when I tried it out again, it gave further trouble. During the earlier break-up, a piece of it had lodged underneath a valve, bending the stem as soon as the engine was started again.

ERA promised delivery of the car in April, but bearing in mind Dick Seaman's experiences of 1935 when his car had been late, I went to see them again. It was the beginning of May and I found the engine was not yet assembled. It was

Previous page: *Cork, the cars lining up for the starting grid. CEC Martin (Alfa Romeo) and B Bira (ERA) on the front row. Bira crashed and Martin pushed over the finishing line to share the team prize. Reggie is in ERA No 8 immediately behind.*

Right: *Start of the first heat at Albi July 1936. At first Lord Howe's ERA led and has disappeared off the left of the picture, but he dropped out after only a lap. He is followed by French driver Marcel Lehoux (ERA No4 R3B mechanic FRW Lofty England later Chairman of Jaguar), Pat Fairfield (ERA 8), and B Bira (ERA 10 R5B Remus), from Bianco (Maserati) Reggie Tongue (ERA 22 R11B) and Veyron (Bugatti). Bira won at 92.19mph (147.99kph), his only victory with Remus. Fairfield retired like Howe with gearbox trouble, and Reggie went out with a puncture. A week later Lehoux was killed in R3B at Deauville.*

then promised for 5 May, and I duly took delivery of R11B with engines 5017 and 5019; one installed in the car and one spare. I did not much want ERA Ltd to look after the car. I had not liked the way Dick Seaman had been dealt with, so I had lunch with Ken Taylor at the Aero Club, and told him I wanted to bring the ERA to him. I had only half-promised to let ERA Bourne service it. Thomson and Taylor had made the chassis, so it seemed reasonable to give them the responsibility of tuning it, and provide mechanics to come to races. It would bring me close to Ken Taylor, Ken Thomson and Reid Railton, and I became one of their best customers. One means of keeping a check on the amount of money I was spending and, in a way, get some of it back, was to take a keen interest in the firm whose finances were if not precarious at the very least sensitive to market changes.

During the week I worked in a stockbroker's office, which seemed prepared to allow me to motor race, provided there was not too much of it and I kept on top of the work. The pay was fairly nominal; I was once called in to see the partners who sat looking grave in their black jackets and striped trousers. I thought they were going to be upset about some Danske Norske 3.5% Bearer Bonds that had been sent by mistake to Scotland instead of Oslo but they were not. They invited me to sit down which was a good sign because they never fired anybody sitting down. Instead they said they were about to award me what they claimed was the biggest percentage rise ever in the history of the firm. On account of the good work I was doing my weekly wage was increased from £1 to 30/- (£1.50). They considered it a great pat on the back.

My involvement with Thomson and Taylor grew as the 1930s progressed and the connection with Reid Railton was responsible for

buying a Railton car. During 1937 I became the owner of a two-seater 28.8hp Railton Drophead Coupe FBP274. As a reliable, comfortable and fast means of travel, it was in a class by itself. It was possible to average 50mph (80kph) on long runs due to the swift acceleration and good braking. On the Continent, where I used it a great deal, it suffered from one persistent fault, which impugned its 100% reliability. It overheated at high altitude on Alpine passes; the petrol boiled in the pump producing an air lock, and the engine lost power. The water pump leaked, even in Britain, yet despite all that my 50,000 miles in the Railton were cheap and thoroughly enjoyable.

I took my uncle's Austin to the Isle of Man for a reconnaissance of the TT circuit, using up several mornings before breakfast learning it, and finding it quite difficult. Together with the editor of the Isle of Man Times and Cowin from the House of Keys I went round the previous three years' circuits used in the car races, then the one to be used in 1935. I told them I did not like the grass banks, since they got in the way of good sight lines through the corners but then blighted my visit by backing the Austin into a lamp-post.

The ERA's shake-down event consisted of short five-lap races at Donington on 9 May and we were delighted to gain a second and two thirds. Railton's chassis was a marvellous design. He was an engineering genius, and although like lots of British engineering the ERA was a little heavy, it did its job admirably. Its next outing was in Ireland, the Cork 200 mile race, and the result exceeded my wildest dreams.

Bira in his ERA was the chief rival and I sat on his tail for lap after lap. Since I had a high axle ratio and he had a low one I never allowed him to get more than two seconds ahead. White nearly put me out of the race when I came round a corner to be confronted with boulders strewn across the track from a wall he had knocked down.

ERA R11B: R E Tongue 1936

May 9	Derby & District MC Meeting Donington		
	5 Lap Handicap up to 1500cc		2nd
	5 Lap Handicap up to 5000 cc		3rd
	5 Lap Scratch Race up to 1500cc		3rd
	10 Lap Handicap up to 5000cc		Unplaced
May 16	Cork 200 Mile Race	Cork, Ireland	1st (85.53 mph)
May 28	RAC Light Car Race	Douglas, Isle of Man	ret (ignition)
June 21	Picardy Grand Prix	Péronne, France	ret. (oil pressure)
July 12	Albi Grand Prix	Albi, France	ret (puncture)
July 19	Develiers les Rangers hillcb	Switzerland	1st 1500cc Class
Aug 23	Prix de Berne	Berne, Switzerland	3rd
Aug 30	Freiburg Hill Climb	Germany	1st in C 8m49.2s
Sept 12	Midland AC Hill Climb	Shelsley Walsh	11th (47.01s)
Sept 26	Irish MRC 200 Mile Race	Phoenix Park, Dublin	6th
Oct 3	Donington Grand Prix	Donington	4th
Oct 17	BARC Autumn Meeting Siam Trophy Brooklands		5th
	Oxford & Cambridge Mountain Race		1st (74.98mph)

Top: *Reggie celebrates in Cork.*

He finished the race with a buckled wheel. Charlie Martin chucked out so much oil that my visor became opaque and when I pulled up my goggles they broke so I finished the race pulling 130mph (208.7kph) on the straight with no eye protection. My car ran marvellously. We decided to stop for fuel on lap 20 after doing a careful fuel consumption test in practice; Hill, Evan Hughes, and Chip Peters were in my pit and we refuelled in 30 seconds. I used Champion plugs instead of KLG because I thought the engine ran more smoothly with no misfiring.

The victory in Cork was resounding although nearly spoiled by an unguarded comment on the radio after the finish. Nobody ever gave you any idea of what to say or told you what not to say. Nobody cut you off, and I unfortunately got into the box and blurted out: "Well, it was a most enjoyable day, I had a frightfully good race, the car went beautifully and I do want to say one thing to people around me. You've got one of the finest circuits in Europe, at least one of the finest circuits I've ever raced over, I could easily say irrespective of world wide, it is the best in the British Isles." I was lucky not to start a revolution, forgetting in the excitement that Cork was in the Irish Free State and strictly not the British Isles.

My exploratory laps of the Isle of Man had been conducted with the next event in mind, the RAC Light Car Race, when I stayed with the ERA people at the Fort Anne Hotel. The mechanics were put up at Mrs Hotchkiss's on Bray Hill on

the TT course. Lord Howe congratulated me on Cork, Harry Carleton my old friend from university came over, and John Dugdale of *The Autocar* asked if he could help in the pits, but he turned up late so I decided not to ask him again.

Practice in the Isle of Man was unsatisfactory. The car was not going properly on either day; engine pickup was poor. I could only hope it was due to the weather, then a stone smashed the windscreen, and I had to have a new one sent over by Green Label parcel service from Bourne on the evening boat. The race was not much better; I had a bad getaway from the start and I was not making up on Wakefield, although it looked as though I might catch Everitt, when the engine began to misfire and I had to call at the pits on every lap. I retired on the sixth. It was a great race and Dick Seaman won but I had a blazing row with Rex Munday of KLG in Putney Vale about plugs.

Top: *the prize-giving at Cork, Reggie in light suit on right, and Powys-Lybbe (centre).*

Left: *Reggie's ERA lines up in front of the Cork pits before the start.*

Right: *Cork, the hairpin, White's Bugatti a lap behind runs wide to let race leaders Bira's and Reggie Tongue's ERAs through. Bira, driving R5B Remus, retired when his supercharger seized.*

Munday prepared KLG advertising following the Cork race, without receiving the customary telegram from me, with the details of what equipment we had been using. I had sent a wire saying "WON CORK RACE. NEVER MISSED A BEAT" and he had been happily producing advertisements to the effect that it was won on KLG plugs. However I had been using Champions after the KLGs had been troublesome in practice. Champion was delighted and produced a suitable advertisement too, so Munday was very put out and demanded to know when I had made the change. I said my mechanic had produced them when I got to Cork, but Munday got to know that I had collected them the previous week. I had also been to KLG then, and reminded him that I was not compelled to use KLG, since I had no contract.

Apparently Munday had had to get KLG to make the plugs I needed specially, as they were out of stock, but that was their fault, not mine. He said the plugs should have cost a guinea (£1.10p) each and I had got them for 2/6 (12.5p) on the understanding that I would use them. There had been no understanding. He accused my mechanic of being in Champion's pocket and wondered what bonus I was getting from Champion as obviously I had not paid for the plugs. I swore that I had no bonus and obtained the plugs in the usual way, managing to keep my temper despite being called a "double-faced swine". It all became very personal. It was a good job I was a good-natured and tolerant man. Munday was always scared stiff of Ken Taylor and so also now probably of me.

I took the car testing at Donington in June to try and trace the misfiring problem. I was getting thoroughly fed up with it, so I tried out the new engine 5019 with the old supercharger. It was only after a lot of fruitless running that I discovered

ERA's foreman had put in soft plugs instead of hard ones. I tried changing from Champion NM5 to KLG 718C but it was no better and we used up all our available fuel to no effect The KLG people were charming, they could not have been nicer and were really sorry that their plugs had not been as good as they should have been at Cork. I went back to London, consoled myself with a drink at the RAC, a room at Berner's Hotel where I had a haircut (the hairdresser was a motor racing enthusiast and knew I was a racing driver which was amusing), changed into tails and was in the Savoy by 7.30pm. There I saw Fred Perry who had just won the Wimbledon Championships and Bebe Daniells before going to a Leslie Henson show.

The engine misfiring remained a worry. The engineering side of the engine seemed sound enough so we went back to Bourne, staying overnight in The Angel, and resolved to try Brooklands again for more continuous running. I began to understand Seaman's disillusionment with ERA. There was just as much faulty running at Brooklands. Both engines had troublesome supercharger gears and the old oil bothers reappeared. When the car was run quickly on the outer circuit the sump filled up and the oil tank emptied, which took a lot of work to eradicate before setting off for the next race at Péronne.

Travelling could sometimes be fraught and on this occasion we got mixed up with French strikers in Calais. They looked a menacing lot, then the Calais-Boulogne road was up, and nobody knew how to get round it. One of the charms of rural road circuits like Péronne was that you could do a bit of unofficial practice and get to know the circuit before it opened for the official sessions. It was a difficult circuit, the car seemed high geared on the 4.0:1 axle, but it was not really possible to go fast because there were so many farm carts. It provided an opportunity to sort out the carburation and check the valve clearances, then after lunch we decided Champion plugs were no good, and went back to KLG.

Almost as soon as official practice began we ran into trouble. As I got to the end of the straight there was a fearful clattering noise. I felt it through my feet and thought at first that it was the gearbox. It turned out to be the blower drive that had broken again, and the bang caused by the fracture, had been transmitted right through the engine and gearbox. My T&T mechanic Jimmy worked all night to fit new blower drive gears and get the car ready for next day's practice.

Unfortunately when we started in the morning I could not get any oil pressure worth speaking of. The gauge should have been reading 100lbs but it would only reach 60lbs. We were still using the new engine and I managed to do one lap fast enough to get me on to the third row in the second heat. Jimmy again worked hard but could find nothing wrong, so in the afternoon I took it out to get the carburation right, for conditions at the same time of day as the race would be.

Our luck was out from the beginning of race day. When I arrived at the pits the front nearside wheel kept locking on even though I was not pressing the brake pedal. Howe's and Seaman's mechanics kindly came to lend a helping hand to eradicate the problem, which was due to a brake connection, and I was able to get away in the second heat. I was up with the leaders, lay fourth at the end of the first lap, and was just about to pass Raymond Mays when he retired. The engine now required quite a lot of nursing but despite that I finished third behind

Dick Seaman (Delage) and Lord Howe (ERA). In the final the oil pressure was falling away on corners, and although I kept in fourth place when I was running, had to retire due to the scavenge pump giving out and the sump filling with oil again. It was yet another race in which we had had bad luck in no uncertain manner

Afterwards I had champagne with the man who kindly lent me his garage and then went back to dinner at St Quentin with the Dobsons and Cyril Paul. Bira and Chula were having dinner with Mays, Peter Berthon, and Humphrey Cook and his wife at another table. Although we all played billiards together later you could not help but get the feeling that there was an inner and an outer ERA clique.

In the morning I collected the Péronne starting money and sent Jimmy back to England with the car. Mays and Berthon had asked me to send the ERA back to Bourne, not to Thomson and Taylor, so that they could put the new engine in properly, an implied criticism of T&T. Yet they had to admit that the blower gears had been faulty and not up to specification so the new ones were fitted free of charge for both engines. When I got back at the end of the month I went to see Ken Taylor at Brooklands and he told me the car was still at Bourne and there was no sign when it would be ready.

In the meantime I went off to the French Grand Prix with Dick Seaman, the Dobsons, Cyril Paul, and Pat Fairfield who said that somebody might give me a drive. They did but not in the way he expected. We argued with the Paris hotel over the price of our rooms, a matter of five francs or so, and we had a cheap dinner resolving not to go out to any wild parties. Anyway we all weakened and before midnight had all spent about 500 francs making the five we worried about at 8pm look a bit absurd.

The 1936 French Grand Prix at Montlhéry was a sports car race. The 1935 race had been pretty well a clean sweep by Mercedes-Benz and Auto Union, which the French press had portrayed as a national humiliation, so a repetition was not to be contemplated. Chicanes on the straights had been brought in, ostensibly for safety reasons but really to slow down the German cars, and they had not worked. If there was no French grand prix car that could be trusted to uphold the glory of the Republic, then the race should be abandoned, or the rules changed. The Automobile Club de France loyally decided, in the interests of French industry, to run the Grand Prix for sports cars with regulations along the lines of the established classic at Le Mans. Entries were invited from manufacturers for three groups, 750cc-2000cc, 2000cc-4000cc, and unlimited, thus ensuring a good enough entry from Bugatti, Delahaye, and Talbot to secure a home victory.

Rupert St George Riley was running the Riley team, and although

no relation of the Riley family, he worked for Riley as its competitions manager and he invited us to stay in their pub if I would share a room with Cyril Paul one of his drivers. At 25 francs a day all in it was fine, and kind of him.

Top left: pictures signed by Shell's representative at Albi, in centre, supervising Reggie's mechanic checking tyre pressures.

Above, top: Reggie, sporting his BRDC badge on his overalls, discusses his car with Jimmy his mechanic before the race at Berne.

Above, bottom: The racing driver's racing driver. Reggie's hero Bernd Rosemeyer with his wife Eli Beinhorn.

Overleaf: Develiers les Rangiers hillclimb Switzerland. Reggie scored fastest time of the day in the 1500cc class, R11B sporting twin rear wheels for extra grip on the long course.

Freddie Dixon's skid marks could still be seen at Montlhéry and also the chips of concrete the Napier Railton removed from the top of the banking. Somebody gave Pat, Dick, Cyril and me complimentary tickets one evening to watch France v America dirt track racing in Paris, a relatively sedate event compared with a couple of nights later when I stayed in Paris and had to pawn my watch to pay my bills. Pat and Paul had to come with me the following day to get it back.

Maurice Falkner and Tommy Clarke had entered an Aston Martin for Clarke and Seaman to drive but the scrutineers would not allow them to start because it was red, not British racing green. Clarke and Falkner were not going to change it, and I could scarcely believe they would come all this way and not take part, yet they seemed quite indifferent, so I resolved to help them.

I went to the garage that evening with some green distemper and a spray outfit, and began getting this car turned from red to green. It was not entirely a work of art and as it got towards ten o'clock the proprietor obviously wanted to go home. He switched the lights on and off as a warning that closing time was approaching. I was not pleased and told him what I thought about him in no uncertain terms. It made no difference. He turned all the lights out. I felt a little contrite the following morning, since I had not behaved quite like a gentleman. I decided to find out how to say sorry in French. I was told the word was 'fâcher.' What I did not know was that you had to put the reflexive with it if you wanted to say "I am sorry." I knew nothing about reflexive verbs and said "Je suis tres fâché" which I later found meant "I am very angry". I finished the car off, and when the proprietor came back we exchanged pleasantries. I felt relieved that he had not understood the strong language of the night before. I had only done it to get worked up and make him see that I was cross. In due course I finished the painting and he said, "It would have been much better if you had talked to me in English from the word go." He had lived in Ealing for 25 years. The Aston retired from the race.

Pat Fairfield, a handsome South African, like lots of racing drivers could be a bit headstrong and unfortunately he and the journalist Tommy Wisdom went off on a binge in Paris. Throughout practice he had not reported by the time drivers were supposed to be in bed asleep and Rupert Riley was cross. Pat turned up in a borrowed – you might say stolen – taxi. Apparently he could find no other way of getting back and Rupert refused to let him drive. He knew he was on a safe wicket because I was there, and he had already put me on standby to take Pat's place.

Left: An Autocar study of Donington, 1936, Reggie's first race with the ERA. Here he leads Peter Whitehead (ERA) Dick Seaman in his first race with the rejuvenated Delage, Rayson (Maserati) and Dennis Scribbans (ERA R9B). Seaman won this 10 lap handicap, Reggie was second and third in the next two 5 lap handicaps, then third in a 5 lap scratch race also won by Seaman.

Top right: Reggie's rival, Bira, at Albi where he scored the only victory in R5B Remus, one of his three ERAs, and stands at attention for the national anthem of Siam. Reggie, in sunglasses, is on the right of the picture.

Accordingly I drove a 1½-litre Riley in the French Grand Prix, with Arthur Dobson, a dashing character who had driven Fairfield's ERA in the International Trophy, but who turned out to be tetchy and difficult during our partnership here. I had never driven the Riley before and it definitely was not as fast as the real works cars. I did not go very fast during practice, getting in six laps to get accustomed to it, but I was glad to have the drive especially as Dobson was paying all the expenses.

37 cars lined up for the Le Mans-type start, and works teams from Aston Martin, Frazer Nash-BMW, Riley, Lagonda, Singer, and a solitary Marendaz contested *The Motor* prize for the best-placed British entry. The race was over 80 laps of the Montlhéry Circuit Routiere, but unfortunately the crowd was disappointingly small. The huge stand was only quarter full. Sports cars, even with a French win in prospect, were less exciting than

full-blown grand prix cars and in any case 28 June coincided with one of France's premier horse races.

Dobson did the first spell but refused to come to any arrangement on the procedure for a pit stop, and would not even say which lap he might come in on. Things were chaotic when he came in; first he overshot the pit and had to be pushed back, and then he leapt out of the car, wasting a lot of time running round because he was too far out for the fuel line to reach. He started to take up the adjustment on one front brake, which being fully compensated Girlings, might have spelt disaster for me. I had to get him to adjust the rest when he had cooled down. He would not tell me anything about the car, rpm, or anything except that I must give two pumps of oil on the hand pressure pump every lap, and also two on the petrol pump to keep up the pressure in the tank.

I ran through my spell and found the car very

slow and always without brakes on the same left hand corner. Pat Fairfield told me later that I was about 7 seconds a lap faster than Dobson. When I came in I leapt out, did the oil and water, cleaned the windscreen and put the fuel line in, while the tyres were changed. Before Dobson went off he did the oil and water again, wasting more time, and went on to finish fourth in the class. The undershield was full of oil at the end.

Still, it was gratifying when Rileys finished first, second, third and fourth in Group I, for cars up to 2-litres, in the order Trévoux/Maclure, von der Becke/Dobbs, and Paul/Sebilleau. Dobson and I were fourth in the class and 17th overall. As I was only a last minute substitute I was delighted. It was a testament to the performance and reliability of Rileys, and although I was happy with the car the suspension was extremely hard. The shock absorbers may have been too tight but it was definitely a car in which a tummy belt was necessary to keep everything in place. Pat Fairfield, Cyril Paul and Freddie Dixon wore them as well.

After Montlhéry I took the ERA to Brooklands for more testing, and since they had fitted a larger pump it now had too much oil pressure, filling the sump after three laps when it should have been keeping it in circulation. Ken Taylor offered to make me up a new pump at the weekend. After Cork we did a Continental Europe tour winning the 1500cc class at Freiburg in the Hill Climbing Championship of Germany, and the 1500cc class at Develiers Les Rangiers. The winning 5300cc Auto Union of Bernd Rosemeyer covered the 7-mile 808-yard course in seven minutes 59.3 seconds, so my time in a 1500cc ERA of eight minutes 49.2 seconds was not at all bad.

The troubles with ERA were mainly with the supercharger and cylinder head. In the former the driving gears sheared due to overloading, and cracked heads were too common because of difficulty obtaining the correct mixture. It was always problematical with the SU carburettors, particularly when using unfamiliar fuels abroad.

The Continentals always seemed to be ahead. With an Alfa Romeo, and particularly the Maserati I had later, it seemed possible to keep the same jets for any fuel and climatic conditions. I could fill up the Maserati in the paddock at Brooklands, run it up on hard plugs, then restart on the handle more easily than with many a 10hp touring car. You could leave the engine idling then go out and do a flying lap without any ill effects.

The use of a Wilson preselector gearbox in the ERA was contentious. I firmly believed that the power it absorbed and its heavier weight far outweighed any disadvantage. Conventional crash-type racing gearboxes demanded too much of a driver's attention, particularly approaching a corner at speed, where the change had to be left until the last possible moment. In a long race the advantage of preselection was enormous through removing strain and allowing the driver to devote all his attention to the road and cornering. After the ERA I was often apprehensive about my gear changes on the Maserati. At Donington in practice for the 1939 Nuffield Trophy, I broke the Maserati's crown wheel and pinion through using the gearbox to help the brakes, which I always could with the Wilson box on the ERA.

The ERA opened up new vistas. I had become quite professional and although still strictly speaking an amateur the van I carried the car in had advertising material on it. I was paid for writing in *The Autocar* and received sponsorship from suppliers of oil, petrol, sparking plugs and accessories. They were all important in bridging the gap between what I could afford and what was necessary to spend to remain competitive. It was an expensive pastime, but as I came into some money I was able to travel all over Europe staying at decent hotels, have a marvellous life racing, and any losses I made could be set against my private income. Accordingly I had little tax to pay.

Away from the track in the 1930s events could take a sinister turn. During the hill climb championships of Germany at Freiburg at the end of August 1936 I nearly got into trouble with the local thugs belonging to the newly elected National Socialists. The Spanish Civil War was at its height, Italy had just declared it had an empire, and the Berlin Olympic games had just given Nazism a huge propaganda boost. Freiburg was not far from Berne where we had been competing the previous weekend, deep in south Germany in the Black Forest, not far from the Rhineland territories the Germans had re-occupied in March.

Top right: *Reggie is pensive in the pits at Berne with Jimmy. At least the Swiss signwriters spelt his name correctly.*

Freiburg was a long climb, there were reputedly 160 bends on the eight mile (12.9km) course in the tradition of Continental hill climbs, very difficult to get right, but we won the 1500cc class with the ERA and set up a new record, although the course was slippery and I had to content myself with trying to beat Seaman's 1935 record. When I came back down to the start line with my huge laurel wreath the crowd, many of whom had been camping out all night, gave me a terrific reception. At the prizegiving I was congratulated by Sportführer Hühnlein who made the customary stirring speech. Afterwards I had a bit of a fight to collect my *startgeld* and prize money.

This was an Alpine-style town with a nightclub bar where you could dance and drink; however the holiday atmosphere was rudely shattered when we saw brown-shirted stormtroopers beating up Jews. It was a repugnant sight and all the motor racing people who saw it were profoundly shocked. I suppose I may have made a mistake talking loosely in the nightclub. I thought what a disagreeable lot the Nazis were generally, and the stormtroopers in particular. One of the Auto Union drivers was Ernst Von Delius, a cheerful man everybody liked, nicknamed Kleiner (little one). He had raced an ERA and warned me of trouble. I could not believe him at first and asked what could happen. He told me in a very matter-of-fact way that what I had been saying had probably been reported to the Geheimpolizei, the Gestapo, and they could arrest me. The Prussian plain-clothes political police had just been reorganised by Hermann Goering, passed to Heinrich Himmler in 1934, and become a subdivision of the SS.

My hotel was close by so I went straight back. An Englishman called Hamilton ran it, and when I explained my predicament he to your room," he warned. "I had best put you in another room and tell them you are out." It was very brave of him, because even though the Gestapo was not yet merged officially with the state security service, it was gaining a fearsome reputation. I kept my head down in this other room, and Hamilton told me that they did come round but they either never found me or decided to take no action. The trouble seemed to blow over, because I competed in the championships without any trouble.

Raymond Mays also had an unpleasant experience here, being awakened by a phone call from someone claiming to be from the Gestapo headquarters in Koblenz, advising him to leave Germany at once. One wonders why they were so anxious to be rid of him. It was said by some that conversations of his had been overheard,

although it was possible they were of a personal rather than a political nature. RM's behaviour could provoke strong reactions.

I had a conversation with von Delius, with whom I got on well, in which he told me about the money the Auto Union drivers received. They divided up the prize money amongst them no matter who had won, but the firm took all the starting money. I also had a long talk with Raymond Sommer who wanted to form a team of ERAs. However he had no money to put up for it so I did not think much about it. He was willing to exchange a 1½-litre Maserati chassis for my spare ERA engine, which would only leave us with one more car to find.

I had competed at Albi, in the south of France twice before, finishing second and third. Setting off for the third time in July 1936 we stayed at

110

caption

Dover in the Lord Warden Hotel and saw the Aston Martin team off on its way to the Belgian 24-hour race at Spa. Peter Berthon of ERA and Pat Fairfield were going to wait for me outside Paris but I got away from Calais late through delays with Customs and they went on ahead. The ERA vans and mine drove together and I pursued Berthon alone in the Ford V8. He was driving a fast experimental Riley saloon with an ERA engine, and we stopped to dine at Montlhéry when it was having a terrific thunderstorm. As I booked into Fontainebleau for the night they were firing guns into the clouds in some bizarre research to try and break the storm up.

It was late the following day when I got to Albi in Languedoc, passing the vans as they arrived, to be met by race officials arranging hotels. I stayed at Le Vigan which was terrible, while the mechanics were put up at the Hotel Chiffre, which was good with pleasant airy rooms, a lock-up for the ERA, and garage space for the van all for 45 francs a day. The club supplied an interpreter who took me round the course. It looked fast but intricate and a bit bumpy with trees bordering the main straight.

During the early practice period when I was still learning the course, only Lord Howe (setting a new lap record), Bira and Fairfield were faster than I was. The car seemed to wander round the road a lot and I had Jimmy look over the steering although I felt it might all be due to me being out of practice and over-correcting. I was not so fast on the second day so I started in the middle of

Left: *The ERA at Berne, 1936. Reggie's album credits the photographer as Humphrey Cook, one of the founders and virtual owner of English Racing Automobiles.*

Overleaf: *A fine shot by Logan of Birmingham of Reggie catching a slide at Shelsley Walsh in the ERA with a deft touch of opposite lock.*

the third row of the grid in the first heat.

The race order was Marcel Lehoux (ERA R3B), Bira (ERA R5B Remus), Pat Fairfield (ERA R4A), then me, until Howe (ERA R8B) overtook just before his gearbox seized and he shot up the escape road. I was soon in the pits. The car was going badly again but new plugs and a different carburettor needle improved it. Even so I could still manage no better than eighth. Lehoux's supercharger seized, and since both Howe's and Fairfield's cars had gearbox trouble they were non-starters in heat two. I kept close to Bira right from the start for ten laps, pressing him hard so that he set a new lap record. I was only a second or two slower, and within a few lengths of him when my rear tyre went on a 120mph bend.

There were no safety barriers. I got into a nasty skid because I had effectively a solid back axle due to the differential locking up when one wheel went 15 per cent faster than the other. The road was lined with people and as soon as I felt the bang I was deeply afraid I was going to mow them down. I did not know if I would be able to master the skid as I had never experienced a blow-out at such speed. The gyroscopic action of the wheel kept the tyre roughly circular at first. There was no drag and no sign of a skid. But when I got down to about 50mph the steering became difficult. The skid marks were over a quarter of a mile long. The slides were gradual at first and I was able to counteract them, but as I got slower they became more prolonged and faster, and by the time I got to about 30mph (48.2kph), I could not control the car at all. I was lucky to miss a telegraph pole and a house.

Somehow I pulled over and that was it; I was out of the race. I walked through the crowd, which was obviously relieved that I had not gone off the road, so pleased in fact that as I made my way back to the pits they started slapping me on the back quite hard and quite often. There were quite a lot of them, so that when in the pits I received the usual kind enquiries: "Are you all right?" I

said I was but for God's sake, don't pat me on the back. I had not hurt myself in the accident but the spectators had raised bruises.

Howe kindly congratulated me on my driving afterwards and in the evening he took me to a dinner party given by Chula along with Lehoux, Bira, Fairfield, and Berthon, celebrating the first and as things turned out the only win Bira ever had in Remus. Chula was extremely pleasant and remarked on how very well a team of three ERAs might do with the right manager. He also asked if I would consider going to a race in Bangkok in 1938 if they were to have one and pay all the expenses. It was a nice gesture and I suppose he meant it, but I was disappointed with the press reports of the race. I felt they scarcely did justice to my fight with Bira or the reason for my retirement. Chula was responsible for *The Motor's* report.

---

12 July: *Albi race day. My luck still seems to be out, or is it very much in as I wasn't killed today. I couldn't go out to the track in the Ford as it was having a new rear spring fitted. I came all the way from Calais to Albi with it broken. The weight of the car pulled the axle casing apart so that all the oil ran out. What a tribute to Ford. The teeth were only a little blued and all was put right by the excellent Ford agent in Albi.*

13 July: *Collected starting money in morning. Paid bills. Collected V8. Left after lunch with Uboldi as passenger, as he wanted a lift to the next event at Develiers des Rangiers hill climb in Switzerland. Ford gave up the ghost. It was the coil this time and we got a tow into Béziers where we stayed at the Station Hotel. Uboldi and I had just started dinner when the lorries arrived. The Italian mechanics could only with difficulty be persuaded from addressing me as "Sir Tongue".*

It was a good idea of Uboldi's to go south through Carcassonne, Narbonne, and Avignon to pick up the good road to Lyon.

14-15 July: *The lorries left before us as we stayed behind to get a new coil. After only a short distance the petrol pump gave up and I had to take it to pieces. We caught up with the vans just before Montelimar where the Italian van had a puncture. Jimmy and I stayed in Lyon at the Hotel Angleterre then he took the van off to St Julien before me but it was some time before I caught up. The V8 wouldn't start in the morning so once again I had to go to a Ford agent, this time to have the petrol pump repaired.*

When we eventually arrived at Develiers les Rangiers near Geneva we found a rather longer hill than the Shelsley Walsh to which I was accustomed. We put twin rear wheels on the ERA to provide more grip over several kilometres of hill. There was plenty of urge with the 4.5:1 axle ratio, although not surprisingly it was difficult to get over the loose stuff without swinging about a lot. In practice the ERA was 2sec faster than anybody to the top of the first col but thereafter a long straight soon had the engine over-revving in top.

18 July: *The straight was a mile long so with the engine at 6000rpm I had to take my foot off. Most people gained on me here, in particular Biondetti in the 2.9-litre Alfa Romeo with its Dubonnet independent suspension. On the third run I decided to take it up to 7000rpm in the gears when I noticed the oil pressure fail on the first corner. There was no oil in the tank. When the tyre blew-out at Albi the axle thrashed about, and the prop shaft had bent the oil tank, so that the filler cap had touched the chassis.*

Going round a fast corner had once again caused the filler cap to be opened and all the oil was thrown out. Decided to wire the cap down to stop it opening tomorrow. Got hold of the Shell man who promised me a supply of Aeroshell, very heavy and difficult to get, if I drove him to Basle in the morning.

19 July: *Obtained the oil in Basle but made a bad getaway in the hill climb. I pumped the pedal too much in first, so it was binding when I got off the line and I went off in a series of jerks, nearly stalling. I took the revs up but it still cut out on the straight and I could only manage 5800rpm. Anyway we won the class and set a new record. Prize giving and dinner in the evening. Got silver bowl. Learnt Lehoux had been killed at Deauville in the 2-litre ERA, in a collision with Farina's Alfa Romeo.*

10 August: *Finally decided cannot eat with Jimmy anymore. He "clacks" his false teeth and eats with his mouth open. At Genoa I took over the driving. Jimmy v. dangerous.*

Bureaucracy in the 1930s could be aggravated by international tensions. Grievances over Customs procedures were strongly held and Reggie sent a telegram to the Royal Automobile Club of Italy (RACI) threatening never to race in Italy again if his lorry was not allowed to enter the country freely. The RACI, mindful of its domestic difficulties, wired back a reply the gist of which was: "Right so don't." Pragmatism won and Reggie replied that having slept on the matter would they kindly organise the necessary permit from Rome. On the way to compete at Pescara in August by way of Menton he fell victim to Italian regulations that forbade the use of British vans in retaliation against political sanctions. The special permit had not arrived from Rome and they had to await it, guarded all the time by vigilant Customs officials who were friendly and apologetic but unmoving. It was while making up time on an all-night drive from Ventimiglia across Italy that Reggie's patience with the mechanic Jimmy finally snapped. See diary entry for 10 August.

The next race at Pescara on Italy's Adriatic coast brought little cheer. Bira's R2B Romulus spoiled its reliability record by catching fire in the pits as a result of a cracked cylinder head provoked by a broken oil pipe, and Reggie's R11B had to be retired when the supercharger drive sheared. Dick Seaman (Delage) won here and also at the following race, the Prix de Berne, in which Reggie came third behind Nicky Embiricos (ERA R2A).

Mays was having trouble with the handling of the new Zoller-supercharged works ERAs, and was so upset about the speed of the Delage that Ramponi reported: "After Dick won at Pescara we went to Berne, where we found that Raymond Mays and Ernesto Maserati had protested to the AC de Suisse that the Delage was fitted with a 2-litre, not a 1500cc engine. We had two more races to do, the Prix de Berne and the JCC 200 at Donington, and I didn't have time to strip the engine to prove that it was only 1500cc so I asked the AC de Suisse to put two seals right round it, and the international sporting representatives from Paris agreed to accept the car at scrutineering for the next two races."

Reggie's relief on getting safely back to Britain was boundless. He savoured the calm atmosphere and familiar friendly faces at the Midland Automobile Club's Shelsley Walsh meeting in September. He sprinted up the 1000-yard hill 11th fastest that day in 47.01 seconds. It was already the oldest hill-climb course in Britain, having been first used in 1905, remaining challenging for its gradient at the Esses, and the speed that could be reached between the corners.

The ERA was doing over 100mph after Kennel, and a lot more over the finish line. Raymond Mays made Shelsley something of a speciality and was first in the 1½-litre class, with 43.91 seconds in his ERA R4D, and the following June under 40 seconds with 39.09 for Fastest Time of the Day. Mays left the record in 1939 at 37.37 seconds with a 2-litre engine in R4D.

Later in September Reggie took the ERA to Phoenix Park in Dublin for the Irish Motor Racing Club's 200-mile race. Phoenix Park was composed of roads within a public park, where the Irish Grand Prix had been held from 1929 to 1931. A circuit of about 4½-miles (7.25km), it had a 2mile (3.2km) straight along one side. The 1931 Grand Prix was the last great international event of the 1930s, races in the following years being shorter handicap events supported by local or British drivers.

Bira produced his ex-Whitney Straight 2.9-litre Maserati for this race, finishing second, and Reggie was sixth behind Peter

Whitehead in R10B. It was then off to Donington Park in the East Midlands for one of the last meetings before the 1937 improvements that brought in the loop to Melbourne Corner and stretched the track to 3.125miles (5.03km). It was still the pretty wooded circuit passing the farm at Coppice Corner, still with its impossible-looking bottleneck between the pillars of the bridge after Starkey's corner. Reggie finished fourth in the Donington Grand Prix, an historic victory for Dick Seaman and Hans Ruesch in the 3.8-litre Alfa Romeo.

On 17 October the ERA went to Brooklands for two races at the Brooklands Automobile Racing Club's autumn meeting. These were the Siam Trophy and the Oxford and Cambridge Mountain Race on a circuit devised in 1930, demanding more braking and accelerating out of slow corners. It took competitors up the finishing straight that bisected the banked track, went right-handed on to the Member's banking, then hairpinned back on itself to regain the finishing straight. There was nothing mountainous about it, but since it encompassed the Members' Hill that gave the best view of the track, it was known as the Mountain Circuit and was given its own Mountain Championship. In 1937 the Campbell Circuit was brought in to create something still more in the style of a road, winding its way across the infield to the middle of the Members' Banking. Reggie was fifth in the ERA-only race and won the Oxford and Cambridge Mountain Handicap from AFP Fane's Frazer-Nash BMW.

The Siam trophy was one of two races on the Mountain Circuit that the BARC put on for ERA cars only. Seven cars entered for the ten-lap 1936 race, Prince Bira in R2B, Dennis Scribbans in R9B, Arthur Dobson in R7B, Douglas Briault in R6B, Raymond Mays in

Top: Jimmy accompanies
the ERA to the start of the hill
climb at Freiburg for the Grosser
Bergpreis von Deutschland.

R4B, Peter Whitehead in R10B and Reggie
Tongue in R11B. Bira withdrew before the
event owing to trouble with new pistons, and
Whitehead also non-started. Mays won after
a good scrap with Dobson, and Scribbans
was third. A similar race in 1937 was limited
to five laps and only four cars took part; it
was won by Dobson in R7B from Johnny
Wakefield in R14B, Billy Cotton in R1B with
Reggie fourth having been slowed by brake
trouble.

Far left: Clerk of the Course
Morgan talks to the drivers.
Hanson, Dobson in dark glasses,
Johnny Wakefield (dark glasses,
white cap), Geoffrey Taylor,
Chris Staniland, Wilkie Wilkinson,
Earl Howe; Lord Avebury, Lace,
Charles Follett and on extreme
right Reggie Tongue.

17 Oct 1936: *The Inter-Varsity
mountain race was a satisfying
event. I had always wanted to beat
Raymond Mays, particularly on this
occasion, because he had a 2-litre
engine and I only had a 1½-litre.
I didn't think I stood much of
a chance but I hung on to Mays
as well as I could and was just close
enough to make him put his foot
down a bit too hard. He came to the
hairpin bend on the last lap and as
we turned into the final straight he
skidded into some barrels marking
the edge of the circuit. I was able to
pass him and go on and win.*

I got great pleasure out of not making the same mistake as he had. Reggie was competitive and his results were commendable, although he was ready to admit that he was usually behind Mays and Bira, to whom he gave credit grudgingly. For Johnny Wakefield on the other hand his praise was lavish. The driver he admired most was probably Dick Seaman and while disparaging those he called "wild drivers" he could not withhold admiration for Tazio Nuvolari despite his brush with him at Pescara. Bernd Rosemeyer he admired for his stylish driving but in a 1936 talk to the Oxford University Motor Drivers Club (OUMDC) he firmly put Ernst von Delius among the wild men of motor racing most likely to crash. Prophetic words. In the 1937 German Grand Prix von Delius died in a spectacular 130mph (210kph) accident on the finishing straight at the Nürburgring, recklessly crashing his Auto Union off the course on to a nearby road, taking Dick Seaman's Mercedes-Benz with him.

Bira, according to Reggie, never gave up, while Count Carlo Felice Trossi was "an artist" on corners as well as an accomplished engineer. The talented Scuderia Ferrari driver Marquis Antonio Brivio was, "...charming but not too steady", while Dr Giuseppe Farina, who went on to become the first world champion driver in 1950, Reggie described as precisely the opposite.

Below: *Following the race Reggie pulls the ERA into the pit road opposite the stands.*

118

Crashing Along At 130 Miles Per Hour

R. E. Tongue Wins Thrilling Cork Race: Bad Luck Robs Prince of Chance of Victory

MERVYN WHITE'S AMAZING ESCAPE

AFTER an intensively thrilling tussle over the six miles Carrigrohane circuit on Saturday, three of the fastest cars in the event fought out the finish of the Cork Two Hundred Miles Road Race, three English drivers taking major honours.

Of the twenty-four starters eight finished within the time limit, five Englishmen and three Irishmen. They were:—

		H'cap.	Time h. m. s.	Speed
1. R. E. Tongue (1,488 E.R.A. s/c)	s/c)	2 laps	2 12 22	85.53
2. A. Powys-Lybbe (2,336 Alfa-Romeo s/c)		2 laps less 1m.	2 15 43	84.03
3. A. Dobson (2,905 Ford)		1 lap less 2m.	2 16 25	63.65
4. J. Toohey (933 Ford)		9 laps less 3m.	2 20 46	66.74
5. I. Peters (1,496 Frazer-Nash)	s/c)	6 laps	2 27 46	74.11
6. Sir A. W. MacRobert (1,087 M.G.		4 laps less 1m.	2 29 20	60.48
7. C. H. W. Manders (995 Adler)		8 laps less 1m.	2 31 58	60.48
8. D. C. MacLachlan (1,089 Riley)		6 laps	2 31 59	64.89

LIST OF AWARDS.

Millfield Trophy and £200 (1st on handicap)—R. E. Tongue (Eccles).

Merchants Trophy and £100 (2nd on handicap)—A. Powys-Lybbe (Bradfield).

Martin Trophy and £50 (3rd on handicap) J. Toohey (Dublin).

O'Boyle Trophy (first Irish driver up to 1,100 c.c.)—Sir A. W. MacRobert.

R.I.A.C. Cup and £50 (fastest up to 1,500 c.c.)—R. E. Tongue (Eccles).

Egan Cup and £50 (fastest up to 2,000 c.c.)—A. Dobson (Surrey).

Brennan Cup and £50 (fastest over 2,000 c.c.)—C. Martin (Alfa-Romeo 3,200), (Surrey), 4m., 91.31 m.p.h.

Cosgrave Cup and £50 (fastest lap)—C. Martin (Alfa-Romeo 3,200), (Surrey), 4m., 91.31 m.p.h.

I.M.R.C. Silver Plaques (other finishers)—I. Peters (Bristol), C. H. W. Manders (Dublin), D. C. McLachlan (Cork). Mangan Cup and £50

Roche Cup and £50 (fastest up to 850 c.c.)—No finishers.

fastest up to 2,000 c.c.), and Team Prize—No finishers.

CAUTION AND DARE-DEVILRY

THE course hardly proved as fast as the satisfaction of being the faste... had been anticipated, for though J. Toohey, in his 1933 Ford, m... speeds up to 130 m.p.h. were attained effort to maintain an early la... in the two mile straight, the back and though the Dublin man is t... in skill around the bends t...

R. E. Tongue, the winner of the Cork car race.

E. R. Tongue (E.R.A.), the winner of the Cork Motor Race yesterday, cornering at Victoria Cross.

Englishmen's Win In High-Speed Cork Race

1, R. E. Tongue, Eccles, Manchester ....(E.R.A.).
2, A. Powys-Lybbe, Bradfield, Yorks ....(Alfa-Romeo).
3, A. Dobson, Surrey ....(Alfa-Romeo).
4, J. Toohey, Dublin ....(Ford).

These were the placings in the Cork motor race yesterday. Tongue won by a margin of 3 mins. 23 secs., and his average speed was 85.53 miles an hour.

The fastest lap was done by the scratchman, C. E. A. Martin, Surrey (Alfa-Romeo) at a speed of 91.31 miles an hour.

Cork Race Takes Heavy Toll
E. R. TONGUE SCORES BRILLIANT WIN
ONLY EIGHT OF TWENTY-FOUR STARTERS FINISH

CONDUCTED BY THOMAS H. WISDOM

Cork, Sunday.

SO far as organisation went the Cork Race, run over the 6-mile Carrigrohane Circuit on Saturday, was the nearest approach to the Irish Free State Grand Prix meeting at Phoenix Park had yet made.

The race was won by R. E. Tongue, in an E.R.A. which never missed a beat. He got fastest lap as the race progressed, and his best lap was 88.91 m.p.h. He drove with exceptional judgment, and never got an error in his driving in the 200 miles. Martin, on a 3,200 Alfa, was the real speed merchant, making c... his p... page half in the first lap...

FIRST-CLASS SCRAP

Tongue and ... were having a first-class scrap be... when Tongue, who...

impression upon A. Powys-Lybbe, now in second place (Alfa-Romeo, 2.3), ... Gamble (2,275 White ... Bugatti) ... cannoned off the road, cutting hard into race, and finally came only himself in the D. C. MacLachlan was near fading of O'... John O'Donohue ... who ...

This on the C... half ... who had ... travelling at 130 m.p.h. Martin use his... running into the race E. K. Rayson (Bugatti) ... cap, but he had to retire.

THE PLACINGS

1, R. E. Tongue (1,488 C.C. E.R.A. S), rec. 2 ...
2, A. Powys-Lybbe (2,336 Alfa-Romeo, S), rec...
3, A. Dobson (2,905 Alfa-Romeo, S), rec...
4, J. Toohey (933 c.c. Ford) ...
5, I. Peters (1,496 Frazer-Nash), rec. 6 laps ...
6, Sir A. W. MacRobert (1,087 M.G.), ...
7, C. H. W. Manders (995 Adler), rec. 8 laps...
8, D. C. MacLachlan (1,089 Riley), rec. 6 laps ...

E.R.A. WINS CORK CAR RACE

Victory for R. E. Tongue at 85.53 m.p.h. Powys-Lybbe and Austin Dobson (Alfas) Second and Third

THE Irish Motor Racing Club's race at Cork, last Saturday, provided the marque E.R.A. with another victory, the winner being R. E. Tongue, who, in a 1½-litre car, averaged 85.53 miles per hour and finished over three minutes in front of A. Powys-Lybbe, who was second in a 2.3-litre Alfa-Romeo. The fastest finisher was Austin Dobson, who was third and who averaged 86.95 m.p.h. in a former Nuvolari Alfa-Romeo. The Alfa-Romeo team, consisting of Powys-Lybbe, Dobson and C. E. C. Martin, were awarded the team prize, although Martin actually pushed over the line after the race had been declared at an end.

The general standard of organization was the nearest approach to the Irish Grand Prix that the Racing Club yet has produced, and there was a very big attendance of spectators. It is useless to attempt to guess the number, but they were as numerous as the most optimistic could have expected.

A. Powys-Lybbe (Alfa-Romeo), who drove a fine race to finish second at 84.03 m.p.h.

The race was run in a very hot sun, which caused the tar to melt, and this resulted in hectic skidding at some of the corners.

At the start of the race W. M. D. Montgomery (747 Austin, S), with a generous handicap allowance, took the lead, followed by J. Toohey (933 Ford) and C. H. W. Manders (995 Adler). Martin, the scratch man, made rapid progress and shook off those who started in the same group, the others, of course, having a smaller number of laps to complete.

The course proved very fast, and the two and a half miles Carrigrohane "straight" soon started to have its effect, pit stops with overheated engines becoming numerous after the first few laps. Montgomery became a victim of this trouble and Toohey went into the lead.

THE RESULTS.

1, R. E. Tongue (1,488 E.R.A., S.), h'cap 2 laps; time 2 hrs. 12 mins. 22 secs.; speed, 85.53 m.p.h.
2, A. Powys-Lybbe (2,336 Alfa-Romeo, S.), h'cap 2 laps less one minute; 2 hrs. 15 mins. 45 secs.; 84.03 m.p.h.
3, Austin Dobson (2,905 Alfa-Romeo, S.), h'cap 1 lap less two minutes; 2 hrs. 16 mins. 25 secs.; 86.95 m.p.h.
4, J. Toohey (933 Ford); 65.65 m.p.h.
5, Ivo Peters (1,496 Frazer-Nash); 66.74 m.p.h.
6, Sir A. W. MacRobert (1,087 M.G., S.); 71.41 m.p.h.
7, C. H. W. Manders (995 Adler); 66.48 m.p.h.
8, D. C. MacLachlan (1,089 Riley); 64.89 m.p.h.

Outside Time Limit.
C. E. C. Martin (3,165 Alfa-Romeo, S.), 78.55 m.p.h.

"Bira," in his 1,488 E.R.A., made notable progress in the first few laps, but gradually he fell back to Tongue, and a great scrap between the two of them developed. This lasted for 21 laps with "Bira" always in the lead, but often by less than a second. The two E.R.A. drivers were beating their handicaps to a greater extent than any other competitors, and their progress through the field was rapid, particularly when a good proportion of that field was spending a lot of time at the pits.

"Bira," however, retired with a choked petrol pipe, and a few laps later Tongue passed Toohey to take the lead. Martin, at about half-distance, put up the fastest lap of the race at 91.31 miles per hour, and soon afterwards broke an oil pipe, following which his progress was spasmodic. Powys-Lybbe and Dobson were, in the meantime, making up a lot of leeway. E. K. Rayson, 2-litre Bugatti, had been beating his handicap and looked fairly sure of a place when he retired somewhere along the straight. C. Mervyn White (Bugatti) overturned his car at a corner and damaged the steering. He attempted to continue in the race, but upon reaching the pits had to be treated for severe cuts and bruises. This was the only crash of the race, although there was an anxious moment when Martin, T. O'Shaughnessy (Talbot) and D. C. MacLachlan (Riley) almost got abreast on the straight—which was scarcely wide enough for three cars when one of them was travelling at 135 m.p.h.

As the race neared its close Dobson was drawing closer to the leaders. Powys-Lybbe, in third place, was threatening Toohey, who was driving with great skill and cornering fast.

Tongue thought it better to take no chances and did a lap at 88.37 m.p.h. The two Alfa drivers, however, were able to pass Toohey.

Austin Dobson, third and fastest finisher at 86.95 m.p.h., in an ex-Nuvolari Alfa-Romeo.

A very sporting action, which was greatly appreciated in Ireland, was performed by the Duke of Grafton. He was debarred from starting owing to his failure to complete the necessary qualifying laps in practice. He at once gave all his fuel to D. C. MacLachlan, who had been unable to obtain a similar type of fuel from England in time.

7 1937

The racing season started with a terrific rush, and according to my plans I discovered that on successive weekends I was likely to be racing at Donington, Turin, Naples, and Brooklands. At first I thought that it would not be possible, but upon consideration decided that it could be done if I travelled with the mechanic in the van. I had some trouble in the British Empire Trophy at Donington on 10 April then set off for the Turin Voiturette race a week later. This was the first time that Eugen Björnstad had driven an ERA. The first one he saw was Ian Connell's R6B at the Swedish winter grand prix, a spiked tyre event, whereupon he decided he had to have one.

ERA R11B: R E Tongue 1937			
10 April:	British Empire Trophy	Donington	flagged off
18 April:	Turin Voiturette Race	Turin	3rd
24 April:	Naples Voiturette Race	Naples	unplaced
1 May:	Campbell Trophy Race	Brooklands	flagged off
22 May:	Cork 200 Mile Race	Cork	5th
3 June:	RAC Light Car Race	Isle of Man	4th
13 June:	13 Florence 1500cc Race	Florence	5th
20 June:	Milan 1500cc Race	Milan	4th
27 June:	Picardy Grand Prix	Péronne	ret.
11 July:	Albi Grand Prix	Albi	3rd
15 Aug:	1500cc Race	Pescara	ret (accident)
28 Aug:	JCC 200 Mile Race	Donington	ret (engine)

He won the Swedish race in his 2.6 Alfa Romeo, but persuaded Connell to buy him R1A as soon as it got back from the Vanderbilt Cup race in the United States. Björnstad's techniques were more suited to ice-racing than road racing, and he spun off on his second lap at Turin after very little practice. He got going again and after more wild manoeuvres drove on to win. I was reported in

Top: *The ERA at Florence where it finished fifth behind the new Maseratis. Trees beside the road were deemed a natural hazard in the 1930s. Following the death of his friend Pat Fairfield at Le Mans the following week the dangers of motor racing were never far from Reggie's mind.*

Owing to the Customs papers having been issued for entry into France at Dieppe only, we were not able to leave England after the British Empire Trophy until the night boat from Newhaven, on Monday 12 April.

Tuesday 13th: *Customs formalities were soon dispensed with and by 11.30pm we reached Chalons sur Saône where we stayed the night.*

Wednesday 14th: *We were called at 6am and had left by 6.45am. We stopped at Macon for coffee and rolls and were away in 20 minutes. After lunching at Montelimar we had an uneventful journey to St Raphael where we arrived at 7.30pm.*

Thursday 15th: *We now thought we would have an easy run to Turin arriving in time for dinner. Unfortunately, we were delayed at the Italian Customs for about six hours and did not leave the frontier until 5pm. After leaving Imperia and turning north we climbed continuously until eventually we arrived at the top of the Coll di Nava at about 9.15pm. As the van steadily wound its way to the top, non-stop in second gear, we could see the snow on the mountainsides in the beam of the headlights. We were both extremely hungry by this time. In the village at the summit I saw a light some distance from the road and it looked as if it might be the type of place where we could obtain something to eat. Upon entering I was immediately welcomed by the landlord, who called his wife and daughter and soon*

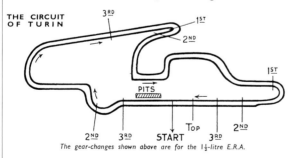

THE CIRCUIT OF TURIN

The gear-changes shown above are for the 1½-litre E.R.A.

we were eating a most excellent meal. Eventually the landlord told us that his name was Cav Abdon Cabras and that he was an engineer, but was obliged to live there for the sake of his health. Before we departed he insisted on our having a bottle of his own special wine and also his own liqueur, which he kept for special occasions. When we were ready to depart, a large crowd had gathered round the van and before we drove away several villagers climbed into the van and examined the ERA by flashlight. As we drove away we could frequently hear in their conversation the words "bella machina". It was now my turn to drive, and with

terrific energy I drove down the winding pass to arrive in Turin at 1.30am.

Friday 16th: *This was the last day for practice and so we had to be out of bed shortly after 6am again. We found a garage, and by 7.30am everything had been unloaded. Unfortunately, we could not get the van out of the garage again, as now that the weight had been taken out, the roof of the van would not clear the garage doorway. Consequently I drove the ERA to practice and my mechanic came after me in a taxi with a few tools etc we required. The fuel I had ordered had not been sent to the pits, and I had only a few gallons left in the tank from after the Donington race. Fortunately the circuit was easy to learn and after three or four laps I felt that I knew all I wished and felt that I must be content to watch the others practising. When "Bira" heard of this he insisted that I should have more practice and very sportingly offered me some fuel, which we pumped from his car's tank. Consequently I was able to do a few laps more practice and so obtain an adequate place at the start. The rest of the day was spent in doing several small jobs on the car.*

Saturday 17th: *After scrutineering we took the ERA on to the Autostrada in order to do our final tuning. Marinoni was also there with one of the Ferrari 12-cylinder Alfa Romeos. So we "blinded" up and down the Autostrada, in spite of the normal traffic, at about 125mph. The thought of the Alfa doing speeds in excess of this on the open road in England is difficult to visualise.*

Sunday 18th: *The story of the race at Turin has been reported in the Press. A plan of the circuit with the gear changes marked has been included on this page.*

Monday 19th: *We left Turin in the rain at about 11am and felt that we had plenty of time to get to Naples for the practice on Thursday morning. After a fairly easy day's motoring we arrived at La Spezia at 9pm and spent the night there.*

Tuesday 20th: *This was another uneventful day and we arrived at Rome at 7.30pm, stopping there for the night.*

Wednesday 21st: *We were now very desirous of getting to Naples as soon as possible and so once again we rose at 6am and arrived in Naples at noon. After some lunch we set out in the rain to find the circuit. This took a considerable time, and on seeing it I was very disappointed. They were in the middle of resurfacing and it was very bumpy and twisty. I was also told that there would be no practice until Saturday* *afternoon, as the circuit would not be finished until then.*

Thursday 22nd: *Spent day checking over the car.*

Friday 23rd: *In the morning I went round the circuit with the Swedish driver Björnstad, to learn the course. In the afternoon we took the ERA out for a little unofficial practice. In spite of the road sweepers, steamrollers, carts etc, it was possible to put in about eight laps at a reasonable speed, in an endeavour to get some idea of the course.*

Saturday 24th: *In the afternoon there was official practice, but it was badly organised. The car seemed satisfactory and the circuit quite easy although tiring. The three ERAs were all together in the third row at the start of the race by virtue of their practice times.*

Sunday 25th: *The race has been reported in the press, we were unplaced, and a plan of the course is included here. Immediately the race was over we packed the ERA into the van and left Naples by 5pm. By midnight we were in Rome, but unfortunately wasted nearly two hours by taking the wrong road and becoming completely lost. By now it was raining, and as the tyres had no tread it was necessary to reduce speed very considerably. However by the time Portobello was reached the moon was out and it was a perfect night.*

Monday 26th: *We drove through the night and all next day stopping for meals and a half hour sleep by the roadside. About 20 miles from Livorno we stopped briefly for breakfast, and we were in La Spezia by 10.30am. Climbing out of La Spezia we were passed by Rovere and one of the Maserati brothers in the former's Rolls Bentley. They had both been to Naples, but probably had not been compelled to travel all night. We stopped for lunch at the top of the pass before dropping down to Sestri Levant. Eventually we arrived at the frontier at Grimaldi between Menton and Monte Carlo at 9.15pm. During the latter part of the journey from Genoa the road is very twisty and narrow and it seemed as if we would never reach the frontier. Anyone who knew that road in pre-Autostrada days will appreciate the achievement with a fully laden van containing a racing car and spare engine. We carried spare parts and pit equipment so we were heavily laden, yet the Dodge was still capable of 60mph (around 100kph).*

Tuesday 27th: *At French Customs we had to be issued with a new set of papers, as they were only valid for one entry and exit for a racing car in France. So we did not succeed in leaving the French frontier until 6pm and could get no further than St Raphael, where we arrived at 8.40pm.*

Wednesday 28th: *We were awake at 6am and soon away. After lunching at Montelimar we pushed on and took dinner at Bar le Duc. It was now dark and when we came back to the van after dinner the battery was exhausted and all the lights were out. Fortunately it stood on a steep hill. By running it to the bottom it was just possible to generate enough current to start the engine and so we drove on to Avallon where we arrived at 10.45pm. The porter had the audacity to ask me if I was a commercial traveller in English clothes. This is the first time the van had been mistaken for a vehicle being used for such a purpose, although I have on occasion been asked if I was carrying dead bodies.*

Thursday 29th: *When we came out of the hotel at 6.30am the battery was completely flat. However we*

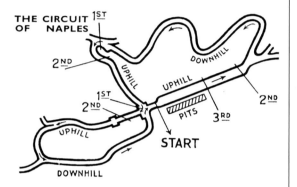

THE CIRCUIT OF NAPLES

succeeded in borrowing a battery to start the engine, switching to the other which immediately began to charge. We had to be on the quay at Dieppe by 5pm. We arrived at 4.35, still possessing four francs and half a gallon of petrol, only to find that the cargo boat was not running. It had been taken off to deliver potatoes to one party or the other in the Spanish war. We took the ERA out of the van and put it on the deck of the passenger boat and telegraphed for a van to meet us in the morning at Newhaven.

Friday 30th: *We journeyed up from Newhaven and arrived at Brooklands in time for practice for the Campbell Trophy race. In practice it was not possible to obtain any revs on the ERA and on the very lap before I was to do my qualifying laps the top came off a valve. Owing to the generosity of Peter Whitehead I was able to qualify on his car. As I had not used my own car however, I was compelled to start on the back row.*

Thanks to the help of others I succeeded in carrying out a very hectic programme and, tiring though it was, I would do it again tomorrow.

the ERA Club Magazine of March 1938, following a talk I gave to the Club, as describing Björnstad as a most dangerous driver but a thoroughly pleasant individual. He did three laps with his shock absorbers slacked right off and went faster than anyone. He maintained he always took the engine to 7000rpm. "No more. No less." And he said he went off the road only once on every race just to find out where the limit was. Experience suggested this was a hopelessly optimistic view.

On the starting grid of the Turin race I could see that his back wheel was interlocked with the front wheel of the car next to him. When the flag was dropped both went straight up in the air with a loud crash. I wriggled past the resultant traffic jam although at one stage I was broadside across the road. Somehow despite the mix-up on the start line Björnstad got going again and I saw him later leaping along on top of a line of straw bales. I have no idea how he extricated himself, but he soon came up behind me. I watched him fascinated in the mirror, shooting from side to side of the road, cannoning off everything. He may have been a charming individual but I believe Ian Connel eventually had to repossess R1A after Björnstad's short but eventful career. When he did get it back it required a substantial rebuild.

The Naples race on 24 April started badly. The man with the starting flag did not seem to know what he was doing, holding everybody up on the grid until half the cars were well on the boil. We got off to hopeless starts. Björnstad turned up with fat tyres on the front and narrow ones at the rear, none with any tread to speak of. His car's cylinder head was so badly cracked that when he took a plug out he had to stuff a rag in as quickly as possible to prevent a pool of water collecting in the cylinder. In spite of this the car was very fast. I toyed with giving my cylinder head some sharp blows with a hammer to see if I could reproduce the effect.

I had come to believe wholeheartedly in careful preparation of the car. Invariably drivers are not clever enough to prepare their own car; it was necessary to have a good engineer, which was one good reason for relying on Thomson & Taylor. Rudolf Caracciola never laid a hand on his car whereas Piero Taruffi was so busy with engineering problems that sometimes he would not drive.

Left: Reggie returned to trials from time to time between races. Here he discusses prospects for the Inter Varsity Trial with Chip Peters who often helped in his pit. The car is a borrowed MG NE Magnette.

Top right: ERA inner circle Humphrey Cook in R12C No 4 and Raymond Mays at the wheel of R4C No 2 at Albi in July 1937. Cook drove the second works car at Albi following Pat Fairfield's death. Reggie was second in the first 20 lap heat, behind Villoresi's Maserati and ahead of Cook, fourth in the second, and finished third overall.

The Campbell Trophy turned out to be a close-fought duel between Bira and Lord Howe that ended unhappily with Howe's bad crash. He was in the lead and looked round to see how close Bira was behind him, with the result that he failed to take the corner before the Vickers bridge, skidded and hit the earth bank and wooden fence, then the car rolled down the bank back on to the track.

I liked Francis Howe enormously. Once going along the Route Nationale south from Calais to Le Mans he overtook in his Alfa, stopped and flagged me down. "When you get about another five kilometres down this road you'll see my car parked on the roadside. There's a restaurant there; stop and I'll buy you some *fraises du bois* and we'll have a drink." I had never heard of *fraises du bois*, although I had done quite a bit of French. I did not know how delicious those lovely little wood strawberries could be.

It was a delightful start to a hot summer morning and the beginning of a long friendship. Before the war we sat on the same committee at the Royal Automobile Club, deliberating how to get government assistance to motor racing, because we

were doing it out of our own pockets. Howe was passionate about getting a British car to drive. He badgered Lord Nuffield to support the Mille Miglia MG team, and encouraged ERA all he knew, but there was no official help forthcoming. Racing in other countries was subsidised in any number of ways, if not through individuals, then through the factories that made the cars or the state itself. We felt we were rather at a disadvantage. I was glad when he recovered from his injuries, which had looked life-threatening at the time.

An incident before the 1937 Cork 200 in May that I like to think was pure chance, occurred after practice. While I was in the bath there was a knock on the door, and much to my surprise, Prince Bira came in. I said "Sit down on the bath stool, what can I do for you?" He said "I wondered if you would like to come to dinner with us tonight?" He had never asked me to dinner before, and I don't think he ever asked me to dinner again, but I duly accepted and joined his party at the Blarney Castle Hotel.

If you went up to the top of the old castle, you could put your head through a hole in the wall, lean out and kiss the Blarney Stone. You had to be held by your legs to prevent you falling, but traditionally if you managed it you were then supposed to be able to lie convincingly and never be found out. It was a lying licence for ever. We underwent the ritual with Chula or Bira holding my legs, and as I had beaten him the year before, I did consider momentarily the possibility that he might let go. Anyway he did not, and we went back to the hotel and played with model aeroplanes. They were not remote controlled, but you could set the ailerons so that they flew in circles. We were all boys at heart and had a lot of fun.

Dinner was served informally; the food was not put out with the vegetables separate, for one to serve oneself. It was already prepared

on the plate and put down in front of each diner. There seemed some confusion over mine. There was a certain amount of juggling the plates round but I had a very nice dinner, the conversation with intelligent princes of the Siamese royal family was pleasant, and I went back to my hotel and slept soundly.

Next day in the pits Bira unaccountably collapsed before the start. He was terribly ill with stomach trouble. A doctor and nurse were sent for and they patched him up and he was able to race but crashed. He and I had had a bit of a tussle for some time because as always he was keen to win.

Top: *Reggie with mechanic Jimmy at Albi, 1937.*
Right: *Working with Reid Railton its designer at Thomson and Taylor, Reggie chose a Railton convertible as his road car.*

There was some paddock gossip that the dinner had been designed to put me out of the running. I do not think it was like that, but you could see how prejudice could be stirred up against rascally inscrutable orientals. I accepted it as entirely coincidental.

The race was won by HB Prestwich in an MG and I was fifth after a lot of plug trouble. Back on the Isle of Man I had a better result in the RAC Light Car Race than in 1936, finishing fourth ahead of Peter Whitehead and Peter Walker in R10B. In June we faced the new Maserati 4CM for the first time, a car brought out in direct competition with the ERA. This Maserati rivalry with ERA had prompted the introduction of the 6CM in 1935 with independent suspension to make up for its new 6-cylinder engine producing only 155bhp (115.6kW) against the 180bhp (134.2kW) from the Jamieson supercharged ERA or the 230bhp (171.5kW) from the Zoller supercharged works cars of that year.

I was first ERA behind the Maseratis in fifth place, then came fourth in Milan the following week. I really felt we were beginning to get somewhere. At Albi on 11 July I came second behind Luigi Villoresi in a Maserati and ahead of Humphrey Cook in one of the new C-type ERAs in the first heat, fourth in the second, giving an aggregate third. Alas the tragic news of Pat Fairfield's death at Le Mans on 21 June cast a pall over everyone connected with ERA. An inexperienced French amateur spun his old Bugatti on the fast bends before the pits, rolling it in front of a BMW. Pat's Frazer-Nash BMW then hit the Bugatti and was rammed by a Delahaye. He sadly did not survive the night and we lost a fine driver and a good friend.

Reggie returned to the Continent in 1937 with only slightly less success than in 1936, his best placing third at Turin in April, before coming to picturesque sun-drenched Pescara. Enzo Ferrari had put its white-walled houses, fringing Italy's Adriatic coast, on the motor racing map in 1924 when he drove an Alfa Romeo to its first grand prix victory. He became manager of the official Alfa Romeo team under the Scuderia Ferrari. Alas it was also where Guy Moll, his most promising driver, was killed just after winning the Avus and Monaco Grands Prix. Pescara's passion was motor racing. In Siena they raced horses, in Pamplona bulls; Pescara's love affair was with cars.

The annual grand prix was as crucial to Italian motor racing as the Targa Florio (begun in Sicily in 1906), or the Mille Miglia (Lombardy in 1927). Pescara's undulating coast road and sinuous mountain tracks made it one of the longest and most dramatic circuits in Europe. The triangular course measured 15.27 miles (25.58km) and corkscrewed into the mountains, a dramatic counterpart to the Nürburgring in Germany or Pike's Peak in America.

Pescara was a driver's circuit, its grands prix fired the emotions, although by 1934 even its most ardent advocates had to concede that it was not safe. Nuvolari held the lap record at 91.3mph (146.8kph) in an Alfa Romeo, notwithstanding speed curbs imposed where the mountain section ran through Spoltere and Cappelle, before the downhill helter-skelter back to the sea front at Montesilvano.

Right: One of the greatest drivers of all time, Tazio Nuvolari, whose presence on the track could be intimidating.

When I competed at Pescara the pits were down by the sea front. It was a narrow tortuous circuit and the grand prix cars and the voiturettes were all on the circuit at the same time. Tazio Nuvolari, often judged the greatest driver in the history of motor racing, was at the same hotel. He did not speak much English, just enough to come to me in the evening and say: "I heard this afternoon at practice you think you going to die?" So I replied, "As a matter of fact when you passed me I did." He seemed to think this was terribly funny. I did not find it much of a joke, on the mountain road when he came right up alongside me on the inside, edging me towards the outside. There was about a thousand-foot drop, and no barriers. I really thought he was going to push me over. Only a part of the circuit round the sea front was properly surfaced tarmac, the rest was unmade with flints and dust and flying stones. They were the sorts of cart tracks that had been serving the local farmers and peasants perfectly well for hundreds of years, but were not best suited to modern motor racing. Dick Seaman described Pescara as two very fast straights of about five miles each, joined by a twelve-mile section of extremely twisty and undulating road. Nuvolari's humour was a bit perverse yet I always liked him despite his sardonic side.

World of Sport

Edited by "Pilot."

Raymond Mays on a "works" E. R. A. leading "B. Bira" and Pat Fairfield down Broadway and on to the Promenade in the first lap of the International car race.

FIRST home in the International car race which was held in the Isle of Man on Thursday of last week was "B. Bira" (E.R.A.), who averaged 70.69 m.p.h. for the 195 miles. Second and third were the works E.R.A.'s handled by Raymond Mays and Pat Fairfield. This year's course, which started at the T.T. stands in Glencrutchery Road, and proceeded down Ballaquayle Road to Broadway, along the Promenade to Port Jack, along Royal Avenue to Onchan, and down Governor's Road and over Glencrutchery Road to the stands again, was considered to be the best yet found in the vicinity of Douglas and seemed to meet with general approval.

The original entry of 22 was one of the best received for a race of this type for many years, but a series of misfortunes reduced the number of actual starters to 15. I have to record with regret that P. F. Jucker (Alta) lost his life in Tuesday's practices.

At the end of the first lap the order was "Bira," Mays 50 yards behind him, and then, strung out, Fairfield, Tongue, and Villoresi. Walker then came in for a change of plugs, and the American-Swiss, Du Puy, came in to the pits and promptly retired. On the completion of the second lap the order was the same, but "Bira" had increased his lead. At four laps he had piled up a lead of over half a minute, while Mays had fallen back.

At this stage the order was "Bira," Fairfield, Tongue, Mays, and Villoresi, the Burmese putting in the fastest lap in 3min. 20sec.,

equal to an average speed of 70.22 m.p.h.

At the end of the 30th lap, the E.R.A.'s came into the pits the one after the other, and spectators were treated to a new form of speed—lightning refuelling.

Even this slight delay, however, cost "Bira" his lead, Mays snatching it from him, and as they roared past the stands on the 35th lap,

Bira was less than a hundred yards behind the leader, and a terrific duel commenced in which "Bira" recovered his lead on the fast stretch at the Promenade.

This stirring duel ended in the next lap when Mays stopped to refuel and "Bira" went on to regain a comfortable lead, while Mays slipped back into third place, Fairfield lying second.

Mays regained second place on the next lap, and at the completion of the fortieth lap the order was:—

		Average Speed. m.p.h.
1.—Bira		70.68
2.—Mays		70.28
3.—Fairfield		70.17
4.—Tongue		69.56
5.—Whitehead (who had taken over from Walker)		68.19
6.—Graffenried		66.51

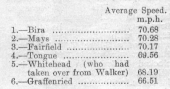

Only 58 seconds divided the first three cars, but the Italian car was two laps behind the leaders. Mays continued to reduce the gap between himself and the leader and when they set out on the last lap of the race there was only 44 seconds between them, and Fairfield was only a few seconds

Raymond Mays (E.R.A.) at Shelsley Walsh.

behind Mays. The final placings in the race were:—

1.—Bira; time, 2 hours 45 mins. 34 secs.; average speed, 70.69 m.p.h.
2.—Mays; time, 2 hours 46 mins. 16 secs.; average speed, 70.39 m.p.h.
3.—Fairfield; time, 2 hours 46 mins. 53 secs.; average speed, 70.04 m.p.h.
4.—Tongue; time, 2 hours 48 mins. 5 secs.; average speed, 69.63 m.p.h.
5.—Whitehead; time 2 hours 50 mins. 30 secs.; average speed 68.64 m.p.h.

Four women, driving a standard Ford V-8 "30," have been putting up an amazing performance at the Montlhery track, near Paris. After ten days and nights of strenuous driving, the car was stopped according to schedule, and it was found that, subject to official confirmation, fifteen International Records and ten World Records had been broken. All records from 10,000 up to and including 20,000 miles had been smashed, the latter at an average speed of 141 kilometres per hour. Amongst the ten World Records broken were the 20,000 kilometres, 15,000 miles, 30,000 kilometres, 35,000 kilometres and 20,000 miles. This is the first time in motoring history that four women have competed for and won any of the arduous long distance records, and the four members of the "weaker" sex are to be congratulated on their remarkable performance.

At Shelsley Walsh on Saturday, Raymond Mays had the satisfaction of breaking his own record. He drove a 1,486 c.c. E.R.A. and his time for the 1,000-yards climb, the average gradient of which is 1 in 8.9, was 39.09sec., representing an average speed of 52.32 m.p.h.

His record in this classic event is brilliant. His list of successes began in 1923 when, driving a Brescia-type Bugatti, he tied in 52.4sec. with M. C. Park at the wheel of a 3-litre T.T. Vauxhall. His next win was in 1929, when he clocked 45.6sec. in a Vauxhall Villiers. In 1933 he was best in 44 4-5sec. with the same car, and since the September meeting has been unbeaten with his E.R.A. Yesterday's victory was his sixth successive win, making his total nine out of the 38 climbs held by the M.A.C. since 1901. Worthy mention must also be made of H. L. Hadley, whose camshaft Austin Seven made second fastest climb with 40.83 seconds. Incidentally, this is by far the fastest time recorded by a car of this capacity. Third best time was made by A. P.

F. Fane with his twin supercharged 1½-litre Frazer Nash.

Quite a fair number of Scots competed in the Blackpool Rally at the week-end, but none of them managed to take a premier award back to Scotland. G. L. Broughton (Singer) won the Glasgow Control prize, while J. G. R. Watson (Ford V-8) annexed the S.S.C.C. award.

Of the 60 cars (maximum allowed) entered for the 24 Hours Le Mans race, taking place June 19-20, 23 are British, representing 10 different makes; 31 French, of 9 different makes; 4 German, of 2 different makes; and 2 Italian, of the same make. The honour of "closing the circuit" will be entrusted to the firm which last won the contest, and this ceremony will be performed by A. P. Good, of the Lagonda concern.

All the experience gained during the past six years has been concentrated upon the 1937 Riley "24," regulations for which are now available. The Riley "24" is essentially a sporting week-end suitable for standard Riley

motor cars—all chassis-damaging and wing-denting sections and tests having been avoided.

For the first time it will not be necessary to motor round the greater part of the British Isles in order to reach the final control. From Paris to Leeds the routes take you direct to the semi-final control, so that everyone may be sure of at least seven hours sleep at the Royal Hotel, Scarborough, on the Friday night. Inclusive terms of 30/- and 35/- have been offered by this hotel for the week-end.

The awards list is inspiring. In addition to the usual trophies there are the three silver cigarette boxes for the special tests, and engraved hunting flasks for everyone completing the course in accordance with the regulations. The trials section is entirely novel and does not involve a large mileage, while the country traversed is among the most beautiful in Yorkshire. Finally, the entry fee has been substantially reduced. Particulars from R. E. C. Jennings, whose address is Eastwood Lodge, Binswood Avenue, Leamington Spa.

(Continued on page 380, column 3).

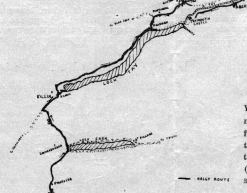

With typical thoroughness, those responsible for the organisation of this week-end's rally of the M.G. Car Club (Scottish Centre) have sent this plan of the route to all competitors.

From 1930 a race for voiturettes took place as a curtain raiser to the Pescara Grand Prix. The main event remained a testament to Italian motor racing supremacy, but other nationals were allowed in to elevate the status of the meeting to international. In 1933 Whitney Straight won the minor event with the MG Magnette Reggie Tongue raced two years later. The following year Hugh Hamilton won again for MG in another Magnette, then watched in awe as Campari, Varzi, Nuvolari, and Fagioli added their names to the distinguished list of winners of the Gran Premio di Pescara.

The title of the voiturette race was changed to Coppa Acerbo, to honour one of the Fascist regime's heroes, Captain Tito Acerbo. Competition between the Pact of Steel coalition Mercedes-Benz, Auto Union, and Alfa Romeo brought a new ferocity to Pescara with speeds on the main straight reaching 180mph (288kph).

In August 1937 Reggie Tongue brought his ERA to Pescara hoping to repeat Richard Seaman's wins of 1935 and 1936. A year younger than Reggie, by 1937 Seaman was graduating from gifted amateur to outstanding professional, after a career competing at Reggie's level. Seaman won at Pescara with his disappointing ERA R1B, then with the venerable Delage. Reggie's ERA R11B was newer and better than Seaman's had been but when he got there the portents were not good. Seaman withdrew injured following a practice crash, and the field was made up largely of inexperienced Italians. Among the drivers were Vittorio Mussolini, son of *Il Duce* and Vito, his nephew.

The race had barely got under way when Pasquino Ermini, in a Maserati, crashed into one of the marker stones edging the rustic roads. Reggie was immediately behind Ermini and saw the red Maserati cut a swathe amongst the crowd. It was a traumatic experience and for Reggie the consequences looked ominous.

Left: *Nuvolari in a Scuderia Ferrari Alfa Romeo P3 at Coppa Acerbo cutting it fine with the inside front wheel on the grass.*

Below: *"a word with Uboldi before the start."*

Mussolini decreed that Italy should have a class of cadet racing drivers learning how to conduct themselves. They were pretty irresponsible, a bit wild and excitable, but we had to put up with them. None of the regular drivers liked these cadets because they were a danger, although since they usually started well back on the grid they were mostly well out of the way behind the main field. The cars allotted to them were never very fast so they got in each other's way more than they did ours. At 15 miles Pescara was such a long circuit you never lapped them, but in 1937 I had a bad practice time so I was near the back of the starting grid. This meant that some of the cadet drivers were ahead of me so when the accident happened I had a ringside seat.

Ermini's Maserati struck a stone kilometre marker just after the end of the first straight, where we turned inland to go up through the mountains. He bounced off backwards amongst cars still closely packed after the start, and they began to cannon off each other. Some were sent flying off the road; others were tossed into the air. I went clean underneath one which was upside down above me with the driver still in the seat. When I came to a stop my car was still upright. I was a bit dazed and thought the race would be stopped. There were no barriers and I could see where the Maserati had gone into the

crowd. The place was strewn with the dead and bits of the dead. I climbed out of the ERA confused. I remember picking up a bit of stocking and saying it might belong to the girl drenched in blood lying by the roadside. She alas was beyond needing stockings ever again. Just when I thought I was going to pass out, a woman came out of a house, and in an act of extreme kindness put a chair under me.

Top above: *Reggie's second race at Cork was less successful. Here he is feted on arrival by Major McNeil and Rory O'Flynn of the organising club.*

Bottom above: *En route to Pescara, Reggie's racing car transporter was scarcely luxurious but it had sufficient billboard space to advertise Brooklands steering wheels and Smiths MA instruments to help defray costs.*

Three women and a Blackshirt militiaman lost their lives on the spot, Ermini was badly injured, and five of the 20 injured spectators died later. Reggie was lucky to escape with his life but he was by no means out of danger. This was a totalitarian state, and he knew the police were not beyond applying popular, perhaps rough, and not invariably officially authorized justice.

As soon as Reggie got back to the pits Tony Birch, Dick Seaman's racing manager sought him out, warning: "This accident is being blamed on you. They think you have been taking drugs." The Spanish civil war was at its height, Hitler and Mussolini were leading a right-wing revolution in Europe, and ill-feeling against outsiders like the British was easy to incite. Birch had to be taken seriously. Seaman regarded him highly; he had been business manager at ERA and Hugh Hamilton's manager up till the time of his death at Berne.

I slowly realised what had happened. Before a long race I regularly took orange juice with Glucodin for stamina and energy. Somebody had seen me, and Glucodin being a white powder, they thought the worst. It was perfectly legitimate, but once I knew the finger of suspicion was pointing at me, I could not sit back and do nothing. It would have been ludicrous to allow the Italians to blame me when it was not my fault. I was a victim of the accident not its architect.

I immediately found Commendatore Corrado Filippini, head of the RACI (Royal Automobile Club of Italy) and complained to him bitterly, threatening dire consequences that unless the rumours were immediately quashed, I would bring legal action against the club for defamation. He spoke good enough English to know that I was extremely angry, and after I had finished he said, "Look, we've been very pleased with

Above: Milan. Racing in a city where a non-Italian victory would have been something of a catastrophe for the local car manufacturers. The opposition from Maserati 6CMs, produced only a few hours drive to the south in Bologna (and soon to move closer to Modena), proved too much. Reggie finished fourth ahead of Peter Whitehead in ERA R10B. Straw bales and a fence protect the spectators.

what you have done. You have been to Pescara several times over the last two or three years, and whatever had happened today, we had decided to give you a special prize. Whether you won or lost you deserve recognition for your endeavours on our behalf."

"When do I get this prize?" I asked suspiciously. There was never any official prize-giving at Pescara. "Go along to the RACI office at six o'clock and they will have it ready for you", he told me. So just after six, I drove to an imposing building in Pescara decorated with Fascist symbols, and introduced myself. "I believe you have a special prize for me." There was some consternation at first but I decided this was understandable since counter staff could not be expected to know everything. They talked animatedly about this special prize then came back and asked, "Who told you this?" I told them it was Filippini. This had the effect of making them agitated but after a time they came back with a large heavy and imposing bronze statuette. It had obviously been wrenched off a plinth and was inscribed with the names of previous winners. I did not look at it very carefully until I got it back to the hotel. It was a female form with wingsoutstretched, a little like the Spirit of Ecstasy on the radiator of a Rolls Royce. I thought it might be Minerva. She was standing with her feet on a globe held in a large hand.

Apparently the hand was modelled on Mussolini's and the globe was supposed to represent the world. It was full of heavy Fascist symbolism but when I looked at the relief round the base, it read, "Il gran Premio Motocyclisto." It was the prize for the winner of the motorcycle Grand Prix, and obviously not a trophy that was ever given away. It was supposed to be awarded in perpetuity. Anyway I took it. It was obviously quite valuable and I thought I deserved it.

I put the statue in the back of the car and wrapped it in a rug to save it from damage. When I got to the hotel Filippini asked if I had received the prize. I said "Yes I have". So he said, again indicating that he did not know anything about it at all, "What have they given you?" When I opened the boot and showed him what was wrapped up in the rug the consternation on his face was almost unbelievable. He was quite taken aback by what they had done but relieved to find they had fulfilled the obligation."

The MG NE Magnette had been developed for one of the most important events on the calendar, the RAC Tourist Trophy on the Ards circuit in Northern Ireland. The 1936 regulations banning superchargers had thrown the factory team into disarray, plans to enter K3s were abandoned and it was decided to use 6-cylinder Magnettes instead. A swift development programme led to the NE with narrow lightweight aluminium body, engines with almost unheard-of compression ratios, high-crown pistons, and a new camshaft with a lot of overlap. Seven cars were built and six entered for the TT, Charlie Dodson driving one to MG's second consecutive TT victory by a narrow margin, a bare 17 seconds after six hours and 465 miles (748.3kms) of racing from Eddie Hall's heavily handicapped 3669cc Bentley.

A surviving NE, JB 4748, had been sold, but as the new owner was in France and not likely to return for some time, the firm that sold it agreed to Reggie Tongue borrowing it in the winter of 1937 for the Inter-Varsity Reliability Trial.

Top: *Racing car of a new generation. Out of racing for a year, Reggie took delivery of the Maserati 4CL, seen here at Albi at the beginning of 1939.*

I set off feeling like a thief in the night, wholly confident about returning it intact. However after a day or two I was unimpressed by it. It seemed short of power, rather heavy and rough. Moreover it had an uncomfortable seating position quite unlike the N-types that were run in trials by the Evans family. I persevered nonetheless and all went reasonably well until the first hill, where the oil pressure dropped to zero, the engine boiled, and all power was gone. A large boulder had fallen down the bank after the course inspection, and I had driven over it. There was a great hole in the sump. The new owner returned to find his engine in small pieces, but by good fortune did not make a fuss and was given a complete overhaul free of charge. I never knew if he discovered the real reason the vendors were so generous.

What a different proposition an ordinary standard Allard was. It belonged to Adlards Motors, was designed for the job, and did it extraordinarily well. I never had more confidence in a car. It climbed trials hills no one else attempted. We once passed a tractor stuck in the mud and we did not even have competition tyres. The Allard was delightful on the road, it was fitted with full touring equipment, had lively acceleration, excellent cornering and reached a creditable high speed in great comfort.

I was sometimes without a touring car and rode motorcycles instead, although I did once buy a bullnose Morris tourer for £12 to tide me over. It did not have much character although the passing of the years probably endowed it with some. I always thought its exhaust sounded like a motorboat. The mechanical components were satisfactory, but the tyres and electrics were not up to much, so it was soon sold. I expect someone got reliable motoring from it.

My motorcycles ranged from a saddle tank 2½ Matchless and a 490cc Norton, to an R51 BMW. In the motorcycle world the BMW was further ahead of its nearest rival than an Alfa Romeo was over its nearest car competitor. The 2.9 Alfa Spider road car was in a class by itself so this is meant as a sincere compliment

It was through the connection with Thomson and Taylor, who built John Cobb's car, that I went to America when he made his attempt on the World Land Speed record at the Bonneville Salt Flats. I went at my own expense, and since I knew war was getting close, I had to consider the wisdom of going at all. As a Class E Reservist I had undertaken to be on call should hostilities break out, but decided against saying anything to the authorities in case they told me not to go. I felt sure I could always get back quickly if necessary and just hoped nobody would court martial me for leaving the country without permission.

Top: *Motorcycle of a new generation. Shaft drive, telescopic forks, hydraulic rear suspension, the BMW R51 was well ahead of its time.*

Top right: *27 August, 1938 the Junior Car Club 200 miles race on the new Campbell Circuit. Johnny Wakefield won in ERA R14B from Bira's Maserati and Earl Howe's ERAR8C. Reggie was fifth ahead of Tony Rolt in ERA R5B. Here Reggie rounds the right hand hairpin alongside the old Finishing Straight with the Test Hill in the background.*

ERA R11B: R E Tongue 1938

1 Aug:	BRDC British Trophy Invitation Race for ERA.s	Brooklands	5th (2nd Heat 1) ret
13 Aug:	Crystal Palace Cup	Crystal Palace	ret
27 Aug:	JCC 200 Mile Race	Brooklands	5th
12 Sept:	Midland AC Hill Climb	Shelsley Walsh	11th (47.01secs)
26 Sept:	Irish MRC 200 Mile Race	Phoenix Park, Dublin	6th
3 Oct:	Donington Grand Prix	Donington	4th
17 Oct:	BARC Autumn Meeting Siam Trophy	Brooklands	5th
	Oxford & Cambridge Mountain Race		1st (74.98mph)

Below: Inter Varsity
November 1938.
Here Reggie tries
the Allard's independent
front swing-axle suspension.

John Dugdale of *The Autocar* and I drove into the Rockies enjoying ourselves until I found myself landed with a real job of work. I had intended to be no more than a spectator but was talked into doing my bit in the sun. Not long after we landed, R A McDonald, "Dunlop Mac" went home at short notice. His wife was apparently upset at him being out of the country with war and bombing and national emergencies imminent, and she wanted him back. His departure left the team short-handed so I had to lend mine to get tyres and wheels ready for the record attempts. The trial runs took place at about 5 o'clock in the morning when the salt was still quite hard after the cool of the night. Once the sun came up it grew unsuitably soft and mushy.

We stayed at Wendale on the Salt Flats. Sam Gilmour, of Gilmour Lion Oils that was sponsoring Cobb, spent about £1,000 a day on hospitality, providing us with breakfast and looking after VIPs. The Napier-Railton had no water circulation system. It had two big tanks filled with enough ice for one run, by the end of which it had melted. I had to take time off tyre preparation to break up ice for the engines. It may not have been a glamorous assignment but it was quite rewarding

to be there on a record attempt at the frontiers of speed.

The record was duly broken, and we went back to the hotel in Salt Lake City. It was a subdued celebration because Salt Lake City was dry – no alcohol could be obtained without a licence. Only one bottle of whisky was permitted at dinner and no wine. I bought the whisky, having taken the precaution of obtaining a licence in advance from City Hall, allowing me to buy it from a drugstore. Alcoholic drink was not allowed on the table when we were eating; it had to be kept out of sight on the floor, and glasses filled unobtrusively.

Ken Taylor, John Cobb, Reid Railton, Tim Rose Richards (the spare driver), John Dugdale and I were the celebrants at this dinner party. Still it was a good hotel, marvellously comfortable, and the first place I ever had really good cornflakes for breakfast. They came with fresh sliced peaches. American breakfasts with really good eggs and bacon were perfection.

Motoring a small Chevrolet sixty-odd miles along a dead straight road between Salt Lake City and Wendover gave me plenty of time to ruminate on cars. The Chevrolet was comfortable and economical although not very fast. It would only do 65mph and without being unkind had the character and individuality of a telephone. It did its job, which was as much as could be expected of it, but I could not help recalling fondly cars I had driven that did have character and personality. I remembered those that seemed to come alive, such as the 2.3 Alfa Romeo of Charles Penn-

Hughes, various Frazer Nashes, my Derby Bentley, the Atalanta, and the 12-cylinder Lagonda. I even rated the TT MG Magnette among the highlights. I recalled the treasured day in Switzerland in 1938 when I drove a Mercedes-Benz 14hp saloon over the Furka, Grimsel, and Klausen passes from Lucerne. It was quick, cornered beautifully, and seemed animated. The driver felt like part of it on that never-to-be forgotten lone day's drive.

Old Frazer Nashes on the road and in competitions were always fun, provided you enjoyed fresh air and did not mind repairing and adjusting things most days. Driving the rear wheels with exposed chains was a crude but surprisingly effective form of transmission when it worked, and frustratingly difficult when it did not. On a Gloucester Trial I had to mend chains without a chain link extractor on a hillside in the dark. It was not easy. The owner told me this tended to happen if the chains were not running in line, an emergency that cropped up all too often, due to worn key-ways on the back axle and sprockets. Frazer Nashes I decided were designed strictly for the enthusiast.

Although never engendering the affection I could feel for an Alfa Romeo, Frazer Nash, or my Allard, the Derby Bentley I owned operated beautifully. The switches for the ignition, lights and minor controls had a beautifully precise Rolls-Royce action. Some designers went to great lengths to engineer tactile switchgear, controls and buttons and levers; keys that clicked reassuringly when they were being operated, but Rolls-Royce

made all theirs like that just by building them superbly. You could start a warm engine on the Bentley by switching on the ignition and flicking the magneto advance and retard lever on the steering column. Like some human beings it was too refined and genteel to have personality however, and it had its weaknesses. On the long straight downhill stretch between Cheltenham and Chippenham, holding it at over 100mph, the 3½-litre's crankshaft broke. It also had an unpleasant front wheel patter so I never rated the high-speed roadholding much.

I drove many Bentleys after the 1930s and the prototype Crewe-built V8 of the 1960s was a

Near left: *June 20 1937. Milan. Reggie shares pit counter with wealthy Swiss Hans Ruesch, whose 3.8 Alfa Romeo Dick Seaman shared to win the 1936 Donington Grand Prix.*

Bottom left: *Reggie relaxes on cross Channel steamer with Dennis Poore who campaigned the famous Ruesch/Seaman Alfa Romeo in post-war hill climbs.*

Top right: *Beautifully proportioned Maserati at 1939 International Trophy, Brooklands (**lower right**) at Albi and (**below**) at International Trophy with the tail painted yellow to ward off following drivers. Photographs from Reggie's collection by Louis Klemantaski.*

revelation. The old troubles of the front suspension were thoroughly eradicated by modern coil spring and wishbone independent front suspension. In the Derbyshire hills I reached 100mph (161kph) in no time although between 30mph (48.2kph) and 75mph (120.7kph) it was less lively. It was a big car so it hardly had the agility to please the real enthusiast, and in contrast to the Derby, Bentley had a great deal of pressed steel and too many fairings.

The V12 Lagonda was ideal for fast road motoring but like the V8 Bentley, too large for British winding roads and heavy traffic. It was better suited to American or Continental straight fast roads.

Yet for really high average speeds on the continent the Surrey Dodge Van I bought from Whitney Straight took a lot of beating. It had a forward control cab, cornered well on winding roads, and covered enormous distances. Although it was slow, by keeping moving all the time and keeping the wheels turning, stopping only when absolutely essential, remarkable average speeds could be achieved.

What with failing exams and one thing and another I was rusticated. That meant I had to live more than 20 miles outside Oxford so I found a convenient place at The White Hart Hotel at Nettlebed run by James and Vi House. Part of the arrangement was that I should lend a hand in the hotel and I lived there quite often, doing more walking round the lanes than working, although I still went to lectures. I spent five years at Oxford, and despite having come down without a degree felt that one way and another I had learned a lot.

Staying at The White Hart meant I became involved in running it. James and Vi never got much time off. She did a lot of the cooking and much of the other work, while he ran the bar, no mean task when the ploughmen or the farm workers came in. They still relied on Shire horses, Clydesdales & Percherons for quite a lot of the work, and what a beautiful sight they were. These men did a fine job of ploughing, harrowing or carting, handling big horses and carts capably and dextrously. They measured out the headlands, got everything straight, and ploughed right up to the hedge expending a great deal of energy walking in heavy soil behind a couple of Shire horses. They came into the taproom at about 10 o'clock in the morning, brought their bagging, and had a pint or two of mild beer. They deserved it, they could take it, and they were really thirsty.

Next event of White Hart routine was the first customer coming back from London. This was generally somebody who had been away overnight and wanted a pick-me-up or a cure for a hangover. After one or two like that, people arrived for lunch, a continuous affair that went on until early afternoon. The last customer could be there at 3 o'clock, and then you had to start thinking about afternoon teas, which went on until well after 5.

At 6 o'clock the bar opened again, and people came in sometimes until quite late, then we did dinners. These had to be prepared during gaps in other activities during the early morning or afternoon, ready to be cooked and served from about half past seven until half past nine. Just as it was getting to the end of the day the ashtrays had to be emptied, the bar tidied, swept up, and the last pints in the taproom served. Following that everything was cashed up, locked up and finished and just as you were relaxing, there would be a pull on the bell from somebody looking for a room for the night.

If you had a bed you would accept. He would then sit in front of the fire and ask you to have a drink. So you would open the bar again and listen to what a hard day he had had London, not left till late, and he was terribly thirsty and could he have another large Scotch before going to bed. He would buy you one and you would sit there chatting, by which time it would be about midnight, and just before you went off to bed he would say "Oh I have got to make an early start. I would like to leave at 8 o'clock please." This meant getting up at half past seven, cooking breakfast, seeing him off and away he would go at half past eight. You ate your own breakfast, served it to the others who had stayed the night, and then it was back with the farm labourers again. It was impossible to refuse work or turn anybody away, because it was difficult to make a decent living at The White Hart.

The Houses took me under their wing, partly because they had never had anybody they could really trust, but in the end I grew disillusioned when they started going out of an evening leaving me in charge. Then they asked me to nip down to Breakspears the Brewers with the order, or with money to pay for the beer. I was getting too involved and the end came when they went away for a weekend. It was an interesting and enlightening experience, but I wanted no more of it. It banished any thoughts I might ever have had of wanting to own a pub.

However at Nettlebed we had ringside seats when we witnessed two men planning the attempt to kidnap Lord Nuffield and hold him to ransom (kidnapping for money was not entirely unknown in the 1930s). The men – one quite pleasant, but the other a rogue and an opportunist – often came to The White Hart for lunch and gave a big tip in order to eat late when the dining room was empty. They did not realise that their conversation could be overheard through the serving hatch. When the Henley police came asking questions we alerted them, then we agreed to report the mens' movements and find out where they were going so that they could be tailed. Once the police discovered the kidnap plot and that their quarries had guns, they began to worry.

The kidnap plan included spending the night before at The White Hart. Talking to the pair casually round the fire it was difficult to believe the magnitude of what they were planning – supposing we betrayed our suspicions, they might produce their guns. They were to gain access to Nuffield on some pretext, arranging an interview at 6pm, to be in secret after everybody left the factory. Nuffield was appraised of their intention, which was to take him blindfolded and with sticky tape over his mouth to a yacht at Pin Mill, a quiet cove on the Orwell not far from Ipswich, and thence into the North Sea. In the end the men decided to change arrangements and stay the night at the Randolph in Oxford, and by the time they set off, plain-clothes police surrounded the whole of the Cowley works.

The accomplice meanwhile had become thoroughly alarmed at the scale of the operation and kept the police informed; when the pair reached the Cowley Road he said, "I think we ought to telephone Nuffield and tell him that we'll be there in a few minutes." He went into a telephone box, called the police, and the would-be kidnappers were apprehended outside the Morris works. The ringleader got a hefty sentence after his colleague turned King's Evidence.

The plan to kidnap Lord Nuffield came to a head on 21 May 1938 with a letter addressed to Viscount Nuffield signed "RC Wilson", who claimed to be writing a series of articles on prominent businessmen in England and Europe for publication in America, and asking for an interview. Thanks to the duplicity of the accomplice, and the intelligence gathered by the police through Reggie and his friends at The White Hart, Nuffield was forewarned and agreed to set a trap.

RC Wilson, also known as John Bruce Thornton, then about 50, was Patrick Boyle Tuellman, with a record for blackmail from which he had made £82,000 over some 18 years. His plan was to drive Nuffield to the coast, put him aboard a yacht sailing off the Suffolk coast, and force him to write a letter of credit for £100,000. A small yacht, the Pierette had been hired, and Thornton had equipped it with surgical instruments and hypodermic needles in case his victim needed to be kept quiet, and sailed it from Harwich to nearby Pin Mill.

Thornton prepared a letter intended for production at the interview arranged for 28 May at Cowley. It said "Read this carefully before passing any remark and do not show it to any other person. I am packing two automatic pistols of large calibre and will immediately shoot you through the guts if you attempt to raise alarm or suspicion." It gave Nuffield instructions to cancel any appointments, walk to a car, not to attempt to make a run for it, "smile, chat, and be cheery." He was to pass Thornton off as a close personal friend, dismiss anyone in the office, and even offer his captors a cigarette before the car started.

Nuffield apparently agreed to the police plan. One can only speculate whether he really wanted to play a more active part than he was allowed, and was as intensely interested and excited by the whole affair as recounted by the Chief Constable of Oxford, CR Fox. Fox recalled Nuffield's annoyance because he would not allow him to be actually kidnapped. "Nuffield would have liked to have dealt with that situation himself," Fox claims in "The Life of Lord Nuffield" (PWS Andrews and Elizabeth Brunner, Blackwell, 1955).

In the event Thornton's plans went wrong anyway. The eleventh hour telephone call from the accomplice to the waiting police was to say they were behind schedule, Thornton had a hangover, and wanted to postpone the whole thing. The police had to decide whether an attempted kidnapping charge would stick if the kidnapper was still a quarter of a mile from the kidnappee, but they pounced nonetheless. Thornton was found with an automatic pistol in a shoulder holster and another in the car. Neither was loaded, but since the car had false number plates, Thornton a wig, gold teeth caps, and various items necessary for disguising himself, the police felt they could make a case. There was also a telegram form addressed to Nuffield's secretary that read: "Unavoidably called away. Cancel all appointments for next week. Writing. Nuffield."

Thornton was convicted at Birmingham Assizes on 22 July 1938 and sentenced to seven years' penal servitude for carrying firearms with intent to endanger life, together with incitement to assault and falsely imprison Lord Nuffield. Attempted kidnapping carried a maximum sentence of only two years but for firearms it was 14 years so both charges were preferred. Thornton died soon after his release in 1942.

In 1938 I was diagnosed with Menier's Disease, a condition of the middle ear that affected my balance, so I had to take the best part of a year off motor racing. It started with partial deafness and attacks of vertigo, and it was no consolation to know that venerables such as Julius Caesar, Martin Luther, and Dean Swift also suffered from it. Although treatment was successful it meant writing off my career prospects for most of 1938. I was especially sad at having to turn down an invitation from Filippini, who seemed to harbour no ill feeling towards me over the motorcycle trophy, to race in Tripoli. Lord Howe wrote to me in February enclosing a copy of a letter from Filippini: "I am very pleased to be able to tell you that the management of the motor races in Tripoli has amalgamated with the Lottery, and all participating motor racers will now receive a starting premium to be taken from the sale of Lottery tickets. To be quite precise 3% of the total amount realised will be distributed in equal parts among the racers starting, the number of whom may not exceed 30 in total." This meant that between 15,000 and 17,500 lire, about £165 to £170 per car, would be available to cover expenses, with more available for special cases.

It was nearly the end of the year before I managed to sell the ERA to the Hon Peter Aitken, Lord Beaverbrook's son, who had been racing a 1936 Maserati 8CM. It went for £1,500, which was not much less than I had paid for it two and a half years earlier. Peter was unable to pay at first, and as I happened to know that his father kept him a bit short, this was no surprise. However I was worried about getting the money safely until he arranged to pay me at the Ship Hotel in Weybridge one Saturday night.

It was near closing time when two men came in looking furtive, asked me my name, and said they were here to pay for the ERA. I knew the landlord of The Ship quite well and took them to his sitting room to deal with the transaction. I decided against dealing with them at the bar, as they had brought the £1,500 in cash. Used notes. This concerned me. They were indeed heavies, thick set and threatening-looking, and I still had to walk back to my flat in Pine Grove. They could easily follow me into the night and pinch the money back or simply lie in

wait by the flat. I was left with no option but to have all this cash about the house for the whole weekend. It was something like a quarter of a million pounds in end-of-the-century money, so I divided it up, spreading it in different hiding places so that in the event of a raid nobody would be likely to escape with it all. I was relieved to get it safely in the bank on Monday morning, although it meant I was without a racing car until May 1939, when my Maserati arrived in time for my comeback race, the International Trophy at Brooklands.

The Maserati 4CL was a great advance in the design of 1½-litre racing cars; it was beautifully made and right from the start never gave the slightest trouble, unlike its predecessor. Designed and built for a single purpose, long distance road racing, it met its objectives well. The 1½-litre Alfa Romeo 158 produced more power per litre, particularly at later stages in its development, but with the exception of it and highly efficient Mercedes Benzes like the Tripoli W165, the Maserati was far and away the best car in the class.

It was sad to see such a splendid racing car used later for short sprints and hill climbs; it was long and elegant, highly geared for long straights on Continental circuits, far more at home doing 150mph (240.8kph) on sweeping high-speed bends than on little twisty turns. Its steering lock was quite unsuited to small-scale courses.

The Maserati's results spoke for themselves. I would not want to compare its handling and performance with the ERA; they were just different. There were three essentials for racing, roadholding, braking and steering, and the Maserati left nothing to be desired in any of them. The steering at high speed was minutely accurate and thanks to the independent front suspension entirely free from kick-back. It was heavy on sharp corners at low speeds but pin-sharp and precise.

Top left: *Inter Varsity Speed Trials, Grantham. Reggie drives Tony Hurst's MG.*

Right: *The Maserati on delivery.*

Overleaf: *Albi, France, 16 July 1939. Start of the first heat. Johnny Wakefield (Maserati) the eventual winner, is on the left while Reggie (Maserati No 22) makes a good start from Bira (ERA No 16). They finished the 20 laps in that order, and the pattern was repeated in the second heat and final classification.*

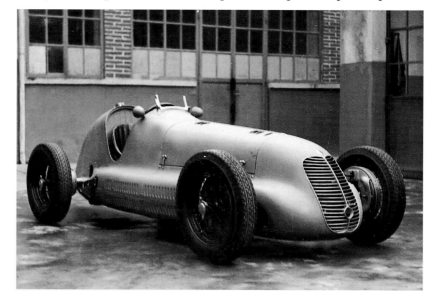

Braking was exemplary, particularly from high speeds, with a smoothness that gave the driver great confidence. The brakes never grabbed or worked unevenly as they did on lots of racing cars, and the suspension gave the driver an astonishingly smooth ride; a great help in a long race.

The most awkward aspect of the Maserati was the gear change. The gear lever was between the driver's legs, tucked under the steering wheel, making it rather inaccessible. It was worse when the change down from third to second had to be left to the last moment. The car's only serious failure took place on the Campbell circuit at Brooklands when the plunger between the brake shoes split and became wedged between the brake shoe and drum just after crossing Howes Bridge.

The result was that the offside front wheel locked. Hideous moment. Yet it was beautifully laid out, the fuel tank taking up the entire tail, and the seat was comfortable and supportive.

Below: At speed at Albi.

Top right: Reggie congratulates Prince Bira following his win in the International Trophy at Brooklands. Professor AM Low, a dedicated motor racing enthusiast is on the left, Bira's cousin and manager Prince Chula in cap, is behind Reggie's outstretched hand.

Lower right: Friends and rivals, left to right Arthur Dobson, Reggie Tongue, Johnny Wakefield.

Brothers Alfieri, Ernesto, Bindo, and Ettore Maserati had been making and driving racing cars on their own account at Ponte Vecchio, Bologna, since 1926. Maserati cars were exquisitely made and it took them only two years to win their first Italian manufacturers' championship. They remained competitive against Alfa Romeo in grand prix racing throughout the 1930s, until the German teams overwhelmed the relatively small Italian operation. Alfieri died in 1932 and in 1937 the surviving brothers sold out to Adolfo Orsi, an Italian industrialist. The resulting refinancing, and the 1938 move to Modena, enabled them to embark on an ambitious programme of grand prix and voiturette racing.

Notwithstanding Orsi's moral and practical support the surviving brothers were as moody, close-knit, and clever as ever. They were most particular that only a handful of specialised craftsmen were ever allowed near their racing cars. For 1938 their grand prix contender was the 8CTF, conforming to Maserati custom with a welded box-section chassis, cross-braced at the rear by means of a beautifully made built-in 6.6-gallon (30 litre) aluminium and magnesium oil tank and cooler. The straight-8-cylinder 2.9-litre engine had cast-iron long-stroke cylinders, and the front-mounted superchargers were gear-driven, like the twin overhead camshafts. Cast in two blocks of four cylinders, it was effectively two 4CM 1½-litre engines laid end to end. The 8CTF was less powerful than the German cars, very nearly as fast, but unreliable. Its best results were in America where it won the Indianapolis 500 twice and might have managed a third but crashed while in the lead.

The 4CL Maserati that Reggie Tongue bought for 1939 was a further development

on the 4CM/8CTF theme with the cylinder dimensions now squared-off at 78mm x 78mm. More significantly it also had the new 4-valve-per-cylinder layout with which the Maseratis hoped to keep their German rivals at bay. Designed under Ernesto Maserati, the lightweight multi-valve gear enabled it to run up to 7000rpm. The chassis of channel-section steel was given extra stiffness by the customary aluminium casting forming the oil tank, beneath the driving seat, and the independent suspension was similar to the larger car with longitudinal torsion bars and wishbones. The rear suspension was by splayed-out quarter-elliptic springs held in place by radius arms. The 4CL was a strikingly well proportioned car with modern sleek bodywork, a Maserati divided air intake grille at the front, and a shapely tail.

Reggie's first race with it was the JCC International Trophy at Brooklands in May 1939. The event was run on the Brooklands road circuit as a handicap race in which the different classes of car negotiated chicanes laid out across the track, the faster cars taking a longer loop than the slower one in an effort to even things out. Bill Boddy, the charismatic editor of *Motor Sport*, wrote that everyone hoped the new E-type ERA would run, but it did not appear at Brooklands until the day before the race. Mays drove it for two laps only at, "… a hopelessly low speed." The Brooklands silencing system was blamed. *Motor Sport* observed it was: " … a great disappointment to those who had subscribed to the British Motor Racing Fund to further the future of these cars." As a consequence, Boddy wrote: "Interest centred on Reggie Tongue's 16-valve 4CTL (sic) Maserati, the latest from Italy, and said to give about 220bhp (164.06kW) at 8000rpm and to weigh just over 12cwt (609.6kg). Thomson & Taylor are to service the Maserati for Tongue."

John Cobb's V12 Lagonda acted as pacemaker for the rolling start, and as it pulled off Raymond Mays led off in the works ERA, ahead of Bira in the older 2.9-litre Maserati. His lead was short-lived however and he came in with his engine and Mays' normally immaculate clothing smothered in oil. The engine was wiped down, more oil rushed in from the Esso pit, and in 2½ minutes Mays resumed, but it could not go on like that and after two more laps he retired. Percy Maclure, the previous year's winner in an unsupercharged Riley with a useful handicap, was second. Reggie's gleaming new Maserati led briefly when the leaders had pit stops and finished third.

Boddy wrote later: "Rain was now coming down in torrents so that Ken Taylor in Tongue's pit removed his shoes – how I remember those soaking days at Brooklands – Maclure snatched a fresh pair of goggles

from his pit without stopping and Tongue came in for his replenishment stop. Fuel went in, both rear wheels were changed and Taylor snatched up the offside of the bonnet. The splash-sheet didn't properly cover Tongue, the mechanics got rather excited, and two minutes five seconds elapsed before the Maserati resumed the race. Tongue's brakes became less effective in the wet so Bira ran on to another victory. That, had we known it, was to be the last long-distance car race ever held at Brooklands."

The British Motor Racing Fund referred to by Boddy was launched early in 1939 with the objective of subsidising ERA. The instigators were Desmond Scannell and Fred Craner of Donington, following the announcement by Humphrey Cook that he was unable to continue financing ERA as he had for the previous four years. Since its foundation in 1933 Humphrey Cook had backed ERA to the extent of about £75,000. Scannell and Craner got together and asked themselves what to do, because to operate ERA during 1939 Cook said would cost about £12,000, and he could not stand being fairy godfather for more than about £4,000 of it. Looking forward to 1940 another £12,000 would have to be found, with again only £4,000 pledged from Cook. Scannell and Craner proposed a public subscription and enlisted three more sympathisers, Captain Phillips of the RAC, A Percy Bradley of Bookhams and RE Tongue, presumably in his role as a director of Thomson & Taylor. This quintet formed themselves into a provisional organising committee under Scannell's honorary secretaryship, and met officially for the first time on 12 January 1939.

I took the Maserati to Albi where I had competed a number of times, only to be beaten into second place by Johnny Wakefield in an identical car. There was not much in it, but anyway he beat me. Johnny was a better driver and he deserved it. Sadly Johnny died in April 1942 in a flying accident while serving in the Fleet Air Arm. My reputation had reached a point where through also being a director of Thomson and Taylor, which was the Alfa Romeo concessionaire for the

Below: *Optimistic noises. Reggie Tongue was in contention to drive an Alfa Romeo 158 in 1940, the fabled Alfetta developed after the war into the most successful car of its time. Thomson and Taylor owned the Alfa Romeo concession for the British Empire and Ireland, and Kenneth Thomson was in little doubt that this was the most competitive 1.5-litre car in the world with the possible exception of the W165 Mercedes-Benz V8 developed specially to compete with the Italians. The opportunity never materialised. By 1940 Reggie Tongue was facing a different sort of challenge.*

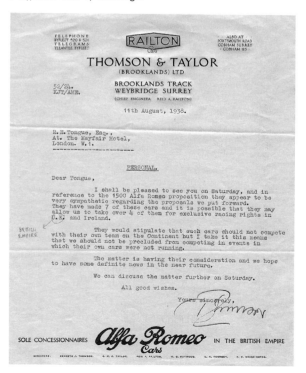

British Empire, it was on the cards that in 1940 I would have a works Alfa 158. This would have put me well ahead of the competition, but unfortunately 1940 never came because of the war, and my works 158 remained a tantalising might-have-been.

When I went off to America with John Cobb, I wanted to see something of the country, and I went to Los Angeles and Las Vegas, that in 1939 had no building of more than two storeys. From there I went to Los Angeles and on to San Francisco, which I thought the most beautiful city, and where I enjoyed every minute. It was clean, perhaps a bit British, and elegant on its hillsides. I then went back to Salt Lake, worrying that as a Class E Reservist I had never obtained permission to go abroad, and with an emergency likely I knew I had better get back to England quickly. I was less concerned about them starting the war without me as anxious not to begin it with a court martial.

Accordingly when I got on an aeroplane from Salt Lake to New York, and happened to sit next to a Vice President of United Airlines, I told him of my plight. He said "I think I could do something for you, but do you mind paying a fairly large fare?" I said I didn't give a damn as long as I got back to Britain quickly, so he promised to see if he could get me fixed up on the one flight a week Pan Am flying boat to Southampton.

I told him I was staying in the Commodore on 42nd Street. What with war in the air and all that I knew it might bring, I thought it quite probable that I might never see New York again. I went out on the tiles. I went to Greenwich Village and had a good root around, then came back late and fell into bed. Next thing I remember was a chap in my room telling me he had done my packing and that I should get up as he had a cab waiting. He told me that provided the driver got me to the Port Washington harbour, from where the Pan Am Clipper flew, then I should pay him. If he failed I shouldn't give him a nickel. Off we went through the streets of New York in the early morning at a hell of a lick. Sure enough he got me there. The aircraft was fully loaded and the engines were running; passengers peered out of the windows intent on discovering whom they were waiting for. On I came with not much luggage, a brief case only, and wearing the strong house slippers I always wore travelling. They looked like bedroom slippers and I must have looked a touch eccentric with no tie and a little dishevelled, because flying in the Clipper was a very up-market way of travelling.

They had a Captain's dinner, a proper printed menu, and a list of all the passengers on board the Boeing 314 flying boat that had started the regular service only in May. However flying was not yet totally reliable. I was anxious to get home quickly and the three-day flight, including overnight stops, was at least a day faster than the Queen Mary. We took off amid worries among some of the passengers that somehow a submarine would surface and shoot us down, much as ship-borne passengers worried about being torpedoed. We set off northwards to Shediac in New Brunswick to refuel.

There we had engine trouble. The starter motor for one of the four Wright Cyclone engines would not work. A new one would have to be flown all the way from New York. The Captain was fretting at the delay so decided to start the engine with a starter motor removed from a good engine, then take the starter motor off while the engine was idling and return it to the first engine. I did not think much of this in case one stopped in mid-air, however he got this done beautifully, all the engines were running then the one they had removed the starter motor from stopped. There was nothing for it but await the arrival of the spare.

Our last stopover before the long haul across the North Atlantic was at Botwood in Newfoundland, arriving safely the following day at Foyne in Southern Ireland. There was nothing to do during these long delays but play bridge, at which I seemed to lose a lot of money. By the time we touched down on Southampton Water I had nothing left; these up-market passengers cleaned me out and I was reduced to giving out cheques. When I reached Victoria Station I had one halfpenny in my pocket and I had to bargain with a newspaper seller to find out what was happening about the war. I had seen the big ticker tape flashing in Times Square New York and it looked as if it was imminent.

I managed to get a taxi to my cousin's digs in Craven Hill Gardens. I knew if she was not in that Miss Morrison the landlady would give me money for the taxi. I was all ready to be called up, but nothing seemed to be happening, so I got in touch with Earl Howe. He came from a distinguished naval family, and I told him I thought I would like to go into the Fleet Air Arm. He felt sure he could arrange something but unfortunately at 27 I was on the upper age limit for operational flying. They did not take fighter pilots over that. The Air Ministry did nothing, so I wrote and told them that as they did not seem to want me, I had applied for the Fleet Air Arm.

I was called up quickly after that.

Below: *Corcovado, Rio de Janeiro, with its gigantic statue of Christ, was the frontispiece for the menu and passenger list on Pan American World Airway Boeing 314 flying boat, in which Reggie flew from America to join the Royal Air Force in 1939.*

International Trophy

(200 miles)

★ THE FASTEST LONG DISTANCE RACE in ENGLAND

A Red letter event in motor-racing!

Organised by the J.C.C.

SEE THE INDIANAPOLIS
MASSED START

Fastest Cars, including the new 160 m.p.h. E.R.A.'s (racing for the first time).

Famous Drivers, including B. Bira, Earl Howe, Raymond Mays, Arthur Dobson, Tony Rolt, Percy Maclure, Reggie Tongue, J. P. Wakefield, Billy Cotton, etc., etc.

ADMISSION 5/- Car Park 2/6. Cars to Course 5/- Cheap Rail and Admission Tickets from S.R. Stations.

The pick of the world's fastest cars, including the latest Italian Maserati and the biggest field of British E.R.A.'s ever seen in one race. The magnificent entry promises BROOKLANDS' most thrilling spectacle, commencing with the Indianapolis Massed Start, flagged off by George Eyston, driven at 100 m.p.h. in the Pilot Car by John Cobb.

You must be there on SATURDAY

MAY 6th

MASSED START 3 P.M.

BROOKLANDS

WEYBRIDGE

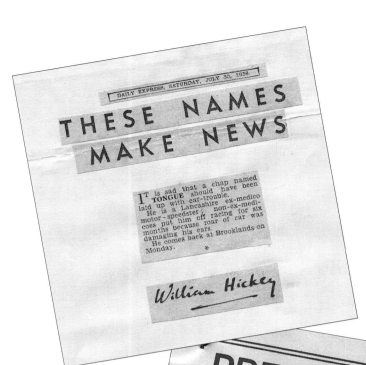

DAILY EXPRESS, SATURDAY, JULY 30, 1938.

THESE NAMES
MAKE NEWS

IT is sad that a chap named **TONGUE** should have been laid up with ear-trouble.

He is a Lancashire ex-medico motor-speedster, non-ex-medicoes put him off racing for six months because roar of car was damaging his ears.

He comes back at Brooklands on Monday. *

William Hickey

PRESS INFORMATION

issued for the favour of Editorial Comment
by The British Motor Race Organisers' Association, 12 Queen's Gate Terrace, S.W.7
Telephone: WEStern 0092

MUSIC IN HIS EARS,- But!
27.7.38
GP/133.

Ear trouble has prevented R.E. Tongue, popular young Lancashire Speedster, from indulging in his favourite sport for the past six months, his doctor having warned him that if he persisted in racing, the roar of his high powered car would aggravate the trouble and possibly result in permanent injury.

Now happily completely recovered, this enthusiast, who gave up medicine to take up motor racing, will make a welcome reappearance in his familiar green E.R.A. at Brooklands on Monday next to run in the British Trophy Race.

Always a popular venue, the Weybridge Track is staging a particularly attractive Bank Holiday program.   Racing starts at 2 p.m. and 75 drivers will compete in the 10 Road and Track events.

----

9 ROYAL AIR FORCE

Since I had flown with the Oxford University Air Squadron (OUAS), and also had my own Leopard Moth with a private pilot's licence, I was already a Royal Air Force Reservist yet I had a difficult time getting into the services. Nobody seemed to want me. As things turned out perhaps it was just as well the Fleet Air Arm turned me down. Instead I went into the RAF in April 1940 as a Pilot Officer, bypassing the customary initial training on account of having had four years in the OUAS, and I was sent to the Advanced Flying School at Hullavington in Wiltshire. Not a great deal happened at first. I gained flying experience on Hawker Audaxes and Harts, pretty in-line Rolls-Royce Kestrel-engined

1920s biplane designs, still being built in the 1930s.

I got on well at Hullavington, despite being about the only officer among the sergeant pilots. There were novel experiences such as being appointed Prisoner's Friend at court hearings. I did not know what a Prisoner's Friend was, but I soon found that I was not allowed to leave the side of the young Pilot Officer who featured in my case. We were not physically tethered but I was not to let him out of my sight. I slept in his room or nearby, and sat with him throughout the day. I had no idea what the case was about and never even heard what happened to him. It had to do with embezzlement or passing dud cheques, so it was referred to a higher court and subsequently a court martial.

The second occasion concerned a pleasant young man whose father owned The Times Furnishing Company. He was a sergeant and kept his Rolls-Royce outside the sergeants' mess. When we were disbanded from Hullavington we had to account for our kit and this poor chap had lost his parachute. Parachutes were regularly stolen to make underclothes and night dresses, such were the clothing shortages in wartime, so a watchful eye was supposed to be kept on them. I was required to bring this sergeant up before the adjutant, a pretty crusty Squadron Leader from the First World War. I duly obtained a guard and he was marched up to the office of the adjutant, who bristled, and gave him a stiff telling-off about losing this parachute.

He could not directly accuse him of theft. In any case he knew the sergeant was extremely wealthy and as we stood there getting this dressing-down the sergeant pulled out his chequebook and said, "Well, how much are they?" There was complete silence. The adjutant told him he could not buy his way out like that and would he please put his chequebook away. Probably charges would be preferred against him. I never knew exactly what did happen but we marched out in great mirth. He was a delightful character. Sadly he went from Hullavington to an Officers' Training Unit, and subsequently into the battle zone, where he did not survive more than a month.

I bought a Fiat 500 when I was at Hullavington. It enjoyed the shortest life of any car I ever owned. It was satisfactory for shopping but quite useless for long runs. The engine would not stand up to hard driving and as a result was soon a sorry mess. It had colossal understeer, the front ploughing straight on when the steering was turned into a corner.

The instructor officers gave me a telling off for driving too fast round the country roads beside the station. Of course they were right. One night we were coming home from a pub, driving pretty fast, and the understeer took charge on the corner just in front of the Mess and we crashed through the hedge. The engine was in the back, and the fan came off, flew through the floorboards and out of the window. It was lucky it did not cut somebody to pieces.

A 1938 Vauxhall 10 (BHR 27) followed the Fiat and how different it was. It gave 80,000 miles of excellent service and I kept it for many years after its useful life was really over. I got it through Bob Keeling, whose uncle Major Godfrey was the Vauxhall dealer in Swindon. He offered me it at very low mileage, and promised it had never been outside the Swindon city limits. It had belonged to the Mayor and I bought it for £160.

In all honesty I had to caution him about the state of the Fiat he was accepting in part-exchange. He very kindly said, "It doesn't really matter about that." It was often quite surprising what people would do for a pilot at that time in the war. I kept the Vauxhall for the duration of the war, did over 100,000 miles in it, had it reconditioned and went on using it in the 1950s. It was still capable of going from the Midlands to London at an average of 40mph (64kph), then I was offered £300 for it, which represented very

Previous page: Michael Royce, known as Scruffy, with fitters attending his Hurricane.

Left: Reggie hiding in trees at Lane House, Fishpool.

cheap motoring for the 20 years or so I had it.

At Hullavington I had to attend parades and do physical training, which I hated. PT took place early every morning supervised by Len Harvey, a former professional boxer from Stockport, and Barnett who played cricket for Gloucestershire and England. They gave the squad a hard time, and while I did not want to seem rebellious, I really did not do it very well. I waited a few days until over a beer at lunch Len Harvey suddenly said: "Tongue, you really are letting the side down. You're making a real mess of this physical training and it doesn't do your rank any good before all these sergeants. We don't like seeing somebody not doing it very well and I think it would be a good idea, if you don't mind, if you did not come any more."

The time at Hullavington was at the height of the invasion scare. There were defence positions all round the aerodrome and the CO was worried about morale. "Would you please go out and chat to them, Tongue. It builds up their confidence. They like to see a pilot, and know that at least we have got some aircraft which will help the defence, if we can get off the ground in time." I went to one of the dispersal points and found airmen armed with wooden sticks and pikes, perfectly willing to take on an armed German paratrooper with a pitchfork.

The aerodrome did come under attack from German light bombers, whose pilots could have seen the chance light at the end of our runway when we were flying. The flares showed the line of the runway and they swooped down and machine-gunned and bombed it. It did not happen while I was flying, which was just as well. We had been told that if all the flares were dimmed and all the lights went out, particularly the chance light, there was no hope of being able to land. We might do more damage by hitting a building or something. We were told we must fly over the Bristol Channel, which we could see quite clearly from Wiltshire even at night, invert the aeroplane,

let it go into the sea and come down on a parachute where a boat would be waiting to pick us up.

I was a bit sceptical about this. I thought no boat was going to find me somewhere in the dark in the middle of the muddy Bristol Channel, the water will be damn cold, and I would be dead by the time anybody got to me. I never expected that it might really happen, until one night while I was airborne, suddenly all the aerodrome lights went out. The place was just black. I knew that if there was a prowling Hun he might see my exhaust flames, get a bead on me, and shoot me down. Well I thought I'm not going to go wandering off all the way to the Bristol Channel and do this stupid thing, even if it means a court martial, which I expected it would because I would be disobeying an order if I did not.

I managed to do a landing very close to the chance light because in the dark my eyes had become accustomed to picking things out. I don't suppose I rolled more than fifty yards before I stopped, thinking, "Now for it, I'll be under arrest." Nothing was said at all, except by some senior officer who growled grudgingly, "That was a good bit of work". When I got my final report on leaving Hullavington it said, "This officer pulled off a marvellous landing in pitch darkness." That I thought of course might spell my doom. Next thing I expected was to be doing these Lysander flights, landing in fields in France with agents. Not a bit of it, nobody in the posting department seemed to pick up this interesting feature of my flying, so I was sent to a fighter squadron.

I was posted to No 3 Squadron at Wick in July 1940. This was in the north of Scotland, a hilltop station on the windswept east coast, just north of the old grey herring fishing port. I obtained permission from the Station Commander to drive there in the Vauxhall with several others together with our kit. There was the customary party in the Mess at Hullavington before we left, so it was late in the afternoon before we managed to get on the road. We only got as far as the Star Hotel in Worcester, a distance of about 65 miles.

By lunchtime next day we arrived at home near Manchester and were entertained lavishly at the Golf Club. I remember it was a Saturday, because lots of people were there, plying us with drink, and we had an extremely good lunch. As a result we did not set off until late in the afternoon again, only getting as far as Blackpool, where we spent another night.

I was beginning to worry about our progress. At this rate it was going to take a week to get to Wick and we might not be well received. I had no idea how urgently they needed pilots. We set off next morning determined to cover a lot of miles, and got all the way up to Aviemore for another night stop, followed by a fairly leisurely run to Wick.

The adjutant seemed surprised to see us: "I don't know what the hell they've sent all you chaps here for, we haven't asked for you, and we don't really want you. We've got a full complement of pilots. You'd better go back." Accordingly we turned round and went all the way back again, a bit quicker this time because the Wick CO would not let us go by car, and I had to leave it in Scotland. Hullavington of course had no idea how such a mix up could have occurred, nobody seemed to want us, and we were duly despatched back to Wick again. After a few days there, we were sent all the way back to Aston Down 5 Operational Training Unit (OTU), near Brize Norton, about five minutes flying time from Hullavington.

This was for an operational training course that turned out to be absorbing, and it was here that I first flew a Spitfire. At Hullavington my rating as a pilot was above average but I am afraid I did less well at Aston Down. They were digging a trench round the aerodrome and piling up all the earth from it. Unfortunately from the air a pile of earth looks quite flat. I always tried to land "dead stick", without the engine pulling. I liked to get as close to the perimeter as I could, because I thought the day will come when I might have to. In due course that day did come, and then I had to do it not once but a number of times, so my practice stood me in good stead. On 2 August 1940 on only the second occasion I came in to land Miles Master M9A N7782, a single 715bhp (533kW) Kestrel XXX-engined advanced trainer at Aston Down, I never saw this pile of earth from the trench. It just looked brown. Next thing I knew was when I hit this most enormous hump. Off came the wheels, the aircraft slid forward on its underside, there was a loud noise of grinding metal and the propeller was all bent.

My Flight Commander was Ken Gough, who had been with 504, an auxiliary squadron in Nottinghamshire, and he was absolutely furious that I had broken one of his aircraft. There were still not many Masters around; it was barely a year since it had first flown and only nine had entered service in September 1939. He gave me a severe wigging and when I left gave me only an average assessment. I met him subsequently during my time in the Air Force and we became good friends but the assessment rankled.

At Aston Down we flew Harvards and Masters, wooden training aircraft that handled a bit like a single-seat fighter, and although the objective of the posting was to train up on Hurricanes in the first few weeks I flew only two and a quarter hours on them, while I had seven and a half on Spitfires. By September when we were then sent back again to Wick I had nearly 24 hours flying time on Hurricanes. At Wick there was not much happening and we spent our time doing sweeps out to sea,

Right: Trevor Parsons, Flying Officer, 504 Squadron on left scanning the sky with a telescope and Tony Rook, Flight Lieutenant and flight commander of A Flight. According to the duty roster it is 20 October 1940, not long after Parsons had shot down a Dornier 17 and shared in the destruction of a Heinkel 111. He was killed just two years later, aged 25, as a Squadron Leader with 264 Squadron.

practising low level flying just above the water. We were billeted in Wick's best hotel, living and feeding like fighting cocks, and altogether it was a pleasant place. We even had some good game shooting. One of our number, Maurice Whinney, who had been with me at Hullavington had an uncle and godfather with an unusual claim to fame. As a child this Admiral James had apparently been the subject of an advertisement for Pears Soap called "Bubbles", a painting of a beautiful curly headed little boy blowing soap bubbles. We got Whinney to send a signal to the Commander in Chief Portsmouth, Admiral James, saying that as the game on his shoot in Sutherland was being neglected, would it be all right for us to do something about it? A signal came back saying: "Yes, by all means, have a good time, but don't forget the Commander in Chief Portsmouth." What he meant was put some grouse on the next aircraft coming his way.

We moved from Wick to a satellite aerodrome called Castletown, along the coast from the Castle of Mey, on Dunnet Bay by Dunnet Head, the northernmost point on the British Isles. Once again we were billeted

in a good pub at Dunnet run by Mrs McKay.

The Station Commander was RLR Atcherley, an identical twin, both of whom were on the station. You could never be certain whether it was David or Richard you were talking to, but despite their reputation for mischief, I was fortunate in having Batchy as CO. He was a delightful man and we had a lot in common. He asked one day if I would like to have lunch in Scapa Flow, the great Orkney fleet anchorage, on an aircraft carrier with the Commander in Chief. The Royal Navy's northern base, surrounded by islands and even then being enclosed by the Churchill Barriers to prevent another Royal Oak tragedy, lay only 20 miles to the north across the Pentland Firth. I pled a previous engagement, suspicious that this may not have been an officially sanctioned visit, and Batchy elected to go off on his own. He took the little Miles Magister, an open two-seater training aircraft we used for ferrying and other odd jobs, and flew off towards Scapa.

The Magister had no radio, so when they saw him coming they fired off signal rockets, flew every flag, and flashed every light to send him away. But he steamed on through the balloon barrage, selected the aircraft carrier and put it down smoothly on the deck. A degree of panic set in because what he did not know was that the lift, which took aircraft from the flying deck to the hanger below, had become jammed in the down position. Batchy was unable to see this on his approach so came trundling across the deck and when he got to where the lift should have been he fell into the hole. The aircraft burst into flames but they put it out quickly and he got away with it. He duly had lunch with the Commander in Chief and a few drinks, but it would have been a disaster if he had set the aircraft carrier on fire, with so much aviation fuel aboard.

Batchy's claim to fame was of course that as Squadron Leader RLR Atcherley he was a member of the High Speed Flight that won the Schneider Trophy at Calshot in 1929. He flew a Supermarine S6 round a triangular course off Calshot, and his lap at 332mph (532.96kph) was a world record for a closed course, that lasted until the 1931 contest. Unfortunately he missed a pylon on one circuit and was disqualified. Schneider Trophy flying was extremely dangerous and Waghorn, Grieg and Atcherley put up a wonderful show to win against the Italians. Batchy and his brother survived the war but both unfortunately died soon afterwards.

One night at Castletown I was duty officer and sitting in front of a cosy fire. Batchy was at the other side of the fireplace when the field telephone rang. A voice said "I'm speaking on behalf of the Air Officer Commanding (AOC) Group. I want to tell you that 'Napoleon' is in operation forthwith". I leaned across and said to the CO "Napoleon in operation forthwith sir". Batchy was unimpressed: "Tell him to get off the line. We've had our legs pulled enough for one week." A short while later there was another call. This time it was the AOC himself and he wanted to speak to the Commanding Officer.

The change in tone was swift. After further calls we had to leave at five o'clock the following morning and would stop at Turnhouse, later Edinburgh Airport, en route for the South where obviously we were going to join in the battle. Someone in the bar told Mrs McKay that we were going. She was quite distraught: "Och ye poor boys. Ye'll a' be kill't before the month's oot. Is there anythin' I can do?" We decided there was. She went to bed and left the bar open.

By five o'clock the following morning nobody was in a fit state to get up let alone fly. Somehow we all made it to the airfield, got into our aircraft, and flew off to Turnhouse. The airfield was literally a field, there were no concrete runways, it was just grass and it had rained a lot so it was muddy. Our boots were dirty, we had no batman, so things did not get cleaned and while discipline was still strict we were a bit cocky. Although we had not seen any action, we felt we could cope with anything, and tended to leave the top buttons on our tunics open in a gesture of insubordination. We went off happily but got the shock of our lives when we reached Turnhouse. The Duke of Kent was coming to inspect us.

Barely half the squadron was fit to be seen. Twelve, that was half, were told to hide in the billiard room and keep out of sight. The other half, which included me, was lined up for inspection even though twelve pilots flying twenty-four aircraft was going to seem a bit odd. Whitney Straight, whom I knew from motor racing days, was Kent's ADC and walked behind HRH on the inspection line. By the time he drew level he was breathless with suppressed laughter. I shook hands with him and reminisced briefly about Brooklands thinking it odd that he should still be wearing his silk flying inner gloves. You never looked down to shake hands with an inspecting officer. You looked him straight in the eye and Whitney duly passed on with no more comment.

I then discovered that my less than dignified pale blue silk pyjama sleeve had crept below the cuffs of my tunic. The slippery material of the handshake was mine, not his. Goodness knows what HRH must have thought. The King's youngest brother, he was only 39 when he was killed in 1942, flying in a Sunderland flying boat to Iceland.

The squadron did not move on from Turnhouse straight away. We thought we would be in the dogfight within a day or two, but it was twelve days before I was posted elsewhere. We remained billeted in a fine mansion on the edge of a golf course. It was really the golf club house and we did not have a lot to do. There were still good restaurants in Edinburgh especially for fish.

We occasionally "scrambled", called out to take off, but never quite knew whether there was an enemy aircraft coming in over the Firth of Forth or not. Either way we never made contact with any.

By the beginning of October 1940 I was posted to 504 Squadron at Filton near Bristol. I went by train via London as I had been told to get there urgently, so I did not have time for socialising on the way. I went by night train and arrived at Filton Station just outside the Bristol Aircraft works in the early hours of the morning. I discovered about 50 airmen with nobody in charge, wondering what to do. They had been posted to Filton as well, so I managed to get them to fall in as a proper squad. I knew little better than they what to do; I had never done any marching or parade work since the OTC at school, and I had not done much of it then. Luckily I got hold of a likely looking Flight Sergeant and said: "Now look here, these men have to be got down to the aerodrome. I think you had better either telephone for some transport, though I doubt there'll be enough to take you all, or else you'll have to march them there."

I was all right because I was met and driven there. Morale at 504 Squadron was good and remained so. It was an Auxiliary squadron, so most of the personnel came from in and around Nottinghamshire, and as they had not had a lot of action they were still pretty well intact. Their Commanding Officer was Squadron Leader Johnny Semple, and he and I got on well. My Flight Commander in B Flight was Barry Royce with whom I remained great friends long after the war. Barry had been with 504 in France in May 1940 and taken command when the CO was killed. He shot down four German aircraft in the twelve days he was there, got a DFC, and finished up as a Wing Commander. Tony Rook was the Flight Commander of A Flight, had been in France as well, and in 1941 went with his Hurricanes on HMS Argus to Murmansk to train

Russian pilots, winning one of the four Orders of Lenin ever awarded to RAF personnel. Barry's brother Michael, nicknamed Scruffy, and I met again in an Operational Training Unit at Usworth near Newcastle in 1941 and spent many years together at Rolls Royce on engine development. Both Royces and Rook survived the war.

A speciality of 504 Squadron was intended to be attacking enemy gun emplacements, so we were tasked to give some practice to the anti-aircraft batteries stationed round the aerodrome, by flying low towards them. Poor "Boosey" Kennett took part but seemed to forget all he ever knew about high-speed stalls. He dived on a gun emplacement and stalled at about 130/150mph (208/240kph) at which he started sinking towards the ground. He went straight through a gun emplacement, fortunately empty by the time he got there, near the Mess scattering guns, sandbags, the lot. He was completely unscratched, the aircraft was not terribly badly damaged, the gun was only knocked a bit askew but I still thought, "He is going to be in terrible trouble for this."

He came back to the Mess and I saw him talking to the CO. I asked him if he was likely to face a court martial. "No," he replied, "The CO sent for the Mess waiter and bought me a pint. He thought I probably needed it". By this stage of the war there was a new attitude. Nobody brought charges or complained unnecessarily about misdemeanours. There was no time. There was far too much to be done.

I spent six weeks at Filton. The Station Commander, Victor Beamish, became something of an RAF legend and led from the front, with a distinguished record against the enemy that won him a DSO and DFC in addition to his AFC gained for establishing the Met Flight at Aldergrove. We played snooker in the evenings and if there was any bombing hid underneath the billiard table. The slate bed of the table weighed about a ton and I do not like to think what would have happened if a bomb had hit the Mess. I am sure it would have crushed us to death.

There was quite a lot of action even in daylight at Filton, because the factory was a prime target and just within range of their fighter-bombers flying from France. The squadron did shoot down a Messerschmitt Bf109, and some bits of twisted metal, and its gun were displayed as trophies in our dispersal hut. The whole squadron were heroes for the day. We were feted, people sent us barrels of beer, the Imperial Tobacco Company sent us masses of cigarettes, we got food, and really the fuss was out of proportion to the success of our endeavours.

The action mostly took place away from the city, and the German bombers were intercepted so far away, that they generally scattered before they could do much serious damage to the aircraft factory. During that time I unfortunately seemed to be on the wrong roster, the wrong flight, or should I say the right one, for whenever I was called to readiness I often never really saw anything. The whole of the Bristol factory area was heavily enclosed with a balloon barrage.

On the afternoon of Wednesday 16 October 1940 we were scrambled to intercept enemy aircraft approaching from the South Coast. The Germans had been making numerous raids with the Bristol Aircraft factory as their target and the squadron was engaged on several occasions. Visibility was poor, but we took off and made a rendezvous, and after I had been airborne for just over an hour the weather grew worse and we all became separated. Aircraft that had been on your wingtip one minute just disappeared the next.

In view of the balloon barrage around Bristol city and the Bristol factory, I decided to make a precautionary landing elsewhere. I had landed at Whitchurch in my Leopard Moth before the war; I had driven past it plenty of times since, and knew the area well. It was now thick fog, visibility was down to about 30-50 yards, and I knew Whitchurch was acting as a parking lot for the aircraft of the old Imperial Airways. They were mostly lying around the perimeter, but I decided it was nevertheless necessary to locate them, so I made several dummy runs, which I think put the wind up the ground staff more than it did me. I eventually decided on a suitable line of approach, parallel to the hangars and past the control tower. I got safely down, passing various obstructions in the fog, including the laid-up Hercules and Hannibal aircraft.

Soon afterwards however I realised that things were still passing by very quickly. In the heat of the moment I had forgotten to lower my flaps, and on the damp grass aerodrome the brakes were not having much effect. Next thing that loomed out of the murk was the perimeter hedge and fence. I went crashing through, crossing the main Bristol/Taunton road, coming to a dead stop amid clouds of steam and much quacking of terrified ducks. Hurricane R4178 was in a duck pond.

Within what seemed seconds a chap appeared with a ladder, and put one end on the bank, and one end on the wing. I climbed out and walked along to the ladder and did not even get my feet wet. I was not so much as scratched and the aircraft was flying again in a few days. I walked

Below: *Reggie never flew this No 3 Squadron Hurricane P3774 but on 22 September 1940 he flew its identical twin P3773 from Castletown in the North of Scotland to Leuchars near St Andrews and on to Turnhouse, later Edinburgh Airport.*

the few feet to the road to be met by the NAAFI wagon and a driver who said, "Would you like a cuppa sir? I have been driving all round the aerodrome wondering where you would finish up, and just happened to be close".

I was not proud of the exploit, however I was relieved not to have hit anything more solid, or done more damage. Upon reflection the humour of the occasion was rather over-ridden by the sobering thought of what would have happened if I had hit the control tower, a hangar, or an Imperial Airways aircraft. The incident is well recorded in the archives of the Battle of Britain at the Imperial War Museum, so there is no need to hide my shame any longer.

The CO Johnny Semple wanted me to stay but squadrons were often split up due to the heavy demand for pilots. He found it difficult to make decisions about who should stay and who should go, and decided to put names in a hat, reducing the chances of me being posted to fifteen to one.

We had some beers in the Mess and duly drew out the name of who was to go on a posting. It was not a very pleasant one; we knew it was in the middle of the London area where everything was happening. My name came out and I was off to Hendon. It was November 1940.

There was not much of an aerodrome left when I arrived at Hendon. It had been blitzed the previous day and there was nobody about. I was not sure what to do so I indulged in some partying and the following day contacted the Air Ministry. I knew that given the casualty rate in Fighter Command, the likelihood of being killed within a 24 hour interval could be great. The Air Ministry sent me to 249 Squadron at North Weald where Robert Barton the Canadian CO had been a great success. He was well known, he gained a DFC and bar (he eventually was awarded an OBE), but I could see at once that he had not taken a liking to me. I only spent a few days with 249 flying with it for a total of fifteen minutes.

Right: It was not far from 9 Flying Training School at Hullavington to the White Hart at Ford, on the old A4 London-Bath road, in somebody's MG TA. Reggie Tongue relaxes with Pilot Officer Maurice Tolley Whinney on left, who accompanied Reggie to No 3 Squadron at Wick, then was put on Special Duties in Bomber Command attached to 161 Squadron. A Squadron Leader, he was made an OBE in 1945 working at the Foreign Office. Peter Kennet from Bexhill-on-Sea on the right also accompanied Reggie to No 3 at Wick, then along with several of Reggie's colleagues embarked on HMS Ark Royal for Malta in March 1941. Within a week or so, after intercepting a Junkers 88, he was surprised and shot down by two Messerschmitt 109s into the sea. He was dead by the time rescue arrived.

Every squadron tried to build up a team and, just like building up a good football team, anybody it did not think would fit in or be successful was dropped. They tried to recruit people who had already achieved recognition or were likely to respond to training. So when 249 Squadron decided it did not want me, 46 Squadron, which operated on the same aerodrome, said it would. It was a resounding success and I spent quite a long time by Fighter Command standards with 46, from 16 November 1940 at North Weald, until it went overseas on 7 May 1941.

I had a short break from 46 when, with a colleague I was posted on attachment for five weeks in March-April 1941 to 71 Squadron, the first Eagle Squadron created before America came into the war. The CO of 46 sent for us one morning, inviting us for a drink with him in the Mess. In view he said, of our record of volunteering for things, this time he had a real job for us. Eagle Squadron was entirely composed, he said rather pointedly I thought, of volunteers.

We were not quite sure at first what we were expected to do, until it transpired we were being sent as Air Training Disciplinarian Officers. Apparently the Americans were not amenable to discipline, and although they had come to England to fight, they were determined to do it their way. They seemed to have an attitude of "Leave it to us. We can win the war on our own".

Their lack of discipline became obvious one morning as I came out of the dispersal hut. A Hurricane was doing aerobatics, mainly loops one after the other, getting closer and closer to the ground. I carefully examined the day's flying log but I knew, as the officer chiefly responsible, that I had not given authorisation for any aerobatics that morning. I asked another of the Eagle pilots what the pilot thought he was doing. The reply was to the effect that if he could get four more loops in before he hit the ground he would clear his poker losses.

I pointed out that he was flying one of His Majesty's aircraft; that they were extremely expensive and hard to come by, and not for playing tomfoolery. Fortunately he backed off before he hit the ground but it proved necessary to get somebody down from the United States Embassy in London to clear things up. They duly sent the Air Attache, a naval man as it happened, Commander Taylor. He gave the pilots a magnificent telling off. He said he knew they were not all heroes. He knew why some of them had volunteered for overseas service. Some of them had left substantial debts in America, some had

legal action pending, in some instances the police wanted to interview them, while some were merely escaping the vengeance of cuckolded husbands. He was extremely outspoken, leaving them in no doubt that unless they accepted the discipline the Royal Air Force demanded, they would be sent back to America to face whatever music was going to be played to them

Right: Examining the cannon from a shot-down Messerschmitt whose tailplane is displayed as a hunting trophy, colleagues from 504 Squadron at Filton left to right Trevor Parsons, "Scruffy" Royce, Charlton Haw, and Douglas Haywood. Haw, then a sergeant pilot claimed a Messerschmitt 109 but was attacked over Bristol, managing to bring his aircraft down at Axminster. In September 1940 Haw was one of a party of pilots sent to Russia to train aircrew how to fly Hurricanes for which he was awarded the Order of Lenin. He completed the war with a DFM and DFC and went to Moscow in 1985 to celebrate the 40th anniversary of the end of the war. Haw died in 1993. Heywood had already had an eventful war by the time of this photograph. Flying the ill-fated Fairey Battles he had been injured in a crash, then wounded when shot down. Flying a Spitfire, he was attacked by Focke Wulf 190s over the Channel and wounded again but managed to crash-land at Dungeness. On rejoining his squadron, on a mission over France his engine failed, and he had to bale out over the Channel. After 17 hours in his dinghy in a storm, he was rescued by a French fishing boat, before being handed over to the Germans as a prisoner of war. Haywood died in 1998.

One of the best pilots and a good leader in the Eagle Squadron was Chesley (Pete Peterson) from Salt Lake City. He became a General in the United States Air Force and was highly decorated. He was well enough disciplined but he was not able, any more than I or anybody else was, to get real discipline into all the pilots in Eagle Squadron. The danger was always of disorderliness spreading, particularly under pressure. We worked hard enforcing order, and towards the end thought we had done a pretty good job. We were stationed at Kirton in Lindsey, just south of Scunthorpe, and twenty miles or so from the North Sea coast at Grimsby. I seemed to be well liked; indeed it was necessary to be so if I was going to achieve anything. One occasion, unknown to us but well known to our controllers, was an emergency flap that may only have been organised to test us out.

We were required to go from Kirton in Lindsey to Speke at Liverpool and the weather was not good. It was thick fog.

A balloon barrage was set up to protect shipping in the Mersey Estuary and I knew the area a bit. Visibility was much better over on the Welsh side, so I took my flight into Sealand, which was an RAF aerodrome in clear weather on the banks of the River Dee. I landed, feeling pleased that I had done a good job. The Station Commander ordered me to take off again and make more attempts to land on fog-bound Speke, so we all got into our aircraft, and took off again into the murk and fog.

I still could not find Speke, but what we did find was the balloon barrage. Suddenly someone shouted to me on the intercom, "Balloons! Balloons!" I looked ahead and sure enough there

163

was a balloon almost on top of me. I had all my flight still in close formation so I opened the throttle and climbed as fast as I could to get over the top of them. I shall never know why one of the aircraft did not hit one of the cables.

The best thing to do was to return to Sealand and explain the situation to the Station Commander, but once again he ordered us into the air, insisting we got into Speke somehow. For the second time that day we encountered the balloon barrage, which was more than enough for me. I did not go back to Sealand; instead I got permission to return to Kirton in Lindsey, while the Flight remained intact. It was a typical example of people on the ground, miles away in a reinforced control room, dictating what should be done without any real appreciation of the difficulties experienced by the pilots.

The Speke balloon barrage incident was a salutary experience. I was extremely fortunate not to hit anything and crash. I felt the Almighty had been looking after us and made sure that we escaped without damage. It was nothing short of a miracle.

Eagle Squadron was certainly a bit unruly but it was a fine crowd to be with. I enjoyed the time that I spent with it and never had a disagreement or even a harsh word. The pilots were great cavaliers and happy-go-lucky. I took the trouble to warn them that when they were posted to Northern Ireland they must fly at a good height because there was a little island in the middle of the Irish Sea called the Isle of Man with a mountain called Snaefell, where later in the war I was distressed to hear that another American plane crashed, killing everyone.

At 46 Squadron I was once again in B Flight. The flight commander was a delightful man called Norman Burnett, who unfortunately did not survive the war, another victim of air combat off Malta after sailing there on Ark Royal. The squadron commander was Alexander Rabagliati. I would have followed either of them anywhere, such was my confidence in their leadership. They inspired me to do the things that really if I had thought about it made me very frightened. He went to the Mediterranean as well and had a distinguished career against the Regia Aeronautica, gaining a DFC and bar, then sadly was lost as wing leader at Coltishall in 1943 on a shipping strike.

One event occurred that we were lucky to get away with. We had been "scrambled" and the cloud base was very low. Rabagliati as CO and leader was with me on the left wing aircraft. We came out of cloud and I knew that we were near the ground because I could see, quite clearly and very close, an Express Dairies milkman with his delivery truck. We were fortunate not to fly into the terrain together. I often wonder how the milkman felt with six Hurricanes roaring out of the clouds almost on top of him. Once again I suffered no reaction at the time, but only later realised how dangerous it had been.

Fear never got through to me much at that age, although I did feel it on the first sweep I did over Calais and Dieppe. We were stoodging along, acting as cover for some bombers below, and I was watching the flak. I had never seen it before, and I thought, rather idly I suppose, how pretty it looked. The stars and shell bursts looked a bit like the Fifth of November. Then other stuff came up from the ground, tracer all in different colours, but little black puffs that looked harmless although they were absolutely lethal. After we had turned round and started back for the English coast my number two, Sergeant Steadman, spotted a gun on the French coast that had got a bead on me. He could see the shell bursts getting closer but just as he was coming up to try and warn me, he must have picked up a stray round that damaged his aircraft and he had to bail out over the Channel. He was rescued by one of our Air Sea Rescue boats, contracted rheumatism from the experience, and wound up commissioned in 1941 as a Flight Lieutenant.

A few days later we were doing another patrol over France, and in mid-Channel we got jumped by nine Messerschmitt Bf109s. We had been instructed that if we ever found ourselves in circumstances where we could not shoot back, we had to get an enemy off our tails. I am sure that in the German records that day I am down as a "kill". The tracer was going right past my wings. I could not understand how none of it hit me. It was absolutely all over the place but Somebody was looking after me and directed the bullets elsewhere. I put the stick hard over to the right and forward and dived. I did aileron turns from about 25,000ft from where all this started, one to the left, one to the right, and of course I then blacked out completely because of the g-force. I must have pulled the stick back instinctively, for suddenly there was no shooting, everything was quiet, and I was climbing again from about 8,000 feet.

There was not another plane in sight. It was an absolutely empty sky but I must have got pretty near the ground. I had pulled off a manoeuvre that quite a lot of pilots did to get away from an enemy in an advantageous position. It certainly saved my life.

Just as I would have followed Rabagliati and Burnett virtually anywhere, I had great confidence in Victor Beamish, my old Station Commander at Filton who took over at North Weald in June 1940. We had one or two pilots in the Mess who were what might be called well connected. There was the old CO of the Oxford University Squadron, one Hill, who was then an Air Vice Marshall in charge of the battle. He came to dine, and some of the people who were more well-to-do succeeded in getting a lot of grouse sent from Scotland, together with some extremely good claret, and we had a most marvellous Mess evening.

Victor Beamish was an accomplished RAF boxer. North Weald was bombed from time to time, and a number of workmen were kept on

hand to fill in the holes as quickly as possible for the station to remain operational. One raid took us completely by surprise, the sirens went but the raid was on before we could get airborne. The workmen had been busily filling holes made by a previous raid, and not surprisingly perhaps, started dashing to the shelters. This was too much for Victor. Without another thought he dashed across, got hold of two of them, and hit them smartly on the chin telling them to get on with it. One was unable to; he was completely laid out. As soon as there was a chance to get airborne Victor, always keen on operational sorties, jumped into his aircraft and dashed away from the dispersal point, but was perhaps over excited and keen. He went smack into a steamroller and took no more part in the fight that day.

Just before Christmas we were sent to Digby, south of Lincoln. This did not necessarily mean we were completely out of things, because we went to Wittering to join up with Leigh-Mallory's Big Wings, doing sweeps over the Channel and the French coast. It was an interesting time; we were a fairly lighthearted lot by then. One afternoon I was off duty, sitting in the Mess reading a newspaper, and some chaps came in wearing green overalls wanting to know where our piano was. I asked them what they wanted it for and they said they had been sent to take it away to be tuned. I thought pianos were tuned on the premises, but they seemed to know what they were doing, so I showed them where it was. I never thought of asking if they had any authority. I did not even know if they needed any. It turned out that they were from Waddington, a nearby bomber station. It had not got a piano and it was having an important Mess night. The green overalls knew we had one so they took it off in a van just like that.

When our station realised the piano had been pinched, they found out what night the party was on, went over when it was in progress and collected every hat from the hat pegs. They put them all into pillowcases and brought them back to Digby. The following day the hats were loaded into an Avro Anson, flown over Waddington, and tipped out.

While with 46 Squadron at Digby I was with Charles Ambrose, who had a DFC after shooting down two Bf 109s, one at Eastchurch, and a Dornier Do17 over Bexley, and baled out of Hurricanes not once but twice. We volunteered for what was euphemistically known as a rhubarb. This entailed taking a Hurricane over enemy territory and destroying a railway engine. Steam locomotives exploded with spectacular results when armour-piercing bullets penetrated the pressure boiler, and although you could not always be certain the trains were loaded with military passengers or material, we were in the business of disrupting railways and transport as much as we could. We hung about waiting for a target but our rhubarb never came about. Ambrose remained in the RAF, qualified in Staff Studies, was made a CBE, and retired in 1972 as a Group Captain

A foolhardy incident from which we were fortunate to emerge with only one minor casualty took place at Digby. Our new adjutant had been a top London divorce lawyer easily imagined, even in his uniform, in court with black jacket, stiff collar and striped trousers. One of the pilots had been killed and his effects and kit were taken to the adjutant, who while he may have been a perfectly good divorce lawyer did not know much about RAF procedure, or for that matter guns. When we took him the dead man's 3.8 Smith and Wesson revolver we made sure there was a bullet in the chamber. The adjutant demanded to know whether it was loaded, or if it was not, how did one make sure. We airily told him the usual way was to point it at a window and pull the trigger. Obediently he duly did so and of course the thing went off with a loud bang. But our laughter ended abruptly when we found two people outside, noisily trying to help somebody, claiming he had been shot in the leg.

The adjutant tried to shift the blame to a sergeant, who had had no part in the episode at all. This was unnecessary as it was I who would have been court martialled. It turned out that the AC 2 who was making all the fuss had not been shot at all but been hit by a piece of masonry, dislodged when the bullet ricocheted off a wall. He had been dozing on a bench outside the equipment store when he heard a bang and felt a sudden pain in his leg. It was probably quite natural for him to think he had been shot.

Not long after my time with Eagle Squadron at Kirton in Lindsey, I returned to 46 Squadron to be immediately posted to Sherburn in Elmet, ten miles west of Leeds near Church Fenton on the main line to York. Not much seemed to be happening until one incident that could have been most unfortunate for me. Acting as flight commander implied some degree of responsibility, so when a VIP from the Air Ministry was with me in the dispersal hut and an AC1 came in, saluted smartly and said, "I've checked the oil in your car sir and I've filled it up with petrol", I nearly died of embarrassment. I had not given him any instructions to do any such thing, and petrol restrictions being what they were there was a risk that the VIP might report the episode. Fortunately nothing came of it and I spent only a fortnight at Sherburn in Elmet before being sent to No 1 PDC at West Kirby on 1 May preparatory to going overseas.

10 AFRICA TO UXBRIDGE, USWORTH TO HUCKNALL

I was unable to find out where I was going until information leaked out that I was bound for West Africa. I had been there as a tourist but was somewhat distraught at the thought of going back. It was the last place in the world I wanted to be. I had forebodings about either falling victim to some terrible disease or drinking myself silly on cheap whisky. Gin was about two pence a nip on His Majesty's Transport, FTF6, that had been in peacetime the Highland Princess.

It was, so far as we were aware, an uneventful trip although the ship's officers were constantly worried about U-boats or surface raiders. We were well fed and there was plenty to drink although I had no idea what was in store at Takoradi. When we landed we moved to the aerodrome at 2nd D, a staging post for transferring aircraft to the Middle East via El Fasha, Midugari, Kharno, Khartoum and on to Cairo. After a day or two we were told that there was a different job in prospect and we were to take Hurricanes from Sekondi up the coast to Freetown. The intention was to form the Freetown Defence Unit, because enemy reconnaissance aircraft were flying over the harbour taking note of shipping movements, and vessels leaving harbour were finding U-boats lying in wait for them in the South Atlantic. I also got a job testing P40 Tomahawks, single-seat American Curtiss fighters with V12 Allison engines, before they were sent to the Middle East. The Allison was smoother running than a Merlin but the Rolls-Royce had better superchargers for high altitudes. I suffered a particularly alarming bird strike in a Tomahawk. A large local bird went clean through the landing light, striking with such force that it bent the main spar, and the entire wing had to be replaced.

Flying Hurricanes to Freetown was not straightforward. There was no proper communications equipment, no long distance radiotelephones, and no real contact with the shore. We did have radiotelephone contact with a Bristol Blenheim that led flights up the coast, but there were no proper maps. To make matters worse I knew suitable aircraft lay on lighters in Freetown. It seemed crazy not to get these aircraft off, assemble them and get them into the air, although probably it was easier to get us to ferry spare aircraft instead. It was certainly unnecessarily dangerous.

I made strong representations about the lack of maps to the commander of the operation. Squadron Leader Holden's response was to call me a weekend flyer, accuse me of shirking my responsibilities, and threaten to have me court-martialled. Later when I had been proved correct in my forecast and seven valuable aircraft lost I felt deep anguish over having my advice ignored. Crews could have been lost as well. It had taken a lot of courage to tell the CO what I felt.

After a lot of chivvying he did succeed in producing a map. It was a tracing on tissue paper of a thousand miles of West African coastline. Flying conditions were difficult in the middle of the rainy season, with cumulus cloud going up to over 20,000ft, and our aircraft were not good in climb, because they carried heavy long-range fuel tanks. Formations were not easily maintained in cloud, nevertheless the first group was set up and flew off led by the Blenheim. We made good progress up the coast, but in the end the task was hopeless, and we had to return to base, after flying for four and a half hours.

If we had reached Freetown it would have been more by good luck than good judgement, because Holden was pretty vague about where the aerodrome was. It was either 100 miles up the railway line or 100 miles up the river, and since the railway line and the river ran in different directions, there would not have been enough fuel to explore both.

After I got back I felt unwell and started shivering, the MO told me I had malaria, so I was sent off to hospital. I got better quickly at first and went to convalesce in the Mess. A second attempt had been made on 21 June 1941 to get the aircraft to Freetown but they had been put down on a beach in Liberia. This was neutral territory, so the pilots risked being interned and they had to set fire to the aircraft so that they were unusable, and walk 72 miles in two days and three nights to the Firestone Rubber plantation 35 miles from Monrovia. It had been a costly operation, and if only I had been listened to, it could have been avoided.

The pilots managed to return on a freighter, although they had difficulty getting into the docks at night because of sentries and watchmen. One was attacked and seriously injured so getting away became urgent. The skipper of a steam coaster brought them all the way back to Takoradi, and they were able to gave us their stories in the Mess. There were no more attempts to fly the aircraft up by this route; it was such a foolhardy operation.

A Nigerian boy brought our coffee every night I was in hospital. He had walked in from the bush to get a job in Sekondi. He aimed to get a job as a stoker on a coastal steamer back to Nigeria, and once he had earned enough money, he would give it all to his family. He brought the coffee in at night with a cheerful grin and say "Very best coffee sir. Made on my own plantation". He was so poor he had hardly a pair of shoes to wear. He got sixpence a week and slept on the concrete outside my bungalow.

Previous page: *Reggie Tongue looking unhappy flying a desk.*

Right: *Squadron Leader Holden's map. Reggie kept the flimsy tracing paper of a thousand miles of West African coastline and when he was compiling his memoirs left instructions for it to be included to illustrate the additional hazards of wartime flying.*

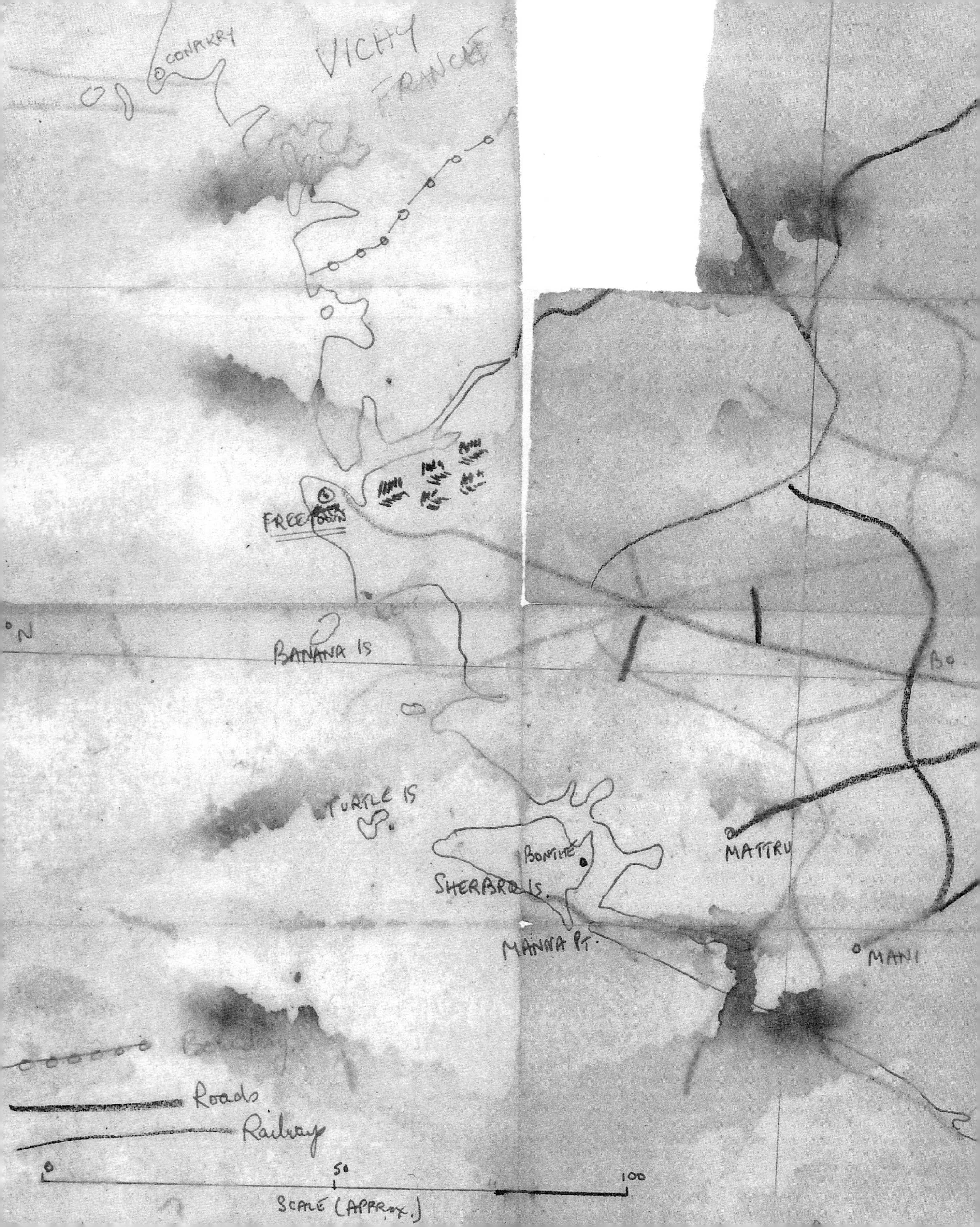

VICHY FRANCE

CONAKRY

FREETOWN

N

BANANA IS

TURTLE IS

SHERBRO IS.

BONTHE

MANNA Pt.

MATTRU

BO

MANI

Boundary

Roads

Railway

0   50   100

SCALE (APPROX.)

My recovery from malaria slowed unfortunately and I contracted a second dose. I really was pretty ill this time, waking up in the hospital delirious, with one of the nurses picking me up. I said to Mike Beytagh in the next bed, "Well, I don't want another night like that, I felt terrible". He told me I had been like that for nearly a week and I had gone down to just under nine stone from about eleven. I once asked him, after we had been in hospital a long time, "What are you going to tell your children when the war's over?" He said, "I'm going to say 'Your Daddy was one of those clever buggers who did not get killed'." It was one of those pithy comments that summed up what a lot of us were thinking.

The doctor was absolutely charming at my next medical check, but told me he was very sorry, I was not at all well. If I remained in West Africa I ran a high risk of more attacks, and also of Blackwater Fever, which would kill me. He told me I would have to go home, not entirely welcome news because the war in the Atlantic was at its height. It took a fortnight by boat from Takoradi to Freetown, where I transferred to an armed merchant cruiser, HMS Cathay for the journey to England.

I was on the quay waiting to go on to the Cathay when a naval officer asked if I knew anything about boats. He wanted me to take charge of the pinnace, a small launch that would take us to the ship. I should have remembered from my visit in 1936 how bad the swell could be in Freetown harbour. The rise and fall of the waves was enormous and the Cathay's gangway was down the ship's side. Without a proper crew to throw fenders, the little pinnace hit the bottom of the gangway really hard, knocking bits off both the gangway and the boat. The other passengers managed to grab hold of something and held on. The navy had an odd sense of humour, because when I did scramble up the heaving walkway, I was piped on board.

For most of the voyage home on the Cathay I slept in a hammock above a metal plate deck. The cargo puzzled the passengers: "Do you know," one told me. "The holds are full of ping pong balls". I did not want to disillusion him by telling him that the huge complement of ping-pong balls was our flotation gear in case a torpedo hit us.

We were pursued by U-boats and underwent a number of course diversions, letting off depth charges whenever the Asdic warned us of underwater predators. It was a hectic voyage, the food was abysmal, and complaints were ignored. The navy said I was always complaining, to which I replied that I had not taken exception to weevils in the rice, but the weevils were beginning to outnumber the rice. The crew's explanation was that they had had to feed a lot of survivors picked up in the Atlantic before setting them ashore. Most of the food they said had gone, but by way of compensation there was plenty to drink.

Top left: *In Takoradi Reggie sported an authentic RAF handlebar moustache. In the mess with fellow officers Curtis on left and Gerrardet on right.*

Right: *The Blenheim sets off for Freetown. The obsolescent light bomber was the Hurricanes' only radio contact as it led the ferry flight along the coast of West Africa.*

It was late August and at one party on board, the captain accused me of being drunk. I could scarcely disagree, but responded that he appeared to be no more sober that I was; as a matter of fact everybody on that ship was drunk quite a lot of the time. Nobody was really fit and I do not know what would have happened if we had had an emergency. As we progressed north and the weather grew colder I complained that a hammock on deck was a poor way for the navy to treat an RAF officer. I obtained a cabin, and life became a good deal more pleasant. The quid pro quo was that I had to go on to the bridge at dawn and dusk and assume responsibility for identifying approaching aircraft. I had to say whether I thought they were theirs or ours.

Unfortunately I had never been trained much in aircraft recognition. I had learnt enough to avoid shooting down the wrong ones during the Battle of Britain, but that was about it. I was rather on edge and found that every time an aircraft approached it did so at a hell of a speed. By the time I made up my mind what it was it could have dropped bombs and shot everybody on deck. Thank God no enemy aircraft came when we were in the South Atlantic, or even the North Atlantic approaching Belfast. All was well but I would have had it on my conscience terribly if we had been hit or anybody killed. I never knew whether the captain realised that I had not much of a clue on aircraft recognition, or whether my advice was any worse than what was already available.

We joined a convoy that had to try and keep together during attacks by submarines. They kept setting off depth charges, and there was one laggard who, in an attempt to keep up, had to burn more coal. Its funnel accordingly belched clouds of black smoke, for which it would get a dressing-down from the commodore for betraying our position. Slowly but surely we reached northern waters, going round the north of Ireland and arriving in Belfast, where the ship was due to have a boiler clean and refit. The journey had

taken 25 days, which was regarded as good going, because we had to take a circuitous route right out into the Atlantic before turning in towards the Western Approaches. It was not possible to come any closer on account of minefields, and despite the welcome vigilance of Coastal Command patrols, we had to come in at right angles from far out.

I arrived on 28 August 1941. Hospital in Belfast did not appeal to me much, so even though the quay was full of Military Police trying to find out where everybody was going, I made my way to the ordinary ticket office and booked myself on to the Heysham ferry. From there I took a train to London, thus avoiding immediate incarceration in hospital, although I was not really fit. I was pretty washed out what with the trip and the after-effects of malaria. Anyway it worked. When I got to London I went straight to the Mayfair and booked myself a palatial room and had some lovely food. Even though it was wartime, drinks were fairly available, and a pilot's uniform with wings opened the door to many things.

Next morning I thought I had better find out where I was going, and to whom I belonged, so I went round to the Air Ministry in Kingsway. They told me I would be posted to Number 1 Depot, Uxbridge, Halton but the first thing the interviewing officer said to me was that he supposed I would be ready for a bit of leave. I told him that I had had no leave for a long time, except sick leave, and that was spent repairing the

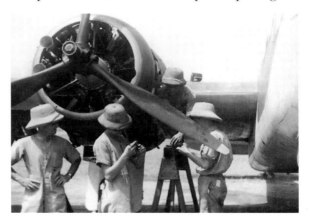

171

damage that had been done by illness. He gave me leave from 29 August to 12 September, a fortnight, and I was going to make the very best use of it. On 12 September I was due to attend Halton Hospital at Uxbridge for treatment for my malaria.

Dr James Jefferiss was on the staff at Halton, and although he was in charge of VD treatment, nevertheless I saw him from time to time at his little cottage. We had been at school together and done a certain amount of medical training with one another at St Mary's. I often stayed at his flat in Spring Street, Paddington, as he was keen on cars and motor racing. He worked extremely hard, and was so successful and respected, that he had a ward named after him at St Mary's Hospital, Paddington.

I remained in a general ward at Halton until 23 September along with pilots who had suffered terrible burns. Engine fires in single-seater fighter aircraft had horrific consequences. These pilots' efforts to shave, when their faces were little more than raw meat, were truly heroic. In the bed next to mine was a patient with a bad back who was suspected of malingering. The staff put him through terrible trouble, and his warnings that he would report their suspicions to his father did not cut much ice. In due course he did report his discomfiture. His father turned out to be Montgomery's protégé and commander of the 8th Army in Italy General Sir Oliver Leese. When the medics were proved wrong they had hell to pay.

After I was discharged I still had to go pretty carefully. I had three weeks sick leave, and another medical to see if I wanted to go back to fight, but I was tired and felt I would not survive very long. My reactions were too slow for combat flying, and although eventually the drugs were doing me good, while I was taking them I had to lie down a lot because of their side-effects.

After my sick leave I got a posting as Acting Flight Lieutenant to 55 Operational Training Unit at Usworth just inland of Sunderland on Tyneside. I found to my great joy that Scruffy Royce, Michael, Barry's brother who had been with me in 504 Squadron, had also been posted there and he was looking after one flight and I was looking after another. Our Wing Commander of Training was Ken Gough, who had been flight commander when I put the Miles Master through the bank of the training airfield at Aston Down.

We got on extremely well but I had not been there long when I suffered a terrible attack of jaundice and was quite ill. We were in wooden huts with stoves for heating, which was not conducive to good health. The jaundice was due to the malaria I had had in Africa, so I needed more treatment, even though I was now flying again. A lot of the work I was doing was formation flying and dual instruction on the Miles Master. There were quite a lot of Polish pilots in the unit, and also Polish service personnel attached to the flight, who turned out to be the cause of much mischief. They discovered that they could float stuff off into the River Wear that ran near the dispersal point, and it would finish up in the adjoining town. It was not long before partly filled barrels of 100 Octane fuel were bobbing off downstream to a backwater on the far side, where they were hauled ashore and sold.

Usworth was a happy station. We had very few accidents and none fatal during the whole time I

Right: *No 55 Operational Training Unit at Usworth had a good safety record until Reggie watched Hurricane W9135 demolish a radio-equipped van placed in the middle of the airfield for air traffic control duties. Fortunately nobody was in the van whose bent steering wheel can be seen under the Hurricane's tailwheel. The van and its radio were a write-off but the aircraft was almost undamaged.*

was there. We did have one spectacular prang right in the middle of the aerodrome. An air traffic control van was prominently placed at the intersection of the runways. I could never understand why, it definitely was an obstruction. I felt sure that one day some student pilot was going to focus on it, become mesmerised at the controls, and not know what to do. It was even more likely that in bad visibility somebody was going to crash into it with a tail-wheel aircraft. When a Hurricane or Spitfire was on the ground, vision forward past the engine was extremely limited. When you were taxiing it was the custom to zig-zag, because with the nose of the aircraft up, you could not see straight forward. It was necessary to squint through the sides of the canopy.

Sure enough I was outside the dispersal hut

one day, saw a Hurricane coming in, and to my horror watched it making straight for the RT van. Like a film in slow motion I watched it hit and go straight through. Curiously the aircraft was little damaged but the van was completely destroyed. Its bodywork was matchwood, taken straight off the chassis, and deployed over the infield. Fortunately there was no one inside at the time but it had been full of electrical equipment and little valves, resistors, panels, wiring and aerials were scattered all over the place. No action was ever taken, because it was a stupid place to leave a van, but it made me take notice of how relatively safe our flying had become.

Quite often I was sent off on attachment. Sometimes it was to the aerodrome at Ouston, inland near Hadrian's Wall, where I met a chum who had been in Africa at Takoradi with me. Jim

Storrar won a DFC during the Battle of Britain, had been a vet in Chester before the war, and was one of the pilots who had been on the fruitless mission to Freetown. We always had plenty to talk about and a lot in common, and I tried to persuade him to let me fly his Lysander. I had always wanted to have a go in a Lysander but I never managed it until much later.

He was CO of 55OTU Annan Gunnery Training Squadron stationed at Ouston, where the army gunnery officer was an old schoolmaster of mine called Badger. He was in the Army, and we started talking about school days and he told me a thing or two which made me realise how lucky I had been at school. The Morecambe incident had not been brought to the authorities' attention even though quite a lot of the masters knew about it. Jim then went to Drem, Scotland in command of 65 Squadron, where he earned a bar to his DFC in action against Focke Wulf 190s.

Newcastle people were extremely kind to station personnel. We got invited to Newcastle United football matches, and were well entertained in the director's box or in the very best seats. We got invited to social occasions and at one dance at the Queen's Hotel my partner was the chief constable of Newcastle's daughter. I had my old Vauxhall 10 but when I called to pick her up the chief constable gave me a stern lecture: "Now I know what you RAF chaps are like. I don't want any nonsense, she's to be back here before midnight, or I shall advise your station commander and you'll probably be put on a charge. Make sure you get her back or something terrible will happen to you."

I went to the dance with Ken Gough, my CO in charge of flying, but when it ended I found to my surprise and horror that Ken had taken my car to drive his girl home. I did not know what to do. Then I noticed a fire station a short distance away. I explained who the girl was and how important it was for her to get home. Could they possibly arrange anything? They said they would

be happy to oblige but they had not got any spare cars. I said what about their fire engines? It was a very helpful and supportive fire brigade to the RAF that night, and they took us both back to the house in the fire engine, on time.

Billy Cotton, an old chum from motor racing days, came to Newcastle Empire with his band so I got tickets for a row of seats in the circle. I sent a message inviting him to the Circle Bar. His banter was as good as ever saying: "You are supposed to be fit and fighting for the country, yet here you are drinking too much beer. You're not as fit as I am". We said he was overweight so he promised to prove to us in the second half of the show that he was nothing of the kind.

When he returned to the stage he did a few handstands and a couple of cartwheels. He really was a great man and I enjoyed his company. I raced against him several times. When the show finished, Billy invited us behind the stage and there he was in his office, with his young son Billy Cotton Junior managing things. The son became a great figure at the BBC right through to the 1980s, and just like his father, full of good nature and good fun.

As my time at Usworth drew to a close Ken Gough was keen that I should take his job because he was going to a post in Norfolk. It would have meant promotion, eventually it would have been a Wing Commander's job, but unfortunately he was disappointed with my pupil returns. They contained no night flying achievement at all. The young pilots had not done any because the weather had been so bad, and I had not felt justified in sending them off flying at night. Had I been able to get more of these night exercises done, I could have had his job when he went. But as I was unable to manage it, I had to be sent elsewhere.

This suited me because I had an alternative. Although I knew there was little prospect of promotion in the job, I was delighted to go to Fighter Command as Liaison Officer with Rolls-

Royce at Hucknall. I went there on 7 March 1942 and stayed until 18 September. I worked for the main Rolls-Royce liaison officer who had been in 504 Squadron, Ronnie Harker. My job was to go out to fighter units and lecture to pilots on how to handle engines to get the best out of them in flight, and particularly how economy could be achieved. Using fairly high revs and coarse pitch was more economical than medium pitch and medium boost. Eventually an interconnecting control for both the throttle and airscrew was devised. This was not terribly popular at first, and my job was to go out and sell them the idea.

Our liaison unit was composed of Ronnie Harker in charge, a chap called Sutcliffe who had been a civilian test pilot with Dunlop, and myself. Ronnie was keen to get this new interconnected throttle and airscrew control adopted and he never knew how I nearly completely ruined his reputation by a stupid error. I was sent down to Fairwood Common in South Wales where there were a lot of Americans. They believed that it was quite impossible to have such a gadget, that you could not override in combat. I had to try and prove to them that it was fully aerobatic.

Aerobatics were not one of my strongest assets in flying. I was a much better navigator and general pilot than I was doing aerobatics. Nevertheless I did my little show, and I thought just to round it off I would do an upward roll, then fly round and land. That should convince them. Unfortunately I had wrongly adjusted the tail trim. So when I got onto my back at about 1,000 feet above the aerodrome, I found I could not hold the nose up in the inverted position, and the only solution was to dive out, which I duly did. Thank God I did not have a high-speed stall. I missed the control tower by a matter of feet, then did a circuit and landed. Everybody rushed up and said, "You've convinced us completely, it's a marvellous thing, what a fantastic display you gave." Actually my knees were knocking to such an extent I could not get out of the aircraft.

I had a commission from people at Rolls-Royce including the CO Harvey Hayworth to go on a shoot in Angus and bring back various commodities that were difficult to obtain in the south, like butter, sugar, and so on. I invariably travelled in uniform because of the complications in explaining why I was able to use a motorcar when petrol was strictly rationed, and as aircrew I got an extra allowance, particularly for leave. On my way back I had a fair amount of game in the car including salmon that you could get without coupons in that part of the world. As I neared the Kincardine Bridge across the Forth, I found a great tailback of cars being examined by the Military Police. I suddenly thought that being discovered with all this contraband would not do my Air Force career much good. I jumped out of the car, went up to the sergeant in charge, and asked him what the hell was going on. I was an Air Force officer with important business in the midlands (which was perfectly true), and it was vital that he let me through as fast as he could. The bravado paid off and he sorted all the traffic out and waved me through. It was a great relief and I just hoped there would be no more checks along the road. The people I obtained all the things for were highly delighted.

I was not with Ronnie Harker's department very long. Shortly after I joined him, he invited me in Rolls-Royce's Miles Monarch to a party at Waddington on 26 March 1942. It was being held to celebrate the first 1000 bomber raid on Germany. The Monarch was a communications aircraft, a version of the Miles M11 design Whitney Straight commissioned FG Miles to build in 1936 as a light aircraft for flying clubs. The 1938 Monarch had three seats and a deeper windscreen, but against the 50 Whitney Straights built, there were only 11 Monarchs of which five were impressed for RAF service and most of the remainder were used as hacks by firms such as Vickers-Armstrong, Phillips & Powis, which made Miles aircraft and Rolls-Royce. It had a 130bhp

(96.9kW) de Havilland Gipsy engine, a top speed of 140mph (225kph) and a ceiling of 17,400ft (5305m).

On our return flight to Hucknall "Babe" Learoyd VC took the pilot's seat. I was in the rear seat and as we flew back the subject of negative G was discussed. Learoyd suddenly said, "I'll show you what neg G is," and pushed the control column sharply forward. I was not strapped in and none of us had parachutes. I left my seat and shot through the Perspex roof. Ronnie pulled me back, which was just as well, because the airstream was taking my breath away. I couldn't shield my mouth as my hands were stuck by my side and I was lucky to get away with nothing worse than a few scratches around my head.

While I was on a stopover at Fairwood Common one afternoon in June 1942, a Focke-Wulf 190, complete with black crosses and swastika on the tail, approached the aerodrome, did a circuit, and landed near the control tower. The pilot had put "red on black" on the compass and flown a reciprocal course over what he thought was the English Channel whereas it was really the Bristol Channel. Nobody had shot at him, and as soon as he stopped he realised what he had done, so he got out and ran away from the aircraft as fast as he could. It was not long before he was apprehended and was asked why he had run away. He claimed the aircraft was equipped with a special device that would blow up if anyone went near it.

We brought him up to the Mess and everybody was nice and kind to him, buying him drinks. He spoke good English, and we sat him at a table in the hall of the Mess and chatted. He seemed a perfectly likeable man. In the meantime they had sent to the Air Ministry in London for some experts to come down and see how the aeroplane was booby-trapped. It was not of course, and we realised that this chap had been having us on. Attitudes to him changed immediately. When he was taken outside to go off to a POW camp the

following morning, he was just picked up and thrown bodily into the back of a truck. I well remember the bang as he hit the floor. By way of compensation however we had his FW 190, so its flying characteristics and the performance of its BMW 801 engine could be evaluated.

Operating out of Hucknall meant I flew all over the place. It was a not very exacting and fairly safe job, and I was not entirely happy in it. At weekends though the chief test pilot Ronnie Shepherd was always short of people to test fly for him – I had always wanted to become a test pilot, and this seemed the opportunity. So as well as doing the liaison work during the week, at weekends I flew test aircraft for Shepherd, and our relationship prospered. He seemed to like what I did and I enjoyed the work, so in the end I asked Ronnie Harker if I could be released, as Shepherd would like to have me full time on the flight development staff. My friend Michael Royce, who had been at Usworth with me, was already on the flight development side at Rolls when I got there, and that again was a bonus.

Although officially with Rolls-Royce on the liaison job until September, I almost completely severed that connection, and joined the development side. In September I was transferred to the Ministry of Aircraft Production and my unit was SDL NO 1 Depot Uxbridge. It was an exciting time because I went to so many different aerodromes and had so many different jobs to do. Often I never knew what the reason for them was. It was sometimes years before I discovered why I had been asked to fly an aircraft at low

Top right: *Tragedy in time of war. The wreckage of Reggie's Halifax. Fuselage and tailplane and part of a wing lie in the partly ploughed field where they crashed. Tractor on right was being driven by the farmer who was killed when the aircraft came down.*

level and very high speeds, with a specially developed engine.

I liked SL (Roscoe) Turner, the Rolls-Royce test pilot. He liked a bit of fun although flying with him could be risky, like the occasion in the High Altitude Wellington, which had fully feathering electrically operated propellers. I was flying it at about 25,000 feet when suddenly I felt it lurch to port. It was a thoroughly dangerous aircraft at the best of times but I quickly realised what had happened. Unseen by me, Roscoe had feathered one of the airscrews, then went on and feathered the second one. Well that would have been fine, but unfortunately we couldn't de-feather them, because the battery that activated them was flat. Fortunately we had enough height to begin taking some action. We dived the aircraft, wiggled it about, and did everything we could by pressing buttons until the airscrews de-feathered of their own accord. It was not hard to imagine investigators trying to figure that one out. Had we survived the crash that looked at one point inevitable, it would not have been pleasant for Roscoe if it transpired that he had been skylarking – literally larking in the sky.

He was an excellent pilot, and I was delighted on 23 September 1942 when the chief test pilot assigned me as number two in a Handley Page Halifax W7814, the replacement for W1009,

which been in such a poor state that it was decreed unsuitable for the development work the Hucknall engineers had in mind. Rolls-Royce was engaged in a programme to improve the performance of the Merlin XX and meet criticisms that new flame-damping ducts badly affected its flying. The RAF was complaining that the ducts, designed to hide the telltale glow of flames from the exhausts, created drag that not only slowed the aircraft's climb but also affected the stalling speed. We set off to undertake a variety of tests on exhaust manifold developments. What we did not know was that Halifax engines were predisposed to go on fire. It was a nice day, and some time into the flight I was in the second pilot's seat, flying the aircraft on a full throttle climb to 20,000 feet over Lincolnshire at 2850rpm 125ASI. Roscoe was sitting in the pilot's seat and we had with us J Steele, an employee of Handley Page, to make observations.

Roscoe suddenly called out, "Port outboard on fire!" I remembered the occasion flying the Wellington with him, and decided he was trying to make me panic. But he said "If you don't bloody well believe me, stand up and have a look." I stood up and sure enough he was right. The engine had flames coming through a hole in the cowling. For a moment neither of us seemed able to do anything except look at it in horror. We tried unsuccessfully to feather the airscrew, whereupon there was an explosion that blew off bits of the cowling, and in order to keep the aircraft level I had on full starboard aileron. I do not know which of us said we ought to abandon the aircraft. We were in our shirtsleeves. I did not have my battledress jacket on, in which I had all my money, possessions and letters and God knows what. So I took off my parachute harness, put my jacket on, and put my parachute harness back on, which took some time. I somehow did not comprehend that the spread of the fire to the fuel tanks could have blown up the aircraft without warning. It did not really cross my mind.

We were at 14,000 feet and obviously Mr Steele had to go out first. He went through the forward hatch and hung there. I was due to go next and I thought he'd lost his nerve and dare not let go, so I put my foot on his fingers until he did. I subsequently discovered that he was hanging on because his harness was not on properly, and he had rather a bumpy landing.

I went next and Roscoe went last. I felt a reassuring tug when the parachute opened and glided down, but as I was getting near the ground, I noticed rows of high-tension cables. I thought, oh my God if I hit one of those, what a disaster it would be after getting out of the aircraft successfully. Roscoe snagged his parachute and damaged it as he left the aircraft, and as a result came down fairly abruptly, finishing up in a tree and breaking his leg. We were safe, but as the aircraft descended it broke up; one of the wings came off, and spiralled down like a sycamore seed. Tragically it landed in a field where a farm worker was ploughing with his tractor. He probably neither saw nor heard it, as it came from behind, and killed him.

I finished up in a farmhouse some way away from the wreckage, where a farmer and his wife were most kind and gave me tea. They had a little boy and I went off and bought some presents for him to thank them for their hospitality. While Roscoe was in hospital the Hucknall pilots visited him. When invited to describe the rapidity of his descent, he famously described it as coming down faster that a whore's knickers on boat race night.

The crash turned out to have been at Kirton Fen near Coningsby, and the investigation showed that one of the rear exhaust stubs on the port outer had fallen off, and flames had made the structure red hot, igniting the fuel. A driver had been instructed to take me to the sick quarters in Coningsby. I was dying for a pint as it was after 6 o'clock, and demanded to be taken to the Mess. He refused, dumped me at sick quarters, and I was made to parade with all the rest of the sick in a row. There was a little old chap next to me, who must have been in the service most of his life, yet still an "Erk". I don't think he had ever received any promotion and never rose above aircraftsman.

When the medical orderly came along he told this chap to roll his sleeve up, stuffed a hypodermic into his arm, and gave me a gargle and an enamel bowl to spit in. The little Erk said to me, "Do you know sir, I've been having a gargle like you had for the last fortnight, and now they go and stick a needle in me". I then realised that they had got their lines switched, he had my anti-tetanus injection, and I had his gargle.

When I got to the Mess, I told the MO what a waste of time the sick parade was and what I thought about him stopping me getting my beer. I had a pint off him as compensation. Next day Harvey Heyworth, the CO at Rolls-Royce, came and took me back to Hucknall and by the end of the month I had been accepted as a member of the Caterpillar Club.

Right: *Open only to individuals who had used a parachute to save their lives, Reggie earned his membership on September 23 1942, when his Handley Page Halifax caught fire on a flight from Hucknall.*

178

One could easily be flying a four-engined aircraft one day, or a jet, then a tiny little single-engined aircraft the next on a cross country. Something that gave me great satisfaction was flying a Wellington, which instead of having a rear gun turret had the first Whittle 2B jet engine in it. It was not practical to put the Whittle jet straight into an aircraft because it was not yet reliable, particularly if it did a flame-out. At altitude the burner sometimes went out, and it was impossible with the facilities then available to relight it. This would have not been much fun somewhere with no aerodromes for a forced landing. They might have lost a terrific amount of development work so they stuck the engine into this Wellington. The Royal Observer Corps kept reporting a Wellington with clouds of smoke behind it looking as if it was on fire. In fact it was paraffin vapour being thrown out.

Flying the jet Wellington was a great joy as I was interested in technical matters. Having been in on virtually the ground floor of jet development made it most rewarding to continue with work on the Gloster Meteor, the pure jet twin-engined aircraft. During development flying you always had to keep alternative aerodromes in view. In wartime, if the engine packed up or you ran out of fuel, the whole country was littered with aerodromes so you were nearly always able to glide down and get into one, probably with a little bit of power left.

We had an Airspeed Envoy, a passenger aircraft that carried four or five people, for moving personnel round the country. On one occasion I took passengers to Boscombe Down, the experimental establishment in Wiltshire, and back. The weather was pretty grim and one of the passengers, something to do with the Air Ministry I

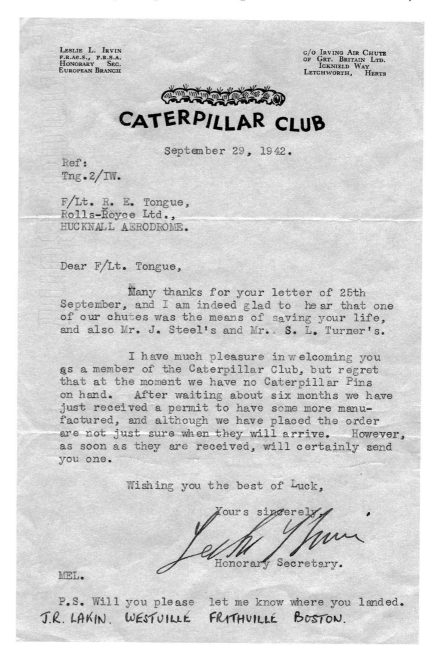

LESLIE L. IRVIN
F.R.AE.S., F.R.S.A.
HONORARY   SEC.
EUROPEAN BRANCH

c/o IRVING AIR CHUTE
OF GRT. BRITAIN LTD.
ICKNIELD WAY
LETCHWORTH,   HERTS

CATERPILLAR CLUB

September 29, 1942.

Ref:
Tng.2/IW.

F/Lt. R. E. Tongue,
Rolls-Royce Ltd.,
HUCKNALL AERODROME.

Dear F/Lt. Tongue,

Many thanks for your letter of 25th September, and I am indeed glad to hear that one of our chutes was the means of saving your life, and also Mr. J. Steel's and Mr. S. L. Turner's.

I have much pleasure in welcoming you as a member of the Caterpillar Club, but regret that at the moment we have no Caterpillar Pins on hand. After waiting about six months we have just received a permit to have some more manufactured, and although we have placed the order are not just sure when they will arrive. However, as soon as they are received, will certainly send you one.

Wishing you the best of Luck,

Yours sincerely,

Honorary Secretary.

MEL.

P.S. Will you please let me know where you landed.
J.R. LAKIN. WESTVILLE FRITHVILLE BOSTON.

supposed, sat behind me during the flight criticising what I was doing. The weather was getting worse and he said we ought to land at Leicester, so I told him to go and sit somewhere else, I was concentrating and since I was captain of the aircraft would he please not keep interfering. He was particularly worried about the oil pressure on the port engine. I told him I was familiar with the aircraft, it was always a bit low on this engine, and not to worry about it.

Scruffy Royce was with me and when we got back to Hucknall it was pretty well total fog. However there was one way of getting into Hucknall in the murk if you knew it. Provided the tops of the brickworks chimneys were sticking up out of the fog you could line up on them, and if you got it right you could go straight in, gradually dropping down onto the aerodrome, which I duly did. I went into the crew office and the duty officer enquired why, given the weather, I had been flying at all that day. It was not my custom to fly in conditions like that. I had to agree that I disliked flying in absolutely awful, horrible weather but I had a good reason to do it today, because I was taking my girl-friend to a dance in Derby and I did not want to miss it. To my horror I turned round to find, overhearing and taking serious note of our conversation, the VIP who had been so worried in the air.

We were always likely to have accidents doing this sort of flying. Some incidents were serious and we were lucky to get away with them, others less so. I was having trouble with the landing lights on our Mosquito – not the landing lights in the wings for night flying, but the warning lights on the flight deck. Sometimes even though they were showing green, to make sure that the undercarriage was down it had to be pumped down. Sometimes the wheels could be down but the lights would be red. I grew tired of this, it was unnecessarily worrying, so one day I went into the flight hangar and found the book that signed off the aircraft as being airworthy. Frierson the engineer kept giving it a clean bill of health and I kept writing against his entry, "You have not given me an assurance that the undercarriage warning lights are operating correctly."

It was just as well. On 1 July 1943 I came in to land as usual with the lights showing green, and had not gone far after touching down when the undercarriage collapsed. The aircraft skidded along the ground and we were extremely lucky not to hit a concrete gun emplacement, missing it by only a few yards. The Mosquito was a write-off but no blame could be attached to me because I had prudently placed on record my concern that the undercarriage warning lights were suspect.

Another aircraft that needed care, with an eye open for alternative landing sites, was a special Mustang with an unusually high supercharger pressure. We did not know what performance of this sort was needed for, but it transpired intelligence information had been gained by code-breakers about the performance of the V1 flying bomb. Various countermeasures were being proposed long before the first one was sent off against the south of England. The V1 or Doodlebug was an early type of Cruise missile with a pulse-jet engine, that flew at about 400mph (650kph) with 850kg (1875lb) of high explosive in the warhead. The plan was to fly alongside, and slowly tilt it over with a wingtip, upsetting its gyroscopic guidance systems so it would crash before reaching its target.

A Mustang needed to go pretty quickly to manage this so it drew in extra air to enhance the power output. It was like the evolution of a racing car; one side produces more power, the other side has to catch up, and so it went on with rival designers and development engineers trying to gain the edge or discover unwanted side-effects. On this occasion we found that the air intake could no longer cope. Enough backpressure built up to collapse the housing, squashing it flat like a sardine tin in a press, and with no air coming in, the engine virtually stopped. It had been working on at least 25psi (1.723bar) and in March 1944 I was doing tests with it at 15,000 feet when there was a large bang. Detonation, when the fuel in the engine ignites violently, set in and as the engine began to self-destruct there was a terrific loss of oil. I had to get the aircraft down quickly and managed to point it towards base but there was virtually no power. It so happened that I had been keeping a wary eye open for places to put down if the worst happened. It was vital to get the aircraft back on the ground intact so that the boffins could piece together the remains and discover what the trouble was and I made it into Debden.

My logbook contains a number of entries about abandoning tests on this particular type of Mustang due to a variety of faults including low oil pressure. They really were highly tuned machines, again just like racing cars operating on the threshold of disaster, and they were not only unreliable but when failures did occur they were usually catastrophic. Some of our work included high altitude climbs without a pressure cabin to anywhere between 38,000 and 40,000ft. This was unpleasant, as although we had oxygen there was no effective heating in the cockpit. The effect of the unpressurised cockpit was that at high altitude your body ballooned, your face became swollen, and it became necessary to loosen the parachute harness to allow your body to expand. There was also a risk of getting the bends through nitrogen in the blood, as afflicts divers. Poor Harvey Heyworth had nasty attacks of it, causing severe pains in the muscles and the joints, but fortunately I was largely unaffected by it.

At 40,000 feet a clear blue sky turns quite black, and taking off on a steep climb you were so nearly lying on your back it became difficult to keep your feet on the rudder bar. The altimeter went spinning round so quickly it was difficult to write coherent records of an aircraft's performance. This process was superseded by cameras fitted in the cockpits, leaving the pilot with responsibility only for flying the aircraft, which was welcome.

Taking a high altitude Spitfire out once, the weather forecast told me to expect a 100mph wind from a northerly direction at 36,000 feet. Unfortunately below me was ten-tenths cloud and when I came back down through it I was completely lost. All my ground references were gone and I had no idea where I was. Instead of giving me the right wind the met office had given me the reciprocal compass bearing, making it 180 degrees from the opposite direction, south. I had been blown much further north than I thought I was.

All ended well once I had found my bearings. We did quite a lot of flying above ten-tenths cloud on a compass course. We had no radiotelephone (RT) and there was always the risk of not getting it right. Going east was generally a safer bet; the coast usually provided a clue to where you were, although you risked being shot at by a seaside anti-aircraft battery. By doing a bit of navigation in your head you could descend in safety into Lincolnshire because it was nice and flat. Providing you kept away from the Pennines there were not many hills to fly into.

We did quite a lot of work at Hucknall with Martin Hurst, whose company specialised in automatic controls that opened or closed the radiator flap in response to engine temperature. His firm designed all sorts of gadgets, and sometimes he would cadge a lift back south. In August 1942 I went with them, Roscoe Turner was the pilot, and the only transport available even though there was some work being done on it, was the high altitude Wellington W5797. This did not have a proper windscreen. It had an astrodome on the top and only the pilot could see out. Nobody else could see anything.

We had been working most of one day until late in the afternoon, and Roscoe took Martin and me to Hendon in this Wellington. In return for the free lift Martin took us to Quaglino's in Bury Street for a delightful meal that included quite a lot of Chateau D'Yquem. The Wellington had poor visibility for landing but was even worse on take off, and Roscoe had to take the aircraft back to Hucknall that night. It was getting late and I was worried, even though in August there was plenty of daylight left. I was quite relieved not to be going with him because Hucknall had no night landing facilities at all. Undaunted Roscoe took off quite late and made it back as the last bit of daylight disappeared.

Flying had its golden moments. It was by no means all white-knuckled danger. I never forgot one memorably beautiful day, when I was doing a test at 36,000 feet, and found at my feet the whole of England like a map. I could see the Welsh hills, the Bristol Channel down to Cornwall, all the South Coast, London, the Thames up to Essex, Lincolnshire, and almost up to the Scottish border. By the end of my RAF career in October 1945, my logbook showed I had flown 36 types of aircraft, a total of 2,098 hours 25 minutes, of which 1,733 hours were on single-engined aircraft.

EPILOGUE

Reggie Tongue's personal life was less perilous than his exploits on the racetrack and in the air; essentially conventional, staunchly Church of England, and deeply conservative, he seriously considered adoption as a Conservative parliamentary candidate after he returned to civilian life. Following his release from the RAF as a Flight Lieutenant in 1945, hunting, sailing and fishing became his principal leisure pursuits rather than the more colourful ones of aviation or motor racing. His business interests widened, and he devoted himself to family life. When he recorded the memoirs on which much of this book is based, he pronounced himself amply fulfilled. He relished telling of what he called his nine lives, viewing them unheroically, yet clearly satisfied with all that he had achieved.

It was hardly surprising that the bereavements Reggie suffered as a child left him, in the words of his second wife Elsie, emotionally tight-lipped. His diaries were comprehensive records, yet revealed little of his feelings, except in areas such as his religious faith of which the redoubtable "Gorty", later the Rev Neville Gorton of Blundells and a future Bishop of Coventry, was the bedrock. Reggie refused to be confirmed until he was over 50, recounting a conversation with Gorty in which he claimed to have found God but was unable to get in touch with the Holy Ghost.

His attitude to motor sport was one reason why Reggie Tongue's recollections and memoirs were a significant record of his times. They gave a lively account of the lifetime of an individual, content to be surrounded by a culture and environment he liked and respected, that also sustained his unwavering senses of duty and responsibility.

In a new millennium it may be unnatural to look on motor racing, or any sport for that matter, as an activity where winning is desirable but by no means essential. Brooklands would not have understood modern professional sport, the term was not

Left: *Reg on "My Hero" at a meet of the Cheshire Forest Hounds, of which he was Secretary. He also established a family tradition of membership of the Worshipful Company of Loriners, ancient manufacturers of horse bits. His son Charles and daughter Louise also became members, and Reg, a member since the 1930s, attained the position of Master.*

yet common currency, a "sportsman" was still an amateur and if his chosen pursuit required a yacht, a horse, or a racing car then he was expected to find the means to pay for it. This was unfair, insofar as lack of inherited wealth effectively excluded a lot of people with talent and ambition, just as in a later professional age lack of sponsorship would too.

Reggie Tongue's world of the 1930s was still emerging from the Great War and the Depression. In Britain the General Strike was a recent memory, and unemployment and anxiety about the renewal of conflict was the background to daily life. Disarmament, rearmament, and apprehension that the Spanish Civil War, with its aerial bombing, foreshadowed a wider European war, gave young people an outlook on life difficult for later generations to comprehend. It was not quite fatalistic, yet there was a strong prospect that one's days were numbered. It was a

Top right: *Reggie and wife Elsie on the hills.*

Below: *Reggie presents the Lookers Cup to the winner of the Cheshire Forest Point to Point. His daughters Emma and Louise are on his right and their friend Heather Seal on left.*

generation short on luck and its apprehensions were, as it turned out, well founded. It was scarcely surprising that Reggie was strongly religious.

Never quite gaining ERA's inner circle affected Reggie. His diaries contain references to being patronised by the aesthete Mays whose blatant homosexuality Reggie would have found distasteful, and the aristocratic Siamese princes, whom he distrusted. By contrast, his friendship with Dick Seaman was well established long before Seaman became well known. They saw one another often during university days and through racing the same sorts of cars. By the time Seaman graduated to the Mercedes-Benz team for grand prix racing, Reggie was one of the select associates who visited him in his lakeside chalet, faithfully recorded in the address book that was also a source of research and information. The entry for Seaman is Haus 12, Ambach, Starnbergersee, Oberbayern, Germany.

It was here that Richard Seaman met and fell in love with Erica Popp, whose father was managing director of BMW, and who he later married against his mother's wishes. Mrs Beattie-Seaman liked Erica but was apprehensive over her son's marriage to a German girl at the height of international tension. Reggie's friendship with the couple had a sequel when, after Seaman's death in the Belgian Grand Prix of June 1939, he became engaged in 1940 to the beautiful young widow. Erica had been married a bare seven months, she was still only 20, and was committed to life in Britain. She told Seaman's biographer Chris Nixon: "I wanted no part of Nazi Germany. I hated the Nazis so much that after Dick's death I left Germany on my own and didn't see my family for fourteen years. I loved my father and my sister but I hated the Nazis, so I had to choose. With Dick the choice was easy there was no question of going back." She had good reason to dislike the regime; it treated her father Franz-Josef badly, accused him of disloyalty, threatened him with execution, and banished him from BMW.

Erica was left with little money. Seaman's estate was worth less than £1,500. He had died before inheriting the family fortune, and his Mercedes-Benz earnings, and property were locked away in Germany. Close to and trusted by her late husband, Reggie Tongue must have seemed reassuring, even though the liaison was not well received by their friends. Erica spent the summer of 1940 in Torquay and Reggie's diaries record some desultory meetings but the relationship was hopeless, the engagement broken off, and Erica eventually sailed for America. Erica never even featured in Reggie's address book in her own right under E for Erica, S for Seaman, or P for Popp. It looks as though Reggie's heart was not in it.

Erica was not the first girl in his life. In 1931-1932 Karen Borgens was the 17-year old daughter of Danish friends of his father's. Borgens Snr built the first margarine factory in England, Reggie recalled, a very able but quiet man whose wife was English and who was fond of Reggie's father. Of Karen Reggie wrote, "We got on like a house on fire," and he took her to the Lake District in his Riley at weekends. They drove there, winter and summer, and walked over Honister, sometimes going for Sunday morning rambles in Langdale, returning home to Hale in time for supper and the customary Sunday night sing-song round the piano.

When Reggie went up to Oxford, Karen was in Bedford at the Froebel Teaching College. "We went out for meals and I spent a few days in Bedford when I was down taking my Responsions examination in Latin. She

was occupied all day; I stayed at the Bridge Hotel, and hired a skiff to row up and down the Ouse at Bedford. It was good exercise, very entertaining, and romantic in the evenings when she came and had dinner with me."

They thought about getting engaged when Reggie was 21 but it did not last. Reggie fell in love with a friend of Karen's and decided to break it off. "It was no good going on with it. I had made up my mind. We had been to Margaret Lendrum's 21st party one weekend in St Neots where she lived, and on the station at Bedford when I was saying goodbye to Karen, I said something like: 'Now I'm afraid this really is goodbye because I can't go on with this.' I could not bring myself to tell her that I had fallen for her best friend."

Reggie describes Karen as "a brick" for being driven uncomplainingly many miles in his Riley. She must have been. It had no weather protection to speak of and very firm springing. "It was a very cosy car, you were on top of one another and one day just going through Preston I put my hand on her knee. She very firmly put it back on mine and said 'Not before lunch!'".

Karen married in 1937. Reggie wrote disparagingly that her husband must have been about 50 years old, and she was barely 21. He worked in Siam and she went back there with him and became a teacher, sending

Reggie a picture of their first child. What became of her during the war was a mystery, Reggie never knew whether she was trapped in the Far East when the Japanese invaded, or made it safely back to Britain.

Other girls came and went in the 1930s including "Languid Ann" met on Reggie's cruise to West Africa in 1935. "She was a very interesting young person if for no other reason that that she weighed only six stone six pounds. She was keen on concerts, the ballet, and she was a socialist. She amused me a lot as her political views were very inconsistent with her mode of life. The man who marries her will have to be agreeable, receptive, and subjective. Her view will always be right."

It was 1941 before he became deeply involved again. Stationed at Digby, shortly before he left England for West Africa, Reggie fell in love with Johnnie Nicholson. It was not a straightforward affair, because she was married to Rex Nicholson, who worked at Rolls-Royce and whom Reggie knew. Her marriage had not been a success but the circumstances worried Reggie deeply. Some members of his family, notably his favourite cousin Delia, counselled him against becoming involved.

After the RAF sent Reggie to Africa, Johnnie wrote almost daily, but by the time he returned months had passed without a word. He had no idea if in his absence she had gone off with somebody else, so when he arrived in London he got a friend to let her know he was back in England. A message came back; she would be delighted to see him, she was in Lincoln and driving military staff cars.

Reggie had lost a lot of weight due to his bouts of malaria, but when they met at Lincoln railway station the romance was rekindled. It turned out that Johnnie's letters had been pursuing Reggie as he moved from place to place. "Despite not receiving letters for some time I always knew she had been writing to me constantly. One morning when we were having breakfast the post delivered a package containing over a hundred of them. They had been redirected from the Army Post Office, APO 1000, Cairo. I got another fortnight's sick leave and most of that was spent with Johnny in Lincoln, although I did go home to see how they all were. A bomb had missed the house by a fraction. Another tiny thousandth of a second on the bomb release button and it would have gone straight through. It finished up in the garden, did not go off but made a very big crater, and the bomb disposal people had to come and take it away. It was a bit of luck that the ground was extremely soft; it was so wet and soggy it had not set off the detonator. Johnnie and I eventually lived together, and when the divorce came through in May 1944 we got married and were very happy. Sadly, after she had borne me a son Charles, she contracted cancer and was desperately ill for years. Yet we had a happy life together. We had a lot of fun, we went fishing, we went on holidays, we hunted together. She was attractive, competent, a good cook, and even a good book keeper. There was not much that she was not good at."

With the war behind him Reggie decided he wanted a peaceful time. He had grown tired of putting his life on the line. Rolls-Royce offered him a job and Strauss Turnbull asked him to rejoin and become a partner, but he did not much fancy either of these and started looking for a farm. It was not a good time. Farms were run-down and dilapidated after six years of war, there was a labour shortage, rationing had survived and looked like continuing for some time. All the farms he looked at seemed expensive yet those that could be bought for £150 to £200 an acre in 1945 were soon going for £1,500 an acre. He enjoyed farming as an adjunct to his motor trade business and a number of enterprises that covered ownership of a small industrial estate in Denton to the manufacture of building industry machinery and production of breeze-blocks. His favourite directorship was of a brewery where elevenses included a sampling of the product.

Among the other business interests Reggie built up before his death in his 80th year in 1992 was as managing director and chief executive of Lookers, one of the leading North of England motor agents. In 1948 he had bought Arden & Bull, becoming governing director, when it was absorbed by Lookers. He was also chairman of Holden & Brooke, the engineering group, in 1983, its centenary year. During the war he became a director of Thomson & Taylor (Brooklands) Ltd, which had been responsible for his ERA, then chairman and joint managing director.

"Thomson & Taylor had premises at Brooklands but it was short of money, and invited me to put up some working capital. It seemed a good idea and meant that when they charged me heavily for their services I might stand to benefit in the long run. It was not long before I was asked to join the board, my first directorship. I accepted as I got on well with them and eventually became chairman. It led to the disagreeable task in the 1960s when it still had the Alfa Romeo concession, but had become hopelessly uncompetitive, of having to sell it off to Jonathan Sieff of the Marks and Spencer family, who amalgamated it with one of his companies."

The interest in motor racing that had engaged him throughout his 20s had all but gone in his 40s, although he took part in the Monte Carlo Rally in 1951 in a Mark V Jaguar. This gave him the unusual, perhaps unique, distinction of having flown two aircraft, the Atlas and the Siskin, with one of the best aero engines of the 1920s, the Armstrong-Siddeley

Jaguar (whose name the Jaguar company took), and also competed with a Jaguar car. Starting from Glasgow with co-drivers his old RAF colleague from 504 Squadron Michael Royce and P E Warr, he finished a creditable 31st in a field of 337 cars. He played an important role, as president of the Mid-Cheshire Motor Club in the creation of Oulton Park, one of the pre-eminent as well as one of the prettiest road-racing circuits in Britain.

Reggie was in constant demand as an accomplished after-dinner speaker for the ERA Club, the Brooklands Society, and his reminiscences were enlivened by his cars, in particular the ERA and Maserati. They featured in historic races and he would sometimes grumble good-naturedly that R11B, one of the most successful of all ERAs, only came good once he had put right all its faults. In 1983 Reggie went to Le Mans 49 years after "A Vincent" distinguished himself as a "Pilote Britannique des Vingt Quatre Heures du Mans".

Reggie's acquaintance with sails began at an early age, with a sand yacht on an old car chassis used on the Anglesey beach at Rhosneigr, where he spent many holidays. The boats he built were usually calamitous, until he went to the Liverpool Museum and measured up the kayaks used by Sir Wilfred Grenfell, the 19th century Cheshire-born missionary in Labrador. Together with his friend Edgar Hickling, Reggie made a replica, carving out the formers, and steaming bentwood rods in his uncle's greenhouse. The framework was secured with copper rivets, canvas was sewn over it, and Reggie being youngest was sent to sea in it, to make sure it remained upright unlike previous attempts.

Reggie did not do much more sailing until he went up to Oxford and bought a 12-foot National called "Restless", which he sailed a lot off Anglesey. A friend at Oxford, Mike Edmondson, had a Bristol Channel pilot cutter on the Hamble, to which Reggie would be invited at weekends. The friendship lasted 30 years and together they took Reggie's National to Anglesey for the Menai Fortnight.

In 1963 Reggie married Elsie, whose family owned hotels in the West Country and in South Africa, and set off for a honeymoon in the Caribbean. The newly-weds went to Antigua looking for a boat to sail to St Vincent, but as with some of Reggie's adventures things did not quite go according to plan. They joined the schooner Alano belonging to a reformed alcoholic, a difficult man who turned out to have little feel either for sailing or bad weather. Reggie on the other hand, sensed the calm before the arrival of Hurricane Betsy, and took his new wife ashore at Martinique just as the storm broke. Alano had two anchors out and the engine running all night in an effort to remain afloat, but pitched and rolled in the mountainous seas, until its owner was bravely rescued by the crew of a tanker and taken to an inner harbour. The severely shocked man trembled for days. The night before the trip ended, a steel band serenaded them from the jetty at the cost of two bottles of rum.

Reggie sailed in Scotland with his friend Tommy Russell, of the Glasgow iron-founding family, who moored his boat at the bottom of his garden at Colintraive in the Kyles of Bute. They sailed the picturesque seaway on the north side of Bute, with its well-marked but narrow channel near Tighabruaich, through which paddle steamers like the Waverley pass with only feet to spare. Reggie recalled his embarrassment after asking Tommy's advice on which side of a buoy to pass. The local man's reply "Either side will do at this stage of the tide," was followed swiftly by a terrible crunch as

their vessel ran aground. To make matters worse, it was dressed overall for Tommy's sister's birthday, providing passing steamers with a risible spectacle as the tide left them high and dry.

Guernsey was another popular recreation ground. Sailing together with daughters Emma and Louise was an important part of the girls' annual holidayswith the couples' friends at St Peter Port where Elsie and Reggie's daughters Emma and Louise sailed in the family's boats, a Nicholson 35 Blue Dolphin and later Parlapippin. Brand new, Reggie set off in her from Gosport, to be met by a huge flotilla coming the other way escorting Chay Blyth on British Steel after its epic voyage. Weaving through it demanded some lively seamanship.

Reggie was sometimes surprised how his exploits, and those of his 1930s track contemporaries, had by the 1960s wrought a motor racing revolution. He would have been even more astonished to find that, around the time of his death, two of the fighter airfields from which he flew in the 1940s had become sites for Japanese car factories. Reggie Tongue's predictable well-ordered world had changed beyond recognition. Yet it was he and his fellow amateurs that brought the world focus of motor racing to the United Kingdom. In the latter half of the century, Britain made the cars and provided the expertise that earned billions of pounds and much respect from every continent. He would have been satisfied with that.

ACKNOWLEDGMENTS

The publishers would like to pay tribute to the perseverance of the Tongue family in their efforts to have Reggie's life commemorated in a book on which he had set his heart. We were grateful for the approach made through the late AF Rivers Fletcher, resulting from his enthusiasm for our Jim Clark biography, and for the great volume of material in Reggie's diaries, photo albums, cuttings books, and memorabilia all of which were freely made available. The book was financed by the family with a contribution from the Michael Sedgwick Trust and is being produced as a special limited edition of 1,000 copies. The Maserati cover picture was painted on commission especially for the Reggie Tongue book by Michael Turner.. The author owes continuing thanks to the proprietors of The Motor, The Autocar, Autosport, Motor Sport, Classic Car, Classic & Sportscar, The Automobile, Automobile Quarterly, and Veteran & Vintage magazine for use of valuable historical motoring research material. The photographs by the late Louis Klemantaski included in the book were given by the photographer to Reggie soon after they were taken and are reproduced by express permission of the copyright holder, The Klemantaski Collection, of Peter G Sachs, Stamford, Connecticut, USA.

As with all Dove Publishing books, our thanks are due to our production consultant David Bann of Microbook and Andrew Barron of Thextension for the jacket design. Book creation, typesetting, and production were by Ruth Dymock.

BIBLIOGRAPHY

Written material used in research for detail included: The History of English Racing Automobiles by David Weguelin (White Mouse Editions 1980); The Le Mans 24 Hour Race by David Hodges (Temple Press 1963); The French Grand Prix by David Hodges (Temple Press 1967); Shooting Star, the life of Richard Seaman by Chris Nixon (Transport Bookman 2000); MG by McComb (Osprey 1978); K3 Dossier by Mike Hawke (Magna Press 1992); The Beaulieu Encyclopaedia of the Automobile (The Stationery Office 2000); The Encyclopaedia of Motor Sport (Ebury and Michael Joseph 1971); The History of Brooklands Motor Course by W Boddy (Grenville 1957); Gorty by John Margetson (Letheringham Books 1998); Aston Martin 1913-1947 by Inman Hunter (Osprey Automotive 1992); The Life of Lord Nuffield by PWS Andrews and Elizabeth Brunner (Blackwell 1955); World Encyclopaedia of Aero Engines by Bill Gunston (Patrick Stephens 1986); Jane's Fighting Aircraft of World War II (1947 as reprinted Studio Editions 1989); British Aircraft of World War II (Aerospace Publishing 1982); Men of the Battle of Britain (CCB Associates 1999); Battle of Britain Then and Now (After the Battle Magazine 1980); MG A-Z by Jonathan Wood (Motor Racing Publications 1998); MG Sports Cars by Malcom Green (CLB International 1997); Dove Publishing archive collections of motor racing and aviation books including The Motor; The Autocar; Autosport; Motor Sport; Classic Car; Classic & Sportscar; The Automobile; Automobile Quarterly; and Veteran & Vintage.

INDEX

192